CAD Books from OnWord Press and Pen & Brush Publishers

MicroStation 4.X

The MicroStation 4.X Delta Book
INSIDE MicroStation
INSIDE MicroStation Companion Workbook
INSIDE MicroStation Companion Workbook
    Instructor's Guide
MicroStation Reference Guide
MicroStation Productivity Book
101 MDL Commands
Bill Steinbock's Pocket MDL Programmer's Guide
MDL Guides
101 User Commands
MicroStation For AutoCAD Users

MicroStation 3.X

INSIDE MicroStation
MicroStation Reference Guide
MicroStation Productivity Book

Other CAD Titles

The CAD Rating Guide
The One Minute CAD Manager

Books By Pen & Brush Publishers
Distributed by OnWord Press
The Complete Guide to MicroStation 3D
Programming With MDL
Programming With User Commands

Cover Art

Image by Jerry D. Flynn and Robert P. Humeniuk, Design Visualization Group, McDonnell Douglas Space Systems Company, Kennedy Space Center, Florida. The images were created and rendered using MicroStation 4.0. A Sony GDM-1950 Monitor and Number Nine Computer 9GX level 3 video board was used for display of images. Originals were shot from screen using an Olympus OM4 35mm camera at F8 with Kodak Kodacolor 200 slide film.

The cover artist would especially like to thank Tony Clarey at Number Nine for the 9GX video board also Raymond Bentley and Brett Yeagley at Bentley Systems for their support during beta testing.

Programming with MDL

The MicroStation Development Language

Mach N. Dinh-Vu

Copyright © 1991 Pen and Brush Publishers.
2nd Floor, 94 Flinders Street,
Melbourne, Victoria 3000.
Australia.
Fax: (03) 818 3704. International 61 3 818 3704.

ISBN 0-646-01679-2

Published in Australia. Printed in the United States of America.

To my parents

Acknowledgements

This book is the result of the support I received from many dedicated people. Thanks to David Wilkinson, who 'corrected' this book. Thanks to Peter Payne, for checking my work and making many useful suggestions. Thanks also to Bill Steinbock for his help with the code and ideas.

Special thanks to all the staff at Bentley Systems, Inc., especially to Keith Bentley and John Gooding. Thanks also to Scott Bentley, Ray Bentley and Peter Huftalen. Many thanks to Katherine Bartlett who always returned my faxes with the right answers. Thanks to my colleagues at OnWord Press, especially Dan Raker and Dave Talbot, for putting up with me. Thanks also to David Hill and Minenco Pty. Ltd.

This book is dedicated to my parents who are always there with support and strength.

About the Author

Mach Dinh-Vu is a Computer Science graduate who majored in computer graphics and artificial intelligence. His initial experience included responsibility for the development and support of Intergraph VAX based CAD systems for Architectural applications and CAD bureau services. In 1987 Mach completed a graduate diploma in Business Technology and in 1988 spent a number of months working in Vancouver with a major engineering firm.

In 1988 Mach joined Minenco Pty. Ltd. to provide CAD software development and support on the PCSA/DECnet and 3Com networks. In August 1989, he wrote and published the book "Programming with User Commands" and in October 1990 co-authored the book "101 User Commands".

Mach has been an active member of the Intergraph and MicroStation User Groups for many years. He is also an active member of the Bentley Systems' Independent Software Development program as well as the Beta testing of MicroStation Version 4.

Table of Contents

1 : MDL Programming Basics

2 : Compiling MDL programs

3 : MDL Dialog Box

4 : Element Search & Manipulation

5 : Element Descriptors

6 : Mathematics and Geometry

7 : Advanced Dialog Box

8 : Input Queue

Appendix A : Include Files

Introduction

MicroStation version 4 introduces a new development tool called MicroStation Development Language or MDL. You may ask "why another language?", when already we have User Commands (UCMs) and MicroCSL. MDL is not just another language, as you will discover from reading this book. MDL requires a new way of thinking.

Anyone who has written a UCM will have said to themselves, "there must be a another way". MDL is the other way. It is based on C, therefore it has all the features of a true programming language. This does not mean that MDL has replaced UCMs. MDL has simply put UCMs back to being a macro language where they belong. If you quickly want to write a simple program to sequence commands, or simulate operator's input, then UCMs are a logical choice. UCM code is IGDS compatible and therefore is the only development language that can execute across the entire range of Intergraph platforms. MDL is designed to be compatible across all MicroStation platforms, and also be platform independent.

MDL is similar to UCM in that it is executed by MicroStation. MicroCSL, on the other hand, executes in stand-alone mode. An example of a MicroCSL application is the design file editor, EDG. MicroCSL is essentially a library of routines linked with either a C or FORTRAN program.

MDL introduces a new concept to the traditional linear C programming of begin, middle and end. Whilst MDL stills has the begin and end, these are inconsequential. The middle has taken over and it is based on an event loop. The loop is a rotary engine that accepts events and generates more events. It is this ability of MDL, to manipulate the event loop, that makes it so powerful. MDL is the future for MicroStation, but it is here now. In this book we will learn how to use MDL.

Basic Requirements

MDL is a full development tool with nothing extra to buy. The compiler, linker, make utility, librarian and debugger are provided with MicroStation version 4. *Programming with MDL* will show you how to access and use these tools.

Although MDL is based on ANSI C, understanding how to program in C is only half the exercise. You must have a very good understanding of the Intergraph MicroStation environment, file structure and element format.

How to use this book

Programming with MDL serves primarily as a tutorial on the MDL language. If you have never used MDL, then it is best to read Chapters 1 thru 5. These chapters provide a solid foundation to the MDL language.

MDL is such a vast and sophisticated language that we expect the reader to be a competent programmer. Therefore we will not be spending much time on programming basics. In the first chapter we will launch into developing an MDL application. Throughout this chapter there are constant references to the C programming language. These should not be used as a guide to learning C, they are used to confirm the understanding of the language between the author and the reader.

In chapter 2 we look at creating our application and seeing it run. Here we introduce the *bmake* utility and, more importantly, the debugger. No programmer should learn MDL without knowing how to use the debugger. The MDL debugger will become your best friend.

We discuss dialog boxes early in the book, as they are a major feature of MicroStation version 4. If you are certain that you will not require dialog boxes then you can skip Chapter 3. Chapters 4 and 5 are the foundation of MDL, therefore it is important that you understand these chapters. The rest of the book revolves around writing as many different applications as possible. This way you can get the 'feel' of MDL and be comfortable with the language.

There are over 1,000 MDL functions available to the programmer. It is beyond
the scope of this book to provide the complete description of all of these
functions. If you need this facility then consult the Bentley Systems' *MDL
Manual* (the words *MDL Guide* appears on the spine) or *Bill Steinbock's MDL
Programmers Guide*. The *MDL-Guides* by CAD Perfect Corporation also
provide this information in an on-line, easy to access, format.

Programming with MDL tries to use as many different functions as possible to
show how they work. Every function used in this book is cross indexed.
Therefore, if you need to use the function *mdlModify_elementMulti* , then
check the index first.

Naming Convention

Filenames used in this book are consistent with the MDL Manual. Filenames
and directories are always shown in their respective cases. Although DOS
does not differentiate between cases, other operating systems, like UNIX,
support both upper and lower case file and directory names. The extensions
are:

.h	include or header file
.ma	MDL application file
.mc	MDL source file
.mke	makefile
.ml	MDL library file
.mo	MDL object file
.mp	MDL compiled program file
.mt	type file
.r	resource source file
.rsc	compiled resource file

MDL predefined functions always start with *mdl* and are shown in italics, for
example *mdlModify_elementMulti*. All functions written in our applications
will be in a different font. For example, `generateImage`.

Accompanying Disk

There is a companion disk containing copies of all source and makefiles required to build the applications. This saves time re-keying the examples, and provides an error free start to your MDL programming experience.

Whilst you can use the applications immediately, we recommend that you rebuild them. Each different host version of MicroStation requires applications to be recompiled and linked.

A floppy disk symbol is used to signify that the specified file is supplied on the accompanying disk.

pbdlg.mc

If you purchased a DOS version then create the parent directory as C:\PROGMDL . For the Unix workstations create */usr/progmdl*. The directory structure of the accompany disk for DOS is shown below.

\PROGMDL\DISK\COMPUCM	COMPUCM.MC
\PROGMDL\DISK\HIGHAP	HIIGHAP.MC
\PROGMDL\DISK\LOCELE	LOCELE.MC
\PROGMDL\DISK\ORCELL	ORCELL.MC
\PROGMDL\DISK\PBDLG	PBDLG.MC
\PROGMDL\DISK\PLBOX	PBDSCR.MC
	PLBOX.MC
\PROGMDL\DISK\PLCIRC	PLCIRC.MC
\PROGMDL\DISK\ROTCELL	ROTCELL.MC
\PROGMDL\DISK\SCANFILE	MODALL.MC
	MODFENCE.MC
	MODSING.MC
	MODSYMB.MC
\PROGMDL\DISK\STRTEXT	STRTEXT.MC
\PROGMDL\DISK\TEXTRMS	TEXTRMS.MC
\PROGMDL\DISK\VIEWONLY	DEMOMODE.MC
	INSTVO.MC
	MESSAGES.MC
	VIEWONLY.MC
	VWCLASS.MC

1 : MDL Programming Basics

Since the MDL language is based on the C programming language, we will look at some C programming basics and how MDL implements them. This chapter does not intend to teach you how to program in C. There are many books available on this topic. We have assumed that the reader is a competent C programmer and therefore only concern ourselves with certain features of C that are required in MDL. We then move on, to consider MDL programming basics.

Basic Concepts

The MDL language is a structured programming language which has a collection of standard commands, functions, and objects that allow us to create an application program. If we were asked to describe MDL in 25 words or less, then our answer would be :-

 MDL is C in structure, has its own run-time library, compiler, linker, librarian and is executed by MicroStation.

As you read through this book, you will find that MDL is beyond a programming language. It is a development tool which taps into the heart of MicroStation to develop seamless add-on applications. Before we start writing MDL code, we should clarify several issues concerning terminology, standards and conventions.

Structure of an MDL program

An MDL program is a collection of statements that adhere to the rules defined by the MDL language. A program statement can have the following:

- Control structure or declaration statement
- Assignment Statement
- Function /Procedure call
- Pre-processor directive
- Comment

This collection of statements (our MDL program) is a text file, stored with a ".mc" extension. We will write an MDL program that will place a box around a text string, and then extend a leader line from the box. We will use this as an example of a 'typical' MDL program. Then we will make a cell out of our newly placed elements. The program will be called *plbox.mc* (refer to Fig 1.1). There are many ways to write code and as you read through this book you will notice several variations on this program. The complete program is listed at the end of this chapter. Here we will go through it step by step.

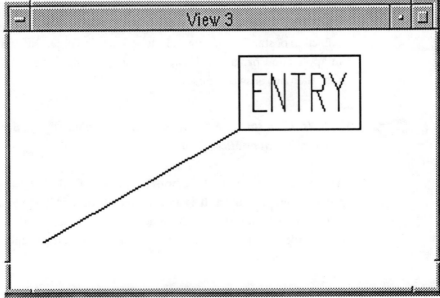

Figure 1.1 The result of PLBOX program

Comments

Comments inform the reader of the meaning of the program code. Comments also remind the programmer of what he has done when maintenance work is required. To start a comment use a forward slash followed by an asterisk (/*). To terminate a comment, do the reverse. That is, use an asterisk and then a forward slash (*/). All comments are ignored by the compiler (more on compilers in Chapter 2). MDL does not support nested comments.

Include Files

An **include file** is a file, containing MDL source code, that the pre-processor reads into our program for use during compilation. Include files are sometimes called header files since they are included at the start of the source code.

We can place commonly used constants into a separate file. We then can include this file into several different programs thus ensuring that the constants are consistently expressed. There are two ways to define an include file:

```
#include    < mdl.h >
```

The convention is to terminate the include file with a ".h" extension. If brackets are used, the pre-processor will try to locate the < mdl.h > file in our MDL include directory, *ustation**mdl**include*.

Alternatively, we can place the filename within quotation marks. This tells the pre-processor to search for the include file in the same directory as the file that contains the include statement.

```
#include    "plbox.h"    /* Generated by "rcomp -h plbox.r" */
```

How do we know which include file to use? The name of each file is shown in the MDL Manual. For example, as we will be using *mdlText_extractShape,* we must include < mselems.h > . The include files delivered with MicroStation are found in *ustation**mdl**include* .

For our *plbox.mc* program we use the following include files.

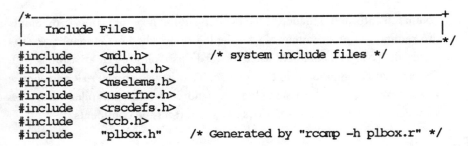

```
/*------------------------------------------------+
|    Include Files                                |
+------------------------------------------------*/
#include     <mdl.h>          /* system include files */
#include     <global.h>
#include     <mselems.h>
#include     <userfnc.h>
#include     <rscdefs.h>
#include     <tcb.h>
#include     "plbox.h"     /* Generated by "rcomp -h plbox.r" */
```

The last include file *plbox.h* is of special interest because it was created by a resource compiler. We will leave the discussion on the resource compiler until Chapter 2.

Variable declaration

Before we can use a variable we must define it. In most cases we will not know what variables are required until we start designing our program. In this section we will assume that we know what variables are required. Since there are many ways to define and use variables in MDL, we will start our discussion from basics.

Definition of a variable

The term **variable** associates a name to a memory location. The amount of memory required to store the variable depends on the variable **type**. The term **address** is the memory location of the variable. For example, the contents of the integer variable *count* is 20 and its address is given by *&count*. That is, the & (ampersand) returns the address of *count* instead of the value of *count*. This is a very important concept. Many programmers have introduced bugs into their programs through misunderstanding the difference between a variable and its address.

 *MDL is a case sensitive language. Keep this in mind when defining variables or function names. For example, the variable **linePts** is different from **LinePts**.*

Variable Type

The **variable type** defines how a variable is stored and also what set of operations can be applied to it. The basic variable types are **short, int, float, double** and **char**. The following table defines each of the MDL types.

Type	Value Stored
short	Integer values from -32,678 through to 32,767
unsigned short	Integer values from 0 through to 65,535
int	Integer values from -32,678 through to 32,767
long int	Integer, from -2,147,483,648 to 2,147,483,647
unsigned int	Integer values from 0 through to 65,535
unsigned long int	Integer values from 0 through to 4,294,967,265
float	treated as a double
double	Floating point values with 6 or 7 digits of precision
char	ASCII character value, or integer from -127 to 128
unsigned char	Integer, from 0 through to 255

Variable Scope

The **scope** of the variable defines the parts of the program to which the declaration of the variable applies. To determine the scope of the variable, the source code of an MDL program is broken into hierarchical blocks. A block may be a procedure or function. The entire file is considered to be a block. Blocks may be nested inside others, therefore a variable defined in the outer block is known to all the nested blocks. A variable declared in an inner block may have the same name as one declared in the outer block. In this case, the variable in the inner block supersedes the outer, but only within the scope of the inner block. These are known as **local variables**. Their values and existence are known only to the function that declares them. **Global variables** are known to every function in your MDL program.

Static and Automatic Variables

Variables are organized into storage classes. These determine how the variable is stored, how long it lives, and to where in a program its name can be referred. If we take no special step when we declare a variable within our function, it is an **automatic** variable. This means that the variable is created automatically when we call the function, and discarded when we leave the function. Sometimes it is desirable for the function to remember the last value assigned to a local variable. The **static** qualifier directs the compiler to store the value of the local variable from one call to the next. By default variables are automatic. Global variables may be static (known to everything within the MDL source module, but not available to other source modules). If a global variable is not declared as static, then it may also be used by other source modules.

In our PLBOX example we need to define two global variables for use in all our functions. We will define *textin* to hold 128 characters. This is significant as there are 128 characters in the "keyin" buffer. The *pntP* variable will hold the data points.

```
/*——————————————————————————————————————————————+
|    Private Global variables                                    |
+——————————————————————————————————————————————*/
static char  textin[128];
Dpoint3d     pntP[2];
```

MDL built-in variables

MDL provides global variables for use in our programs. We can access these variables without defining them as they are built into the compiler. Many of these built-in variables are structures or unions. For example, the variable ***tcb** is a structure containing all the information on the current design file. If a built-in variable has a simple type such as *int*, it is not necessary to include a header file. However, if the built-in type is a structure or union, or is a pointer to a structure or union then it is necessary to include the proper header file. For more detail on the contents of the header files please refer to Appendix A.

Type	Variable	Description
short	dgnbuf[ ]	holds all the information on the current element in dgnbuf. All elements are loaded into this buffer by a locate or element manipulation commands.
MSStateData	statedata	contains all the information on the current state function. Defined in < global.h >
Tcb	*tcb	holds all the information on the current DGN file. Defined in < tcb.h >
Mgds_modes	mgds_modes	contains the mode information about the current execution of MicroStation. Defined in < global.h >

byte	cmplx_hdr[ ]	will be TRUE if an element is a complex header. For example, the following will be true: cmplx_hdr[CELL_TYPE]
char	mgdsPrompt[35]	holds the text for the prompt. The default is "uStn > ".
short	element_drawn[8]	this is a bit mask where each bit is an elements type. If the element is displayable then the bit is set.
short	msversion	the current version of MicroStation, in hex.
short	database	will be true if the database is currently attached.
int	mdlErrno	error number for various MDL functions
int	errno	error number for various operating system functions.
MSGraphConfig	graphConfig	contains the graphics configuration. Defined in < global.h >
long	mdlCommandNumber	contains the command number of the most recently started MDL application command.

MDL Functions

There are two types of functions, pre-defined and those we create. To use a function we must define it before we can access it. To use a pre-defined function we must have the correct include file at the start of our program. MDL provides two distinct sets of pre-defined functions, namely the standard C functions, and those specific to MDL (prefixed with *mdl*).

Explanation of the standard C functions are not documented in this book, as they can be found in the many books available on C programming. Standard C functions supported by MDL are as follows:

File Manipulation, Input and Output: *fclose, feof, ferror, fflush, fgetc, fgets, fopen, fprintf, fputc, fputs, fread, freopen, fscanf, fwrite, fseek, ftell, getc, printf, putc, remove, rename, rewind, sscanf, setbuf, setvbuf, sprintf, tmpfile, tmpnam, ungetc, unlink, vfprintf, vprintf, vsprintf.*

Character Classification and Conversion: *isalnum, isalpha, iscntrl, isdigit, isgraph, islower, isprint, ispunct, isspace, isupper, isxdigit, toascii, tolower, toupper.*

String Manipulation: *strcat, strchr, strcmp, strcmpi, strcpy, strcspn, strlen, strlwr, strncat, strncmp, strncpy, strpbrk, strrchr, strspn, strstr, strok, strupr.*

Memory Allocation, Buffer Manipulation, Data Conversion: *atof, atoi, atol, calloc, exit, free, getenv, malloc, memchr, memcmp, memcpy, memmove, memset, rand, realloc, srand, strtod, strol, strtoul.*

Mathematical: *acos, asin, atan, atan2, ceil, cos, cosh, exp, fabs, floor, fmod, frexp, log, log10, ldexp, modf, pow, sin, sinh, sqrt, tan, tanh.*

Date and Time: *asctime, ctime, difftime, gmtime, localtime, strftime, time.*

Variable Arguments: *va_arg, va_end, va_start.* MDL supports both ANSI and K&R methods of handling variable arguments.

The Main Function

Whilst an MDL program does not have to have the `main` function, it is rare that a program does not have it. In an MDL program the `main` function serves three purposes:

- `main` is the initial entry point.
- it is essentially an initialization function.
- when `main` returns to MicroStation, the MDL program remains resident (unless unloaded by the MDL program).

```
main()
{
 RscFileHandle   rfHandle;
 /* load our command table */
 if (mdlParse_loadCommandTable (NULL) == NULL)
     mdlOutput_error ("Unable to load command table.");
 mdlResource_openFile (&rfHandle, NULL, FALSE);
 mdlOutput_prompt("Key-in in PLACE BOX to execute");
}
```

Our `main` function will load the command table into MicroStation. We will discuss command tables and resource files in the next section.

Displaying Messages

MicroStation's command window is broken into 6 areas where messages can
be displayed. The 6 areas are known as the *error, prompt, command, keyin,
message* and *status* fields. We can inhibit all messages sent to these fields if
tcb- > control.inh_msg is set with a non-zero value. If *tcb- > control.inh_err* is set
with a non-zero value then the function *mdlOutput_error* will not display
messages.

The Message functions are summarized below:

mdlOutput_error **mdlOutput_prompt** **mdlOutput_command** **mdlOutput_keyin** **mdlOutput_message** **mdlOutput_status**	display a message in the Command Window field that corresponds to the specified area.
mdlOutput_errorU **mdlOutput_promptU** **mdlOutput_commandU** **mdlOutput_keyinU** **mdlOutput_messageU** **mdlOutput_statusU**	display a message in the Command Window field that corresponds to the specified area. These functions will ignore the inhibit bit.
mdlOutput_printf	display a message in the Command Window field designate by one of these parameters MSG_MESSAGE, MSG_ERROR, MSG_PROMPT, MSG_STATUS, MSG_COMMAND and MSG_KEYIN.
mdlOuput_vprintf	same as above but the messages are displayed according to a format string.
mdlOutput_rscPrintf	display a message in the Command Window field with the message taken from the MessageList resource.
mdlOutput_rscvPrintf	same as above but the messages are displayed according to a format string.

messages.mc

If we write a very simple program as shown below, we can see where the messages are displayed.

```
mdlOutput_error("This is the ERROR field");
mdlOutput_prompt("This is the PROMPT field");
mdlOutput_command("This is the COMMAND field");
mdlOutput_keyin("This is the KEYIN field");
mdlOutput_message("This is the MESSAGE field");
mdlOutput_status("This is the STATUS field");
```

```
┌─────────────────────────────────────────────────────────────────────────┐
│                  MicroStation Command Window - test.dgn                    │
├─────────────────────────────────────────────────────────────────────────┤
│ File  Edit  Element  Settings  View  Palettes  User                  Help │
├─────────────────────────────────────────────────────────────────────────┤
│ This is the STATUS field              This is the MESSAGE field            │
│ This is the COMMAND field             This is the PROMPT field             │
│ (1) BSTN> This is the KEYIN field     This is the ERROR field              │
└─────────────────────────────────────────────────────────────────────────┘
```

Figure 1.2 Displaying messages to the User

Structures and unions

Structures let us group related values of different types. As we will see in the MDL include files, structures are used extensively because of their convenience. In the example below, we have defined a structure called *elm_hdr* and created a type *Elm_hdr*. The *#if, #else* and *#endif* are pre-processor directives, which we will discuss in the next chapter.

```
/*----------------------------------------------------------------+
|    Element Header structure - common to all MicroStation elements    |
+----------------------------------------------------------------*/
typedef struct elm_hdr
    {
#if !defined (mc68000)
    unsigned          level:6;        /* level element is on */
    unsigned          :1;             /* reserved by Intergraph */
    unsigned          complex:1;      /* part of complex element (cell) if set*/
    unsigned          type:7;         /* type of element */
    unsigned          deleted:1;      /* set if element is deleted */
#else                                 /* bit fields in reverse order for 680x0*/
    unsigned          deleted:1;      /* set if element is deleted */
    unsigned          type:7;         /* type of element */
    unsigned          complex:1;      /* part of complex element (cell) if set*/
    unsigned          :1;             /* reserved by Intergraph */
    unsigned          level:6;        /* level element is on */
#endif
    unsigned short    words;          /* number of words to follow in element*/
    unsigned long     xlow;           /* element range- low (reversed longs)*/
    unsigned long     ylow;
    unsigned long     zlow;
    unsigned long     xhigh;          /* element range - high (reversed longs)*/
    unsigned long     yhigh;
    unsigned long     zhigh;
    } Elm_hdr;
```

To use the structure we must define a variable of type *Elm_hdr* and access it with the dot operator. For example, we define *hdr* of type *Elm_hdr*.

```
Elm_hdr      hdr;
```

To change the level of the element we would use the statement:-

```
hdr.level=3
```

Element Union

There is a special structure called **union**, which allows a variable to store values of several types, but only one value can occupy the variable at any time. In the Fortran programming language these are known as equivalence. The TCB variables - *UCBYT, UCWRD* and *UCASC* are an example of a union concept.

Unions are an extremely powerful feature that allow us to manipulate data with relative ease. Consider the element union *msElementUnion* shown below. We have included every possible MicroStation element plus the DGNBUF. The fixed element header *Elm_hdr* is also in this union.

```
/*--------------------------------------------------------------+
| name            element_union - union of all element types    |
+--------------------------------------------------------------*/
typedef union msElementUnion
    {
    Cell_Lib_Hdr      cell_lib_hdr;
    Cell_2d           cell_2d;
    Cell_3d           cell_3d;
    Line_2d           line_2d;
    Line_3d           line_3d;
    Line_String_2d    line_string_2d;
    Line_String_3d    line_string_3d;
    Text_node_2d      text_node_2d;
    Text_node_3d      text_node_3d;
    Complex_string    complex_string;
    Ellipse_2d        ellipse_2d;
    Ellipse_3d        ellipse_3d;
    Arc_2d            arc_2d;
    Arc_3d            arc_3d;
    Text_2d           text_2d;
    Text_3d           text_3d;
    Cone_3d           cone_3d;
    Surface           surf;
    Bspline_pole_2d   bspline_pole_2d;
    Bspline_pole_3d   bspline_pole_3d;
    Bspline_curve     bspline_curve;
    Bspline_surface   bspline_surface;
    Bspline_weight    bspline_weight;
    Bspline_knot      bspline_knot;
    Bsurf_boundary    bsurf_boundary;
    short             tmp[768];
#if defined (ip32)
```

```
    short               buf[780];
#else
    short               buf[780];
#endif
    Extlev_hdr          extlevhdr;
    Elm_hdr             ehdr;
    Header              hdr;
    } MSElementUnion, MSElement;
```

We can define a variable *el* of type *MSElementUnion*.

```
MSElementUnion   el;
```

When we read an element, we are uncertain which element we have. With the
element union, we can test the fixed element header *el.ehdr*. In the example
below we can check for a line, and using unions we can access the same data in
el.line_2d.

```
if (el.ehdr.type == LINE_ELM)
{
    el.line_2d.start.x += 100;
    el.line_2d.start.y += 100;
}
```

Notice how we extracted data from the union with one union member and used
another to manipulate the information. In this instance we moved the start
point of the 2D line 100 units to the right and up 100 units.

Pointers

Pointers potentially are the most misunderstood feature in MDL. As with variables, we can declare pointers of type int, float, double, and char. Consider a common usage of pointers in MDL.

 Note the definition of the variable, *pString, in the parameter list. Throughout this book we will use the ANSI method of defining the argument type in the parameter list. This method has the added advantage of having type checking on the argument.

```
Private void parseInputString (char *pString)
{
char *pResult;

 if ((pResult = strtok (pString, " ")) != NULL)
 {
 strncpy (oldString, pResult, sizeof (newString));
 if ((pResult = strtok (NULL, " ")) != NULL)
        strncpy (newString, pResult, sizeof (oldString));
 }
}
```

In the above example, we are looking at two character pointers, *pString* and *pResult*. The (*) asterisk tells the program to go to the memory location stored in the pointer *pString* to find the value of the character string.

Passing by Reference

There are two ways to pass parameters, by **value** or by **reference**. When we pass our parameter by reference, we send the receiving parameter the address of the argument. Therefore, any changes to our argument in the called routine will also change the value in the calling routine, as they both share the same memory location. We have to pass character strings by reference. We can do this by using pointers to point to the address of our *string*. We don't require an & as a string is an array of char, and all arrays in MDL are passed by reference.

For example, the declaration of string tells us that we must pass it into `parseInputString` as a pointer.

```
char string[20];              /* definition of string on main program */
.
.
.
parseInputString(string); /* pass the string into our function */
.
.
.
Private void parseInputString (pString) /* pass it by reference */
char *pString;                          /* define pString as a pointer */
```

Looking back at our `main` function, the structure *rfHandle* is passed as a pointer. How can we tell? The ampersand character (&) is the address operator. This returns the address of a variable in memory, not the value of the variable.

```
mdlResource_openFile (&rfHandle, NULL, FALSE);
```

The routine *mdlResource_openFile* is a pre-defined function. When we look it up in the MDL Manual we can see that the first parameter must be a pointer. By using the ampersand in front of *rfHandle* we have provided the function with the argument in the correct format.

Passing by Value

We can also pass our variable by value. This means that the argument is evaluated and its value copied to the receiving parameter. Changes to the variable within the called routine are local. They are lost when the routine terminates. Looking at the example below, the routine will place an arc in view 2. Here, *viewNumber* is passed by value and regardless of what we do to the receiving parameter. There will be no change to the variable when we finish with the call.

```
..
viewNumber=2;
placeArcbyCenter(viewNumber);
.
.
```

```
Private void placeArcbyCenter (int view)
{
  MSElementUnion      arc;
  Dpoint3d            arcp[3];
  double              origin;

  arcp[0].x = 25.;            /* start point */
  arcp[0].y = 35.;
  arcp[0].z = fc_zero;        /* floating point constant */
  arcp[1].x = 55.;            /* center point */
  arcp[1].y = 35.;
  arcp[1].z = fc_zero;        /* floating point constant */
  arcp[2].x = 85.;            /* end point */
  arcp[2].y = 35.;
  arcp[2].z = fc_zero;        /* floating point constant */
  origin = 55.0;

  if (mdlArc_createByCenter (&arc, NULL, arcPt, TRUE, origin, view)
      == SUCCESS)
      {
      mdlElement_display(&arc, NORMALDRAW);
      mdlElement_add(&arc);
      }
}
```

Note: MDL array follows the C convention and starts from 0. For example, in the above definition of Dpoint3d arcp[3], the array indexes are arcp[0], arcp[1] and arcp[2].

Function Pointers

In MDL we can pass the address of a function as an argument. Therefore, the program can call the function by referencing the pointer's value. Function pointers are used extensively in MDL. For example, the function *mdlState_startPrimitive* requires the first two arguments to be pointers to functions.

```
mdlState_startPrimitive(placeBox_firstPoint, placeBox_start, 1, 2);
```

The functions `placeBox_firstPoint` and `placeBox_start` must appear before nay references are made to them. We can do this by defining the function name at the start of the program with:

```
Private void placeBox_firstPoint(), placeBox_start();
```

or have the entire function appearing before any calls are made to it (this is the approach used throughout this book).

MicroStation - The State Machine

MicroStation is an event driven machine. That is, at any point, an event has put MicroStation into a known state, and there are state handlers to process input to it.   We can demonstrate this by calling the PLACE LINE primitive and placing the first point of the line. The second point "rubber-bands" as we drag the cursor around the screen. Instead of giving a second data point, we will pick up the WINDOW AREA command and select our new window. Our line has disappeared when our window updates - or has it? Being a state machine,

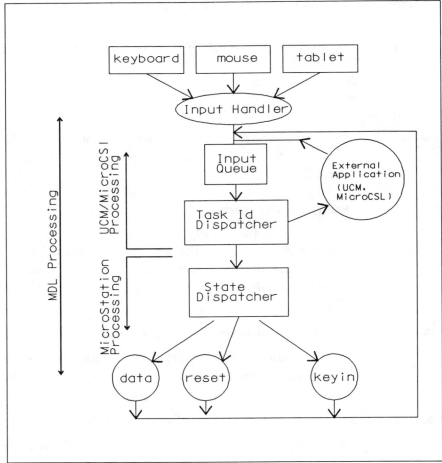

Figure 1.3 MicroStation input loop

MicroStation differentiates between the **command states**. The view command is a different state from the place line command. Therefore, we can assume that our line is still active - and it is. Hitting a reset will take us out of the view command and bring back our line.

We can write an MDL program to establish state functions to process input such as a data point or a key-in. In this way MDL allows us to tap into MicroStation at the "primitive" level. Every MDL application we write will have the benefit described above without any explicit programming.

Other MicroStation programming tools like UCMs and MicroCSL "sequence" MicroStation commands. If we look at Figure 1.3 we can see that UCM and MicroCSL loop between the input queue, task dispatcher and the external application. Therefore, a sequenced application will never get control at the state dispatcher level.

Resources

A **resource** is a group of data stored in a file called a resource file. Typical groupings of data are text strings, error messages, raster icons, and command tables. The purpose of using a resource file is to isolate data from the application source code. There are many advantages with this approach, namely:

• overall memory requirement is reduced since data will only be loaded as needed.
• several applications can share the same resource.
• simplify maintenance. Changes to prompts/messages will not require changes in the application program. For example, converting the application to another language, i.e French.

We will discuss resources and how to create them in later chapters.

Command Table

Our main routine, shown below, loads the application command table from the resource file. The command table defines a command language. For the purpose of this exercise, we will assume that main will load, into MicroStation, the command **PLACE BOX**. Again we will discuss the command table in later chapters.

```
main()
{
  RscFileHandle    rfHandle;
  /* load our command table */
  if (mdlParse_loadCommandTable (NULL) == NULL)
      mdlOutput_error ("Unable to load command table.");
  mdlResource_openFile (&rfHandle, NULL, FALSE);
  mdlOutput_prompt("Key-in PLACE BOX to execute");
}
```

Here, we have told MicroStation only about the existence of our application command, we have not executed our program. This is the beauty of MDL. It allows the application developer to tap into MicroStation at the 'primitive' level. We have now defined a primitive called PLACE BOX.

To activate our MDL program we must enter PLACE BOX at the uStn > prompt. MicroStation will parse user entry, word by word. Therefore, entering PLACE on its own will generate an ambiguous command - MicroStation cannot differentiate it from PLACE LINE. Creating a primitive called PLACEBOX will defeat the purpose of a command table, as there is no command hierarchy and commands cannot get a classification. Getting a command classification is important. It allows MicroStation to determine, or allocate, the current state of the application. We will discuss this in detail when we create our command table for the PLACE BOX application.

When MicroStation successfully parses a user key-in, a command number is generated. A task ID of the application associated with the command table, and the command number, are used to determine the application to execute the command, and hence the function to call. In the routine on the following page, *cmdNumber* associates the function placeBox_start with a

command number.   When we enter PLACE BOX, MDL will start execution
from `placeBox_start`.

```
cmdName        placeBox_start ()
cmdNumber      CMD_PLACE_BOX
{
  mdlState_startPrimitive (placeBox_firstPoint, placeBox_start, 1, 2);
}
```

The routine *mdlState_startPrimitive* will set the state functions so that a data
point will activate `placeBox_firstPoint`, and a reset will loop and
execute `placeBox_start`.   Also it will print message number 1 from
message list 0   into the command output field, and message number 2 in the
prompt output field.   In chapter 2 we will discuss *MessageList* and show how
to create them.

The State Control Functions

An application that sequences MicroStation commands will terminate the last
command before another executes. For a User Command to do a WINDOW
AREA, in the middle of a PLACE LINE command, it needs to prompt
explicitly for the WINDOW AREA. Writing an MDL program as an
event-driven application will not cause the application to suspend. Functions
are established to handle the event. In this section we will discuss the various
state control functions, which are the heart of MDL programming. There are
four MicroStation command states.

Primitive Command State

Primitive commands can create, modify and delete elements. Starting a
primitive command will terminate the last primitive, and is active until another
primitive replaces it. To initialize the primitive command state we must call on
the following.

mdlState_startPrimitive   starts a primitive and is only used
                                               for element creation.

mdlState_startModifyCommand   starts a primitive to locate and
                                               modify elements.

mdlState_startFenceCommand   establish function that will be used
                                       as the fence manipulation primitive.

View Command State

View commands are used to modify or update views. To initialize the view
command state we must call *mdlState_startViewCommand*. Starting a view
command will suspend a primitive command. When it terminates, the
suspended primitive will resume. If a user enters reset, we must terminate the
view command with *mdlState_exitViewCommand*.

mdlState_startViewCommand   start a view command.

mdlState_exitViewCommand   exit a view command.

Immediate Command State

Immediate commands are used to modify a setting (e.g. changing the snap lock
or entering WT=). Immediate commands do not call state functions and
therefore will not affect the state of the primitive or view commands.

Utility Command State

Utility commands perform non-interactive functions, such as COMPRESS.
We need to call *mdlState_startDefaultCommand* when we finish with the utility
command.

The rest of the state control functions are listed here:

mdlState_clear   reset the command state so the no
                                       command is active.

mdlState_checkSingleShot   check if the command is to operate
                                       in single shot mode.

mdlState_dynamicUpdate   specify the function to use in simple
                                       dynamic operations.

mdlState_registerStringIds   specify the prompt to use when a
                                       primitive starts up.

mdlState_restartCurrentCommand   restart current primitive command.

mdlState_setFunction	specify the function to use depending on the event.
mdlState_setKeyinPrompt	specify the string used in the keyin area. Default is "uSTN >".
mdlState_startDefaultCommand	start the default command when the current command finishes.

User Functions

MDL uses function pointers to specify the user supplied function to execute, when certain events occur within MicroStation. Function pointers make programming easier and powerful. For example, the function *mdlState_startModifyCommand*, requires 5 user functions to execute, when certain events occur. These events are the user sending a reset, data point, or to display dynamics. The remaining two parameters, show and clean, are used to display the modified element in DGNBUF. Show and clean are usually paired together, so that clean can undo the previous show function. We can pass NULL for some of these arguments. The following lists the user functions:

 Please note that the function name in italics is not the actual name of the function. Replace it with the function name you use in your program.

userState_clean	function to use for modify function.
userState_commandCleanUp	function to use when cleanup is required before another command starts.
userState_complexDynamicUpdate	function to use to display complex dynamics.
userState_datapoint	function to call when datapoint is pressed.
userState_dynamicUpdate	function to use for simple dynamics.
userState_fenceContent	function to use in processing fence content.
userState_fenceOutline	function to use in redisplaying fence outline.
userState_keyin	function to use in processing a user keyin.

userState_reset	function to use in processing a reset.
userState_show	function used in displaying an element once the modify command is loaded into DGNBUF.

Looking back at our PLBOX example, we need to set up the place box primitive. The first parameter, `placeBox_firstPoint` is a pointer to the function to execute, when the user sends a data point. The second parameter is the function to call if the user sends a reset. In this case we will loop and restart the place box primitive. The last two parameters are used to define the message on the screen. We leave the discussion of *MessageList* to Chapter 2.

```
cmdName      placeBox_start ()
cmdNumber    CMD_PLACE_BOX
{
  mdlOutput_rscPrintf (MSG_PROMPT, NULL, 0, 2);
  mdlState_startPrimitive (placeBox_firstPoint, placeBox_start, 1, 2);
}
```

Event Types

If we look at the function `placeBox_firstPoint`, it expects a data point, which is passed to it from *mdlState_startPrimitive* . We will save the point and set up the state functions to call, depending on what we receive from the user. The function *mdlState_setFunction* requires two arguments. The first being the event type, and the second is the pointer to the function to execute. The possible values for event types are:

STATE_DATAPOINT	when the user sends a data point.
STATE_RESET	when the user sends a reset.
STATE_KEYIN	when the user sends a keyin.
STATE_COMPLEX_DYNAMICS	generate dynamic display, see below.
STATE_COMMAND_CLEANUP	cleanup current command before another starts.

MDL provides dynamic manipulation of elements. This is the rubber-banding seen on the screen when an element is created, moved or modified. **Simple dynamics** is used when we require dynamic display of one element. **Complex dynamics** is used for more than one element. There is a function, *mdlState_dynamicUpdate*, that we use with simple dynamics.

For complex dynamics we must use *mdlState_setFunction*. To determine how to display the dynamics, MDL executes the user function `generateImage`, and displays the elements in highlight mode. Therefore, the elements are written to screen, but not to disk. We will see how this works when we discuss the dynamics used in PLBOX.

```
Private void      placeBox_firstPoint
(
Dpoint3d     *pt,
int          view
)
{
 /* save first point */
pntP[0] = *pt;

 /* Set the datapoint state function for the second point. */
mdlState_setFunction (STATE_KEYIN,keyinText);
mdlState_setFunction (STATE_DATAPOINT, placeBox_secondPoint);
mdlState_setFunction (STATE_RESET, placeBox_done);
mdlOutput_rscPrintf (MSG_PROMPT, NULL, 0, 3);

mdlState_setFunction (STATE_COMPLEX_DYNAMICS, generateImage);
}
```

As we can see from the function `placeBox_firstPoint` we have established state functions for every possible event. The routine `keyInText` will take the text from the input queue and save it in the variable *textin*.

```
Private void   keyinText ()
{
  if (!*statedata.cmdstring)
     return;
  strncpy(textin, statedata.cmdstring, sizeof(textin));
}
```

The function `generateImage` is of special interest, because it is our routine that is called every time we move the cursor. We have told MDL to use this function, in our dynamic operation, in the line :-

```
mdlState_setFunction(STATE_COMPLEX_DYNAMICS, generateImage) .
```

`generateImage` will place the text string and a bounding box, as well as adjusting the line to the corner of the box.

Element Functions

Below is a list of general element functions, which will operate on a single element. We will discuss the manipulation of complex elements in subsequent chapters.

mdlElement_add	add an element to the file.
mdlElement_append	append an element to the file.
mdlElement_appendAttributes	append attribute data to an existing element.
mdlElement_cnvFromFileFormat	convert an element from external to internal format.
mdlElement_cnvToFileFormat	convert an element from internal to external format.
mdlElement_display	display an element in all views.
mdlElement_displayInSelectedViews	display an element in specified views.
mdlElement_extractAttributes	extract attribute data from an existing element.
mdlElement_getFilePos	return element's file position.
mdlElement_getProperties	return element's property information.
mdlElement_getSymbology	return element's display symbology.
mdlElement_getType	return element's type number.
mdlElement_igdsSize	return the element's size in words.
mdlElement_isFilled	return TRUE if the element is filled.
mdlElement_offset	move the element by an offset distance.
mdlElement_read	read the element from the design file to a buffer.
mdlElement_rewrite	rewrite over an existing element.

mdlElement_setFilePos	set the element's file position.
mdlElement_setProperties	set the element's property information.
mdlElement_setSymbology	set the element's display symbology.
mdlElement_size	return the element's size in bytes.
mdlElement_stripAttributes	strip all attribute data from an existing element.
mdlElement_stroke	stroke an element by converting it into a series of vectors.
mdlElement_transform	transform an element by a transformation matrix.
mdlElement_undoableDelete	delete an element so that UNDO can undelete the element.

Element Creation Functions

MDL provides several functions to create MicroStation displayable elements. These elements are created in memory. Therefore, it is important to write the element to the file, using the function *mdlElement_add*. The element structures are defined in <mselems.h>.

It is good practice to use these functions to create the elements as it isolates the code from subsequent element format changes. This is evident with the two new MicroStation elements, dimension and multi-line, where the detailed element structures are not supplied in <mselems.h>.

The following lists the element creation functions:

mdlArc_create	create an arc element.
mdlArc_createByCenter	create an arc element by a centerpoint and 2 end points.

mdlArc_createByPoints	create an arc element using 3 points.
mdlCell_create	create cell header element.
mdlCircle_createBy3Pts	create circle/ellipse using 3 points.
mdlCone_create	create a cone element.
mdlCone_createRightCylinder	create a right cylinder element.
mdlCurve_create	create a curve element.
mdlCurve_createI	create a curve element, using 32-bit integers.
mdlEllipse_create	create an ellipse element.
mdlLine_create	create a line element.
mdlLine_createI	create a line element, using 32- bit integers.
mdlLineString_create	create a line string, shape or curve element.
mdlLineString_createI	create a line string, shape or curve element, using 32-bit integers.
mdlPointString_create	create a point string element.
mdlText_create	create a text element.
mdlTextNode_create	create a text node element.

To create our text string we will use *mdlText_create*. There is nothing special about the way we create the text string, but when we come to display it, we need to consider dynamic display.

Drawing Modes

When we display an element on the screen with *mdlElement_display,* the possible drawing modes are:

Drawing Mode	Meaning
NORMALDRAW	drawing element in its normal color
ERASE	erase from screen
HILITE	draw element in highlight color
TEMPDRAW	draw temporarily
TEMPERASE	erase temporarily drawn
TEMPROTATE	exclusive-or and halftone
XORDRAW	use exclusive-or
SET_ALLOWBGCOLOR	used on the MAC to draw elements in the same color as the background.

The dynamic routine will temporarily draw our image on the screen and erase it as we move the cursor around. When we accept the position with the second point, the function `placeBox_secondPoint` is activated, because we have previously established this.

```
Private void      placeBox_secondPoint
(
Dpoint3d       *pt,
int            view
)
{
 generateImage(pt , view, NORMALDRAW);
}
```

The function `placeBox_secondPoint` makes a direct call to `generateImage` and passes it the NORMALDRAW option. We will create an orphan cell from our PLBOX elements. Calling *mdlCell_begin* will create the type 2 cell header. Every element placed from here on will be part of that cell. In `generateImage` we can see that a NORMALDRAW will add elements to the DGN file.

```
/* Create Text in dgnBuf for MicroStation Dynamics to display */
mdlText_create (&el, NULL, textin, &pntP[1], NULL, NULL, NULL, NULL);
mdlElement_display (&el, drawMode);
if (drawMode == NORMALDRAW)
{
        cellFilePos=mdlCell_begin("plbox", &origin, NULL, 0);
        mdlElement_add(&el);
}
```

Element Extraction Functions

When we create the text string it is still in DGNBUF. Only when we call *mdlElement_add* will it be inserted into the DGN file. The next step is to place a shape around the text string. To get information on any element we can use one of the many element extraction functions. These functions allow the programmer to retrieve information about the element, without knowing how the element format are stored. Programmers are encouraged to use these functions, to protect their programs from possible future changes in element formats.

The following lists the element extraction functions:

mdlArc_extract	extract arc or ellipse element.
mdlCell_extract	extract cell header information.
mdlCone_extract	extract cone element information.
mdlLinear_extract	extract array of coordinates from LINE, LINESTRING, SHAPE, CONIC, CURVE, MULTILINE, or BSPLINE elements.
mdlLinear_getClosestSegment	find a line segment on a linear element that is closest to a point.
mdlSharedCell_extract	extract information on shared cell instance or its definition.
mdlText_extract	extract text element information.
mdlText_extractShape	extract smallest bounding box around text element.
mdlText_extractString	extract character string from text element.
mdlTextNode_extract	extract text node element information.
mdlTextNode_extractShape	return smallest bounding box around text node.

We will use *mdlText_extractShape* to get the five points of the rectangular box (the first and last points are the same). By setting the fourth argument to TRUE, the bounding box is made larger by the current snap tolerance (same as the SET LOCATE key-in). Note that we did not read the string from the DGN file, as we already have the string in DGNBUF from the last operation.

```
mdlText_extractShape(shapep, NULL, &el, TRUE, view);
mdlShape_create(&el, NULL, shapep, 5, -1);
mdlElement_display (&el, drawMode);
if (drawMode == NORMALDRAW)
        mdlElement_add(&el);
```

The next stage of our program is to correct the leader line to match one of the corners of the box. In figure 1.4, the dotted line indicates the line we would have drawn if we took the points as supplied by the user. With simple geometry we will assign the end point of the line to the appropriate corner point, depending in which quadrant the first point is.

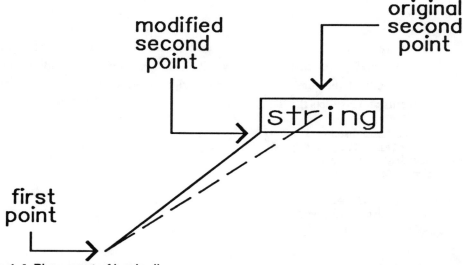

Figure 1.4 Placement of leader line

The arithmetic for our new end point is shown below.

```
if (pntP[0].x < origin.x)
{
    if (pntP[0].y < origin.y)
    {
        pntP[1].x=shapep[0].x;
        pntP[1].y=shapep[0].y;
    } else {
        pntP[1].x=shapep[3].x;
        pntP[1].y=shapep[3].y;
    }
}
else
{
    if (pntP[0].y < origin.y)
    {
        pntP[1].x=shapep[1].x;
        pntP[1].y=shapep[1].y;
    } else {
        pntP[1].x=shapep[2].x;
        pntP[1].y=shapep[2].y;
    }
}
```

Once we have calculated the new end point, we place the line with *mdlLine_create*. We close the cell by calling *mdlCell_end*. This updates the cell header with the number of words in description, the number of component elements and corrects the file pointers.

```
/* place the modified leader line */
mdlLine_create (&el, NULL, pntP);
mdlElement_display (&el, drawMode);
if (drawMode == NORMALDRAW)
{
        mdlElement_add(&el);
        mdlCell_end(cellFilePos);
}
```

Putting together all we have learned, here is the complete listing of our first MDL program, *plbox.mc*.

Optional Disk. No need to type this program in. You can save time by buying the optional disk. You will find an order form at the back of this book.

plbox.mc

```
/*-----------------------------------------------------------------------+
 | Copyright (C) 1991, Mach Dinh-Vu. All Rights Reserved                  |
 | Program   : plbox.mc                                                   |
 | Revision  : 1.0.a                                                      |
 +-----------------------------------------------------------------------+
 | Example MDL function to place a box around                             |
 | a text string with a leader line.                                      |
 +-----------------------------------------------------------------------*/
/*-----------------------------------------------------------------------+
 |    Include Files                                                       |
 +-----------------------------------------------------------------------*/
#include       <mdl.h>           /* system include files */
#include       <global.h>
#include       <mselems.h>
#include       <userfnc.h>
#include       <rscdefs.h>
#include       <tcb.h>
#include       "plbox.h"
/*-----------------------------------------------------------------------+
 |    Private Global variables                                            |
 +-----------------------------------------------------------------------*/
static char  textin[128];
Dpoint3d     pntP[2];

/*-----------------------------------------------------------------------+
 | name         main                                                      |
 +-----------------------------------------------------------------------*/
main()
{
  RscFileHandle    rfHandle;

  /* load our command table */
  if (mdlParse_loadCommandTable (NULL) == NULL)
     mdlOutput_error ("Unable to load command table.");
  mdlResource_openFile (&rfHandle, NULL, FALSE);
  mdlOutput_prompt("Key-in PLACE BOX to execute");
}
/*-----------------------------------------------------------------------+
 | name             generateImage - dynamic function for box.            |
 +-----------------------------------------------------------------------*/
Private int      generateImage
```

```
(
Dpoint3d *pt,
int        view,
int        drawMode
)
{
 MSElementUnion  el;
 Dpoint3d   origin;
 Dpoint3d   shapep[5];
 long       cellFilePos;

 pntP[1] = origin = *pt;

 /* Create Text in dgnBuf for MicroStation Dynamics to display */
 mdlText_create (&el, NULL, textin, &pntP[1], NULL, NULL, NULL, NULL);
 mdlElement_display (&el, drawMode);
 if (drawMode == NORMALDRAW)
 {
  cellFilePos=mdlCell_begin("plbox", NULL, NULL, 0);
  mdlElement_add(&el);
 }
 mdlText_extractShape(shapep, NULL, &el, TRUE, view);
 mdlShape_create(&el, NULL, shapep, 5, -1);
 mdlElement_display (&el, drawMode);
 if (drawMode == NORMALDRAW) mdlElement_add(&el);

 if (pntP[0].x < origin.x)
 {
  if (pntP[0].y < origin.y)
    {
        pntP[1].x=shapep[0].x;
        pntP[1].y=shapep[0].y;
    } else {
        pntP[1].x=shapep[3].x;
        pntP[1].y=shapep[3].y;
    }
 } else {
    if (pntP[0].y < origin.y)
    {
        pntP[1].x=shapep[1].x;
        pntP[1].y=shapep[1].y;
    } else {
        pntP[1].x=shapep[2].x;
        pntP[1].y=shapep[2].y;
    }
 }
 /* Place the modified leader line */
 mdlLine_create (&el, NULL, pntP);
 mdlElement_display (&el, drawMode);
 if (drawMode == NORMALDRAW)
```

```
        {
                mdlElement_add(&el);
                mdlCell_end(cellFilePos);
        }
        return  SUCCESS;
}
/*----------------------------------------------------------------------+
| name         keyinText                                                |
+----------------------------------------------------------------------*/
Private void    keyinText ()
{
    if (!*statedata.cmdstring)
        return;
    strncpy(textin, statedata.cmdstring, sizeof(textin));
}
/*----------------------------------------------------------------------+
| name         placeBox_done                                            |
+----------------------------------------------------------------------*/
Private void    placeBox_done()
{
    mdlOutput_rscPrintf (MSG_PROMPT, NULL, 0, 4);
    mdlState_restartCurrentCommand();
}
/*----------------------------------------------------------------------+
| name         placeBox_secondPoint                                     |
+----------------------------------------------------------------------*/
Private void    placeBox_secondPoint
(
Dpoint3d        *pt,
int             view
)
{
    generateImage(pt , view, NORMALDRAW);
}
/*----------------------------------------------------------------------+
| name         placeBox_firstPoint                                      |
+----------------------------------------------------------------------*/
Private void    placeBox_firstPoint
(
Dpoint3d *pt,
int             view
)
{
    /* save first point */
    pntP[0] = *pt;

    /* Set the datapoint state function for the second point. */
    mdlState_setFunction (STATE_KEYIN,keyinText);
    mdlState_setFunction (STATE_DATAPOINT, placeBox_secondPoint);
    mdlState_setFunction (STATE_RESET, placeBox_done);
```

```
mdlOutput_rscPrintf (MSG_PROMPT, NULL, 0, 3);

/* Setup Rubber Banding function  */
mdlState_setFunction (STATE_COMPLEX_DYNAMICS, generateImage);
}
/*-------------------------------------------------------------------+
| name               placeBox_start                                 |
+-------------------------------------------------------------------*/
cmdName        placeBox_start ()
cmdNumber      CMD_PLACE_BOX
{
  mdlState_startPrimitive (placeBox_firstPoint, placeBox_start, 1, 2);
}
```

Chapter 1 - Summary

Learning a new programming language is always difficult. We believe that the best approach is to launch right into it and look at an example. If by this stage you feel lost, don't be distressed, just remember these points:

- MDL is based on the C programming language.
- MicroStation is a state machine and MDL can take advantage of this by tapping in at the primitive level.
- A state machine means that commands will not run sequentially but parts will be activated depending on events within MicroStation.
- User commands and MicroCSL programs sequence MicroStation commands. MDL can sequence commands also, but its true power is to provide functions to call in response to state transitions.

2 : Compiling MDL programs

In the last chapter we looked at how to write an MDL program, without actually seeing it run. In this chapter, we will discuss the next stage in the development cycle. We will learn how to create command tables. Also, we will look at understanding resource files, compiling, linking and executing our MDL application.

Our MDL source is a set of instructions for MicroStation to perform. It is in ASCII text format. This means that the instructions are readable by us, but not by MicroStation. When we compile our program, it is converted into an object file. This is an intermediate file to link into an executable.

An object file has function calls to MDL pre-defined functions. The linking process will resolve these calls. This creates an **MDL program**. Using the librarian will combine the object, resource and other program files, to produce an **MDL application**. The application is loaded into memory an executed as an **MDL task**.

A very powerful feature of MDL is pre-processor directives. These directives are instructions to the compiler. Therefore we need to understand them before we can proceed.

Pre-processor Directives

Pre-processor directives are part of an MDL program. They are instructions to the compiler, rather than statements that are compiled. Pre-processor directives always begin with a hash symbol (#). We have seen their use in our PLBOX program with *#include* . For example:

```
#include <mdl.h>
```

When the compiler reaches this line, it will read the contents of < mdl.h > into the current file, making it part of our program. Therefore, all of its functions and data definitions are available for use.

Another common use for the directives are constant definitions. The directives assign a constant value to identifier names. When the compiler finds an identifier in the program, the associated value is substituted for the identifier. For example:

```
#define  GRAFIC 1160
```

This is a good method for defining constants, as it uses no memory. Also it makes the program readable and easier to maintain. Consider the example below, where we are updating the type 9 element header with the new graphic group number.

```
.
int      size=1, offset=GRAFIC;
.
.
mdlParams_storeType9Variable(&tcb->graphic,size,offset);
.
.
```

When the compiler scans the file for pre-processor directives, it will replace GRAFIC with 1160.

Conditional Compilation

Pre-processor directives are used also to define conditional compilation. These are instructions to compile a section of code if an identifier is defined. These directives are *#if, #ifdef, #ifndef, #line, #else, #elif, #endif* and *#undef.* The best example of this is a multi-platform development environment, where we need to maintain many different versions of the same program.

```
#if defined (unix)
   short      prompt_color[4];
#else
   short      prompt_color[6];
#endif
```

The above code was taken from < tcb.h > where the data structure will vary, depending on the operating platform. At the start of our program we can put the line:

```
#define unix
```

then *prompt_color* would be an array of 4 shorts. Otherwise it will be an array of 6 shorts. The built-in directives are *mdl, dos, pm386, mc68000, macintosh, vax, unix* and *ip32.*

Compiler directives - #pragma

Pragmas are compiler directives that send special instruction to the compiler. Pragmas are often used instead of compiler options, as they are placed in the source code. The MDL compiler only supports 2, **Version** and **resourceID**.

Version pragma

The pragma **Version** defines the version associated with an MDL program. To use the Version pragma we place the following line in our include file.

```
#pragma Version 4:1:2
```

If we don't specify the version pragma then it defaults to version 4.0.0. The version number must be integers separated by colons (:), if no number is specified, then 0 is assumed.

The value specified with the Version pragma is displayed in the Version field of the MDL Application Detail dialog box. To view the version number of an MDL program, select the MDL Application Detail dialog box as shown below.

resourceID pragma

If we try to put more than one MDL program into a resource file, and none of the programs contains a pragma to change the resource ID, the resource librarian generates the following warning.

```
###Warning: duplicate resource detected -
resourceclass=(0x4D646C49, (Mdll)resourceID=(1296124238, 0x4D41494E,(MAIN))
```

This occurs because both programs have the default resource ID for MDL programs. To avoid getting the warning, we can assign another resource ID to an application by using the **resourceID** pragma. To do this, we place the following statement in our resource source file

```
#pragma resourceID 'plresc'
```

#pragma and *resourceID* must appear as specified. The 'plresc' value may be replaced by any integer expression.

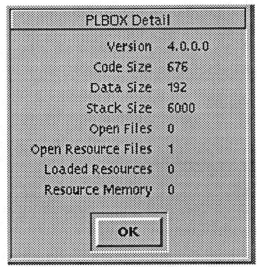

Figure 2.1 MDL Application Detail dialog box

The Development Cycle

To write an MDL program, the development cycle is more involved than that for a typical C program application. We need to consider the command table, resource file and dialog box. Here, we will discuss the development cycle for our PLBOX program which does not have dialog boxes. Dialog boxes are discussed in detail, in the next chapter.

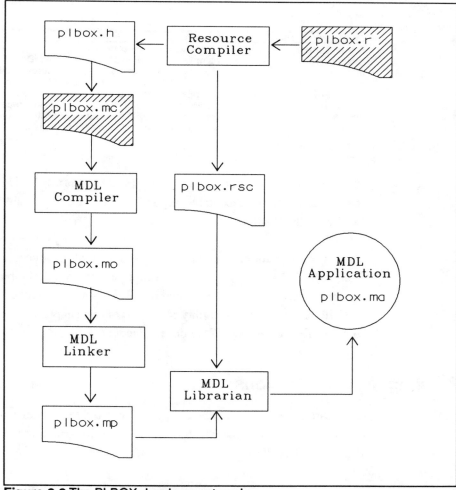

Figure 2.2 The PLBOX development cycle

Development Cycle - Overview

We can break the cycle into 4 main areas. Creating and **editing** the source code with a text editor. **Compiling** the source code to generate an object file. **Linking** the object files. Building the application with the MDL **Librarian**. Tools are used at each stage of the development cycle. These tools are found in *ustation**mdl**bin*\ (for DOS machines). On the UNIX machines, these files are in */usr/ip32/mstation/mdl/bin*. The text editor is any editor that can produce an unformatted ASCII file.

Development Tool	Description
Any text editor	create MDL source code files.
mcomp.exe	compile MDL source files and create MDL object files.
mlink.exe	link object files and create MDL resource/application files.
mlib.exe	create and manipulate libraries of MDL object files.
rcomp.exe	compile resource source file into MDL resource files.
rdump.exe	display the contents of resource files in a readable form.
rlib.exe	create and manipulate libraries of MDL resource files.
rsctype.exe	compiles C type definitions into source files for rcomp.exe

As we can see from Figure 2.2, there are several stages involved in getting from the source file to the executable application. We are responsible for creating the files in the shaded boxes.

There is a program maintenance utility *bmake* that produces an application from `makefiles`. The use of *bmake* simplifies program development. Usually we copy an existing `makefile`, and modify it for the particular development. We will discuss the *bmake* utility at the end of this chapter. For now we need to understand each stage of the development cycle.

Creating MDL applications

To create the source file *plbox.mc*, you can use a text editor and type in the program found in the first chapter. To save time you can purchase the optional disk, which has all the programs used in this book.

Compiling MDL applications

The MDL compiler is a software program that makes sure the MDL source file has not violated any rules of MDL. If the file does not contain syntax or semantic errors, the MDL compiler creates an intermediate file with the extension ".mo". If there is an error the compiler generates a syntax error. Errors in program logic are not found by the compiler.

The command line syntax for the MDL compiler is as follows:

        mcomp [-flag, -flag, ...] input-file

where `input-file` is our source code. If no extension is specified, then the compiler will append ".mc" to the filename.

where `-flag` is optional. Valid flags are:-

-c   Compile only. Used to tell *mcomp* to compile only, and do not
            automatically link. Without this option, a UNIX workstation will
            continue with the link stage, if the compile was successful.
            On PCs, the link is never done automatically.

-d*name*=*value*
            Used to define *name* with a *value*. The name is found in the
            preprocessor *#define* statement.

-g   dump all debugging information to the output file.

-p   display preprocessor output.

-v   verbose, show compiler progress.

-o*filename*
            object output filename. If not specified, then the object file
            will have the extension ".mo" added to the input filename prefix.

-i*dir*   add extra directories to search for the include files.
            The MDL compiler can support up to 40 include directories.

The Operating System environment variable MDL_COMP defines the command line arguments to the compiler. It is used to specify which directories to search for the include files. For example, the following line in *autoexec.bat* (for DOS) will specify two directories to search for the include files.

```
set MDL_COMP = -ic:\ustation\mdl\include  -ic:\include
```

On the UNIX workstations the command line is:

```
MDL_COMP=-i/usr/ip32/mstation/include
```

In practice we don't use MDL_COMP as the search path for the include files. This is better done using `makefiles`, more about this latter. To compile our PLBOX program we would use the following command line:-

```
mcomp -c -v  plbox
```

The above line will compile (-c) *plbox.mc* showing the compiler's progress (-v), and create the object file *plbox.mo* in the current directory.

Creating an Application Command Table

We briefly touched on resource file and command table in the last chapter. In this section we will discuss these two features of MDL in detail. Every command table file must contain the two include files < rscdefs.h > and < cmdclass.h >.

```
#include <rscdefs.h>
#include <cmdclass.h>
```

To create a command table, we first need to build a structure called *Table* that will define the hierarchy of our command syntax. The syntax for the *Table* structure is shown on the following page.

```
Table <tableid>=
{
  <number>,<subtableid>,<commandclass>,<options>,"<commandword>",
}
```

tableid   is a 32-bit unsigned integer. The main or root command
                 word table must be assigned a *tableid* of 1.

number   defines the command number. This number can be from
                 1 to 255 inclusive, for the first three words in a command,
                 and 1 to 15 inclusive for the last 2 words in the command.
                 There can be a maximum of 5 words in the command.

subtableid   this specifies the subtable for the next word in the command.
                 If there are no subtables then use the #define CT_NONE.

commandclass   this specifies the command class. The command class is
                 predefined and can be one of the following:

PLACEMENT	1
VIEWING	2
FENCE	3
PARAMETERS	4
LOCKS	5
USERCOMMAND	6
MANIPULATION	7
SHOW	8
PLOT	9
NEWFILE	10
MEASURE	11
INPUT	12
CELLIB	13
FILEDESIGN	14
COMPRESS	15
REFERENCE	16
DATABASE	17
DIMENSION	18
LOCATE	19
TUTORIAL	20
WORKINGSET	21
ELEMENTLIST	22
UNDO	23
SUBPROCESS	24
VIEWPARAM	25
VIEWIMMEDIATE	26

The other class of interest is INHERIT, which simply means to inherit the last command class as we parse through the command hierarchy. There are 63 possible command classes. The first 48 classes are reserved for MicroStation, and the last 15 are for application use. Going back to our PLBOX example we can see that PLACEMENT is the most appropriate command class for our primitive.

options   The possible options are NONE, DEF, REQ, TRY and CMDSTR(n). These options can be joined with an OR(|), for example DEF | TRY.

DEF   (default) specifies the default value for a particular table.
REQ   (required) tells the command parser that a selection from a subtable is required.
TRY   (try parse) this option will try to parse a value in the subtable. If it does not match then it passes the non-matching portion onto the application program. An example of this is ACTIVE STYLE 3, where the 3 is passed to the application program.
CMDSTR(n)   every time the command is executed this macro will display the string *n* in the *MessageList*.

Looking below at the resource file *plbox.r* (which contains the command table) we can see that the root command word is PLACE, and it belongs to the command class PLACEMENT. The subtable is CT_PLACE and this is compulsory because we have told it so with the option REQ. If the second word is BOX then the CMDSTR will display the first string (1) in the *MessageList*.

```
#include "rscdefs.h"
#include "cmdclass.h"

#define     CT_NONE        0
#define     CT_MAIN        1
#define     CT_PLACE       2

Table    CT_MAIN =
{ /*     Subtable,   CommandClass,  Options,      CommandWord */
  { 1,  CT_PLACE,    PLACEMENT,     REQ,          "PLACE" },
};

Table    CT_PLACE =
{ /*     Subtable,   CommandClass,     Options,            CommandWord */
  { 1,  CT_NONE,     INHERIT,          NONE | CMDSTR (1),  "BOX" },
};
```

Understanding MessageList

MessageList is a pre-defined resource class used to display messages on the screen. The reason for breaking messages from the source program is to simplify maintenance and enhance portability. For example, we may wish to port the application to another speaking language. Using *MessageList* we can make the changes easily, and recompile the resource file rather than the whole application. The syntax for the *MessageList* structure is as follows:

```
MessageList <messageid>=
{
        <messagenumber>, "<message>",
}
```

messageid	is a unique number identifying the list.
messagenumber	is a unique number and must be in ascending order.
message	is the string containing the message.

Combining the *messageid* with a *messagenumber* uniquely identifies a message in the list. Looking at the message list in *plbox.r*, we can see that the following MDL command will display the string "Define start point" in the prompt field.

```
mdlOutput_rscPrintf (MSG_PROMPT, NULL, 0, 2);
```

The *MessageList* used in the PLBOX application is shown here:

```
MessageList 0 =
{
  {
     { 0, "" },
     { 1, "MDL Place Box" },
     { 2, "Define start point" },
     { 3, "Define Box position" },
     { 4, "PlBox complete" },
  }
};
```

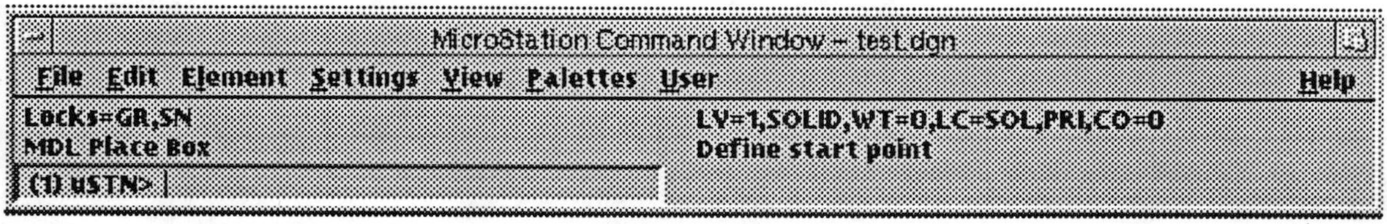

```
+                        MicroStation Command Window - test.dgn                        []
File  Edit  Element  Settings  View  Palettes  User                                   Help
Locks=GR,SN                            LV=1,SOLID,WT=0,LC=SOL,PRI,CO=0
MDL Place Box                          Define start point
(1) uSTN> |
```

Figure 2.3 Prompt display as we start PLBOX

Compiling Resources

File naming convention for the resource source file is to use the extension ".r".
The default extension for the compiled output file is ".rsc".

Command line syntax for the MDL compiler is as follows:

    rcomp [-flag, -flag, ...] input-file

where `input-file` is our resource file. If no extension is specified then the
compiler will append ".r" to the filename.

where `-flag` is optional. Valid flags are:-

-d*name* = *value*
> Used to define *name* with a *value*. The *name* is found in the pre-
> processor #*define* statement.

-h
> generate the header file, usually with the extension ".h". The header
> file has the format of a C include file.

-ho*filename*
> specify the header *filename*.

-i*dir*   add extra directories to search for the include files.

-o*filename*
> object output compiler filename. If not specified then the object file
> will have the extension ".mo" added to the input filename prefix.

-p   display preprocessor output.

-v   verbose, show compiler progress.

To compile our resource file *plbox.r*, we will use the following command line:

rcomp -h -v plbox

The above line will compile *plbox.r* showing the compiler's progress (-v) and
create the header file (-h) *plbox.h* in the current directory.

The contents of the generated *plbox.h* are shown here.

```
#define CMD_PLACE          0x01000000  /* PLACEMENT */
#define CMD_PLACE_BOX      0x01010000  /* PLACEMENT */
```

We have seen the CMD_PLACE_BOX in our source program. When we enter PLACE BOX at the uSTN> prompt, MicroStation generates a command number. By searching a list of command numbers, associated with the application, it determines the function to call. In our case the function is placeBox_start as shown below.

```
cmdName      placeBox_start ()
cmdNumber    CMD_PLACE_BOX
```

Linking MDL applications

The MDL linker combines the object files into a program file, which can be used as an application file. Alternatively, using the resource librarian, it can be combined with other resource files.

The command line syntax for the MDL linker is as follows:

```
mlink  [-flag, -flag, ...]  input-file
```

where input-file is our object file or library file. If no extension is specified then the linker will append ".mo" to the filename.

where -flag is optional. Valid flags are:-

-a*filename*   specify the output application filename. If none is specified then ".ma" is appended to the prefix of the first filename.

-g or -gd   dump all debugging information to the output file.

-gn   provide enough debugging for a meaningful message. This is the default if the -g flag is omitted.

-go   omit all debugging information.

-ml   load map with labels sorted by location.

-mn   load map with labels sorted by name.

-s[*stack size*] specify a stack size. If none is specified, the linker will
                allocate one. If the stack size is too small, then a stack over-
                flow will cause the MDL application to abort. If the stack
                size is too large, then memory is wasted.

-t[*taskID*]   specify a *taskID* for the application. Each program must have
                a unique *task ID* if it is to be merged with other programs.

-v   verbose, show linker progress.

Using the Resource Librarian

The Resource Librarian combines the resource files (".rsc" files) with the
program file (".mp") to form a finished application. In developing an MDL
application it is possible not to use any resources, which in turn would not
require the Resource Librarian. The development cycle then would stop at the
link stage.

The command line syntax for the Resource Librarian is as follows:

```
rlib  [-flag, -flag, ...]  input-files
```

where `input-files` are our resource files, or program files.

where `-flag` is optional. Valid flags are:-

-o*filename*   specify the output filename. If not specified then the output
                file will have the extension ".rsc" added to the filename.

-t <*class*>   combine a particular *resourceclass*.

-r <*resourceID*> combine a particular *resourceID*.

-v   verbose, show librarian progress.

In the PLBOX example, the command line for the resource librarian is as
follows:

```
rlib -od:\ustation\mdlapps\plbox.ma \
d:\ustation\mdl\examples\objects\plbox.rsc \
d:\ustation\mdl\examples\objects\plbox.mp
```

The bmake Utility

A single application program may have several include files, several resource files and several source files. If we were to modify one of these files, we may need to recompile other files. As there are dependencies between these files, it is important to make sure that they are all up to date.

bmake is a program maintenance utility which simplifies the process of applying changes to our programs. There is a *bmake* description file (the `makefile`) that tells which files a program uses, and the specific relationships between those files. *bmake* is a powerful utility to manage the development cycle, and therefore we will use it throughout this book.

bmake works by comparing the dates and times of two sets of files. These are known as target and dependent source files. The target is the file to create from the source file.

The Makefile format

The `makefile` is a text file defining dependencies between source files and target files. When we run *bmake*, it will read the supplied `makefile`. The `makefile` consists of blocks. These blocks list a target, the source, and the command that builds the target.

A typical block may look like the section of code shown here:

```
plbox.mo : plbox.mc
  d:\ustation\mdl\bin\mcomp\
  -c\
  -i\ustation\mdl\include\
  -i\progmdl\disk\plbox\
  -oplbox.mo
  plbox.mc
```

We can see that the target file is *plbox.mo*, which is dependent on the source file *plbox.mc*. If the date of the target file is older than that of the source file (that is, we have modified the source file), then a build command will compile the source file.

Before we use *bmake*, we have to set up the MS environment variable, and look at the file *\ustation\mdl\include\mdl.mki* . To set up the MS environment variable, we can use the following command at the DOS prompt, or insert it into *autoexec.bat*.

```
SET MS=D:\USTATION
```

A listing of the *mdl.mki* file can be found in Appendix A. There are several important lines in this file which are discussed below.

bmake Macros

Macros are a shorthand notation for an expression or group of instructions. *bmake* macros are case-specific, and are executed when it finds "$(*macro*)" in the makefile (where *macro* is the macro name).

Pre-defined Macros

bmake supports the pre-defined macros shown below. When *bmake* sees one of these macros it will replace it with the appropriate file. The appropriate operating system macros *msdos, IP32, unix, macintosh*, and *vax* are pre-defined for us to use.

$@	substitute with the current target file
$?	substitute all dependency files that are newer than the target file
$=	substitute with the newest dependency file
$<	substitute the current dependency file
$*	substitute the base filename of the target file
$%	substitute the directory of the first dependency

Defining Macros

User macros are defined in three ways.

1. In the body of the `makefile`
2. From a DOS environment variable. The MS environment variable is an example of this method.
3. In the *bmake* command line option -d.

To define our macro in the body of the `makefile` we would use the following format:

```
macro = definition
```

For example:

```
msg = |Building $@  from  $=
```

We have defined a macro *msg* , which will display (|) the message "Building *target file* from *source file*". When *bmake* scans through our `makefile` and it sees $(msg), then it will display the above message.

The second way to define our macro, in the `makefile`, is to concatenate a definition to an existing macro, using the following format.

```
macro + definition
```

Defining Macro paths.

Macros are used to define search paths. Consider the following three macros in *mdl.mki*. The macro $(MS) is substituted with *d:\ustation,* therefore we have defined the macro *mdlapps* with *d:\ustation\mdlapps*. Everywhere there is an occurrence of $(mdlapps) then the path will be substituted.

```
mdlapps      = $(MS)/mdlapps/
toolsPath    = $(MS)/mdl/bin/
src          = $(MS)/mdl/examples/
```

Build Commands

These are instructions to build the target file from the dependent files. If there is an error during the build, (that is, a compile or link error) then *bmake* will terminate. If there is no build command for a dependency, then *bmake* will use a pre-defined rule. This is very important. We will see how this works in the next section.

There are several control characters in a build command which have special meaning. These are:-

—	do not terminate if this command returns an error. This is often used to signify an argument.
@	do not echo.
|	echo the line.
>*filename*	this is a redirection of all lines in the `makefile` to the *filename*, until the < sign. This is used to build a link file.
~ current	print the current time.
~ time	use to "touch" the target file with the time of the newest dependency file. This is usually the last line in the build command, to make sure that the files are up to date.

Dependencies

A dependency is a relationship between files, by which modification of one file will mean the rebuilding of the target file. The format of a dependency is:

```
target1 target2 ... targetn : dep1 dep2 ... depn
        [buildcommands]
```

For example:

```
$(objectDir)plbox.rsc    : $(baseDir)plbox.r
```

If any of the *dep* files are newer than the *target* files then the *buildcommand* is executed. If the *buildcommand* is not specified, then one of the predefined inference rules is used.

Inference Rules

Inference Rules are templates that define how the target file is built from the source file, with a given extension. The general format is:

`.[dir1;dir2;...;dirn]source.target:`

For example, the following inference rule tells how to build a ".ma" file, using a ".mo" file.

```
.mo.ma:
        $(msg)
        > $(objectDir)temp.cmd
        -a$@
        $(linkOpts) $%$*.mo
        <
        $(linkCmd) @$(objectDir)temp.cmd
        ~time
```

The most important thing to remember is that the source and target are both file extensions. The *dir1;dir2;...;dirn* are optional. If not specified, the files are searched for in the current directory. The macros $(linkOpts) and $(linkCmd) are both defined in *mdl.mki*.

Pre-defined Inference Rules

The file *mdl.mki* provides pre-defined inference rules that perform these common development tasks.

.mc.mo	compile the ".mc" source file and create an object file ".mo".
.mo.ma	link the object file ".mo" and create an application file ".ma".
.mt.r	read a type file ".mt" and generate a resource source file ".r".
.r.rsc	compile the resource source file ".rsc".
.r.h	build the command include file ".h".

Conditional compilation

bmake supports conditional compilation in the `makefile` by excluding, or including, sections of the `makefile`. The valid conditionals are:

%include   include file as if it is part of the current `makefile`
%ifdef   if the macro exists, include subsequent lines
%ifndef   if macro does not exist, include subsequent lines
%else/%elif   use with %ifdef and %ifndef
%endif   close an %ifdef block

For example:

```
%ifdef msdos
.c.obj:
  $(msg)
  $(CCompCmd) $%$*.c -ob $@
  ~time
%endif
```

The best way of understanding a `makefile` is to look at *plbox.mke*. The first part of the *plbox.mke* is self-explanatory, we are defining search paths for our files.

plbox.mke

```
#----------------------------------------------------------------
# PLBOX MDL Make File
#----------------------------------------------------------------
%include $(MS)/mdl/include/mdl.mki

#----------------------------------------------------------------
# Define constants specific to this example
#----------------------------------------------------------------
progmdl      = d:/progmdl/disk/
baseDir      = $(progmdl)plbox/
objectDir    = $(mdlexample)objects/
privateInc   = $(baseDir)

plboxObjs    = $(objectDir)plbox.mo
plboxRscs    = $(objectDir)plbox.rsc \
                 $(objectDir)plbox.mp
     .
     .
     .
```

The hash symbol (#) tells *bmake* to ignore the rest of the line and treat it as a comment. The backslash symbol (\) tells *bmake* that the line continues to the next line. To avoid the confusion with the backslash as the DOS directory path, *bmake* uses the forward slash (/) to specify paths.

The next step is to define the dependencies. We have not specified build commands for the three lines below, so *bmake* will use the default inference rules, found in *mdl.mki,* for the build command.

```
$(privateInc)plbox.h       : $(baseDir)plbox.r
$(objectDir)plbox.rsc      : $(baseDir)plbox.r
$(objectDir)plbox.mo       : $(baseDir)plbox.mc
```

In writing our own build commands we will be putting the arguments for the link command in *temp.cmd*.

```
$(objectDir)plbox.mp             : $(plboxObjs)
        $(msg)
        > $(objectDir)temp.cmd
        -a$@
        -s6000
        $(linkOpts)
        $(plboxObjs)
        <
        $(linkCmd) @$(objectDir)temp.cmd
        ~time
```

The contents of *temp.cmd* for the link command are shown here.

```
-ad:\ustation\mdl\examples\objects\plbox.mp
-s6000
d:\ustation\mdl\examples\objects\plbox.mo
```

The same is done when the resource files are combined with the program file, to produce the application file.

```
$(mdlapps)plbox.ma               : $(plboxRscs)
        $(msg)
        > $(objectDir)temp.cmd
        -o$@
        $(plboxRscs)
        <
        $(rscLibCmd) @$(objectDir)temp.cmd
        ~time
```

Executing bmake

The command line syntax for the *bmake* utility is as follows:

```
bmake   [-flag -flag ...]   makefile
```

where `makefile` is our dependent description file. If no extension is specified then *bmake* will append ".mke" to the filename.

where **-flag** is optional and can be one of the following:

-a   rebuild all files and ignore dependencies.

-i   ignore errors and continue with *bmake* on error.

-l   used to list the target, before executing the build command.

-n   display the build commands, but do not execute them.

-m   continue even if there are missing dependent files.

-p   print macros as defined.

-s   in silent mode, do not print the build commands as they are executed.

-t   do not use the build command, but set the date of the target file to the date of the newest dependent file.

-w   stop on warnings and errors. Usually *bmake* will only stop on errors.

-d*macro* define a macro. This is the third of the three methods used to define a macro.

Now we are ready to run our makefile. At the DOS prompt, enter :

bmake -a plbox

and this is the output.

```
MicroStation Resource Compiler 4.0
   Generating header file (d:\progmdl\disk\plbox\plbox.h) ... done.
MicroStation Resource Compiler 4.0
Bentley Systems Make Utility. Version 4.2h, 1989-90
Sat Mar 16 13:11:11 1991

[== Building d:\progmdl\disk\plbox\plbox.h,
            (d:\progmdl\disk\plbox\plbox.r) ==]
 \ustation\mdl\bin\rcomp @\ustation\mdl\examples\objects\temp.cmd

[== Building \ustation\mdl\examples\objects\plbox.rsc,
            (d:\progmdl\disk\plbox\plbox.r) ==]
 \ustation\mdl\bin\rcomp @\ustation\mdl\examples\objects\temp.cmd

[== Building \ustation\mdl\examples\objects\plbox.mo,
            (d:\progmdl\disk\plbox\plbox.mc) ==]
 \ustation\mdl\bin\mcomp @\ustation\mdl\examples\objects\temp.cmd
MicroStation Development Language Compiler 4.0

[== Building \ustation\mdl\examples\objects\plbox.mp,
            (\ustation\mdl\examples\objects\plbox.mo) ==]
 \ustation\mdl\bin\mlink @\ustation\mdl\examples\objects\temp.cmd
MicroStation Development Language Linker 4.0

[== Building \ustation\mdlapps\plbox.ma,
            (\ustation\mdl\examples\objects\plbox.rsc) ==]
 \ustation\mdl\bin\rlib @\ustation\mdl\examples\objects\temp.cmd
Stack size = 6000.
MicroStation Resource Librarian 4.0

Sat Mar 16 13:11:56 1991, elapsed time: 0:45
```

We will create a *seed.mke* file, so that we can use it to create future makefiles. This seed file will be restricted to applications that do not use the dialog box user interface.

To create a new makefile, first take a copy of *seed.mke*. Using your text editor make a global change, substituting your new application name for all occurrences of 'seed'.

seed.mke

```
#----------------------------------------------------------------------
#         SEED MDL Make File
#----------------------------------------------------------------------
%include $(MS)/mdl/include/mdl.mki


#----------------------------------------------------------------------
#         Define constants specific to this seed application
#----------------------------------------------------------------------
progmdl          = d:/progmdl/disk/
baseDir          = $(progmdl)seed/
objectDir        = $(mdlexample)objects/
privateInc       = $(baseDir)

seedObjs = $(objectDir)seed.mo
seedRscs         = $(objectDir)seed.rsc \
                        $(objectDir)seed.mp

$(privateInc)seed.h      : $(baseDir)seed.r

$(objectDir)seed.rsc     : $(baseDir)seed.r

$(objectDir)seed.mo      : $(baseDir)seed.mc

$(objectDir)seed.mp          : $(seedObjs)
        $(msg)
        > $(objectDir)temp.cmd
        -a$@
        -s6000
        $(linkOpts)
        $(seedObjs)
        <
        $(linkCmd) @$(objectDir)temp.cmd
        ~time

$(mdlapps)seed.ma            : $(seedRscs)
        $(msg)
        > $(objectDir)temp.cmd
        -o$@
        $(seedRscs)
        <
        $(rscLibCmd) @$(objectDir)temp.cmd
        ~time
```

Executing MDL applications

To execute our MDL program we must load the program, from our application, into MicroStation. An application can have more than one program. When a program is loaded, MDL will create a task. When the program is unloaded, the task is destroyed.

When MDL tries to load an application, it will search for the file with the extension ".ma", in the directory defined by MS_EXE and then MS_MDL. If it cannot find the files then it will search for them, using the extension ".rsc", in the same directories.

If you are using the *bmake* utility, you may notice that the MDL application (.ma) is created in the directory *ustation\mdlapps*. This is the default MDL application directory, defined by MS_MDL.

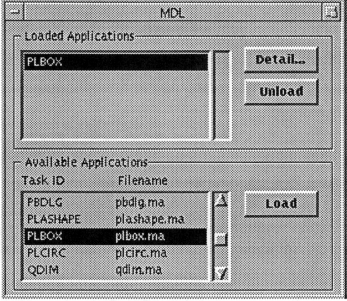

Figure 2.4 Load MDL applications

To load any MDL application we need to be inside a DGN file. We then enter the following:

MDL LOAD *application name*

where *application name* is the MDL application. In our example we would keyin the following:

MDL LOAD *plbox*

We can abbreviate the above line to MDL L *plbox*. Also, we can load the MDL application by selecting the USER palette, and then the MDL Application dialog box (refer to Figure 2.4). MDL can load an application using several other methods also, which are covered in Chapter 8.

The PLBOX program will start executing from the `main` function, loading the command table and initializing variables, so that MicroStation knows about our application.

When we write an application that uses dialog boxes, the `main` function has to publish data structures for the dialog manager, and our application. Also, it needs to set up functions to execute when the application is unloaded. More about this in the next chapter.

Running MDL applications

Above, we have only installed PLBOX. To run it, enter PLACE BOX at the uSTN > prompt.

MDL provides another method of running an application through the command line:

MDL COMMAND *cmdName*

where *cmdName* is the command handler function. In our example, this function is `placeBox_start`. We will not use this method of running the MDL application. Executing the application is better served with command tables.

The Debugger

With the debugger, we have a very powerful tool in developing MDL applications. This is why we have decided to introduce it early in this book.

With traditional programming, it is easy to follow the sequential nature of the code. To debug these programs, we only need several well-positioned *printf* statements and away we go. All this has changed with MDL, due to the event driven nature of the language. Without the debugger it is very difficult, if not impossible, to follow an MDL program. This is because we are never too sure which state we are working in.

The debugger commands are discussed below. These commands are not case sensitive. However, the variable names, passed to these commands, are case sensitive.

The **STEP** facility, of the debugger, steps through our program and executes each line. We can step single lines, or multiple lines, and see the application run.

step/into	will step the debugger into a called function, otherwise the debugger will execute just at the top level.
step/over	will activate the debugger next time a new line of code is executed from the current function.
step/from	will activate the debugger next time an instruction is executed in the function that called the current function.
step/ <count>	execute the number of times specified by count before returning control to the debugger. This is useful in loops, where we can tell the loop, to execute for a certain number of times.

At any stage we can enter a variable name, and the debugger will **DISPLAY** the contents. The DISPLAY command can display the data in **/char, /short, /long, /double** or **/string**, regardless of the implied data type. For numeric data types (all the above excluding /string) the output format can be specified in **/HEX, /OCTAL** or **/DECIMAL**. The argument for the DISPLAY command must be a pointer.

If we are not sure of what variables are defined, then the **SYMBOLS** command will display all known **/functions, /variables,** and **/structures.** For example, the command 'SYM/F/V pla' will display all functions and variables starting with 'pla'.

We can establish a **BREAKPOINT,** which pauses program execution and returns control to the debugger, when the specified line or function name is reached. For example, to set a breakpoint at line 237 of function main we use 'BR main 237'. To remove the breakpoint, we can use BR/DEL, which will prompt for confirmation. We can set the break point also, at a specified interval, with the command /< count >. Here, the debugger will break when it reaches this number.

The break facility can be applied to variables with the **WATCH** facility. This will pause program execution when a variable is modified. There are limitations with the WATCH command, as it only applies to the PC version of MicroStation. We can set up to 4 watch points and each watches one byte.

Once the execution of an application is paused, we can restart execution with the **GO** command. It will run then until another BREAKPOINT, or the program completes.

Other debugging facilities include the **CALLS** command, which displays the history of functions called, to reach the current function. The /< count > option will display only the number of calls to get to the current function.

The **MEMORY** command will display the starting address of the memory used by the application. The **TYPE** command allows us to list any number of lines forward or backward from the current position. The /< count > option will type out the specified number of lines.

Debugging setup

The debugger allows us to step through each line of source and see what it does in our design file. This is an extremely powerful feature, but it means that we need a text screen and a graphic screen active at the same time.

Since the Intergraph workstation is a multi-tasking platform, it will write the text to its own window. For PC systems using a single screen, MDL will spawn a DOS window when it needs to write to a text screen. The DOS window is actually a graphic screen, therefore it is slow in writing text. Also, it takes up screen real estate, leaving less room to work with.

A good solution is to purchase a second (mono) monitor. For example, we may have a VGA (or EGA) monitor, and a low cost mono monitor. We configure MicroStation for a single VGA monitor. Before entering MicroStation, at the DOS prompt, we enter MODE MONO. This will switch screen output to the mono screen. If we enter a design file through MicroStation, we notice that the graphic screen output goes to the VGA monitor. This happens because DOS uses different memory areas for the mono screen, and the VGA screen. Here, we have told DOS to use the mono screen, and MicroStation to use the VGA screen. MicroStation does not check to see what DOS is doing, it writes the graphics to the VGA portion of memory. For this reason we cannot have a combination of VGA and EGA screens, because both use the same memory location.

When we leave MicroStation, we can return DOS to the color screen by typing MODE CO80.

Compiling with Debug

To build the debug information into our application we need to tell *bmake* to compile and link with debug on.   This is done with the -g option at the command line. For example,

bmake -g plbox.

We can specify the debug option in the makefile by defining debug before the call to *mdl.mki*.

```
debug = 1
%include $(MS)/mdl/include/mdl.mki
```

If we don't specify debug, then we cannot check the contents of the variables.

Using the Debugger

Once we have successfully compiled and linked with debugging on, we are ready to debug our application. The debugger needs access to our source file, because it will display each line as it is executed. We can define where our source file resides by setting the environment variable MS_DBGSOURCE with the path. For example, if our source files are in the directory *c:\progmdl\disk\plbox*, we put the following line in *uconfig.dat*:

```
MS_DBGSOURCE=c:\progmdl\disk\plbox\
```

The most efficient way is to make our source directory the current directory, and then call MicroStation. This way we need not concern ourselves with environment variables, especially when working on more than one application. When we are at the mdb> prompt, we can push to the operating system with the ! (exclamation mark). Then we can change directory to where the source file resides. To return to the debugger, we enter **exit**.

Loading the debugger

Assuming we have a two monitor setup as discussed previously, we enter MODE MONO at the DOS prompt. We have now switched to the mono screen. We then enter graphics through MicroStation. At the uSTN> prompt we load up our application with debugging by using the following command:

MDL LOAD DEBUG *application name*

where *application name* is the MDL application. In our example we would key in the following:

MDL LOAD DEBUG *plbox*

We can abbreviate this to:

MDL L D *plbox*

We should get the mdb> prompt on our mono screen. We can start stepping through the program by entering **STEP**. The debugger will display the source line before it is executed. Therefore, to see what the line does, we hit return. The debugger remembers the last command (in this case STEP), and a carriage return will echo and execute it. Also, we can use the up arrow as last command recall, and then hit return.

At any stage in the debugger, we can enter a variable name to see the contents. Don't fall into the trap of seeing the variable name in the source code, and then inquiring as to its contents. It will be incorrect as the line has not been executed. Remember that the debugger has only displayed the line. We need to be at the next line before we know that the debugger has executed the previous line.

After we step through the `main` function. We return control to MicroStation. If we now enter PLACE BOX at the uSTN> prompt this will execute the MDL program, and we are placed back into the debugger. We are now at the function `placeBox_start`. To explain how useful the debugger is, and the event driven concept, we have slightly modified the function by adding the statement :

```
mdlOutput_message("Select position");
```

Our function now looks like:

```
/*------------------------------------------------------------+
| name          placeBox_start (modified)                     |
+------------------------------------------------------------*/
cmdName        placeBox_start()
cmdNumber      CMD_PLACE_BOX
{
  mdlState_startPrimitive (placeBox_firstPoint, placeBox_start,1 ,2);
  mdlOutput_message("Select position");
}
```

Stepping through, notice that *mdlState_startPrimitive* has established a function to handle an event (in this case a datapoint). The next step displays the message "Select position", in the message field. This is out of line with the traditional top down programming technique. One would normally expect one entry and one exit point to a function. The event driven concept means that the state function has established a "middle".

Many programmers have difficulty understanding the event-driven nature of MicroStation. When we use any of the *mdlState_* functions, we have established "handles" to process the events. The more state functions we use, the more events we can handle, hence the more entry points into our MDL program. This stresses the importance of the debugger. Without it, it would be impossible to follow the flow of an event-driven software.

Displaying variable contents

When we display the contents of a variable, we must be sure that we have asked the debugger to display the information that we want. The debugger has a built in C expression interpreter. It will try to evaluate the expression, and perform any assignment we have requested. For example, if we are looping through the program and decide to change loop counter *i* by entering:

```
mdb> i = 5
```

the *i* will have a new value of 5, and the loop will continue with the new value.

When we are displaying variable contents and we get something like 0x126678, we know immediately that we have displayed the address of the variable, and not the contents.

If we wish to display the contents of a text string, then typing the variable name into the debugger will display a character per line. We can stop the display by hitting CTRL-C. This will return us to the mdb > prompt.

Causes of Errors

Syntax Errors

Program errors are broken into syntax or semantic errors and run-time errors. The compiler will trap syntax errors but not run-time errors. The MDL syntax is based on C, therefore we can check syntax errors against a C programming book.

Run-time Errors

Run-time errors are often caused by an error in logic. This is where the debugger can help. By stepping through the program we can verify that the program is doing what we want it to do.

Pointer Errors

Even when our logic is correct we may get pointer errors. MDL makes extensive use of pointers, and incorrect use often will result in the machine locking up. The only way to regain control is to reboot our machine. When the Unix workstations boots, the operating system will automatically do an integrity check on all unclosed files. With the DOS machine we need to run CHKDSK/F. This will create any unclosed files with the extension ".chk" in the root directory. We can delete these files.

When we get a message like "bad memory access", we know that we have passed it a value, instead of an address.

Chapter 2 - Summary

In this chapter we saw the complete development cycle of an MDL application. We were introduced to many supporting tools available with MDL. We suggest that you learn how to use *bmake* and the debugger. Any serious software development will required extensive use of these tools. It is important that you understand them, before proceeding further with MDL.

In the first two chapters we discussed MDL programming basics. If you have problems understanding the C side of MDL, then stop, and consult a C programming book. For the rest of the book, we will assume that you are a competent C programmer.

3 : MDL Dialog Box

In this chapter we will add a dialog box interface to the PLACE BOX program from the previous chapter. We will call this application PBDLG, and the result is shown in Figure 3.1.

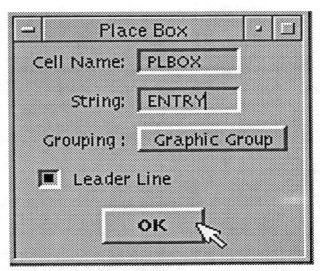

Figure 3.1 PBDLG dialog box

The Development Cycle

Typically, the development cycle for applications using dialog boxes, as shown in Figure 3.2, is very involved. This stresses the importance of the *bmake* utility, and its ability to maintain and update all files associated with an application. In Figure 3.2, we are responsible for creating the files with the box shaded.

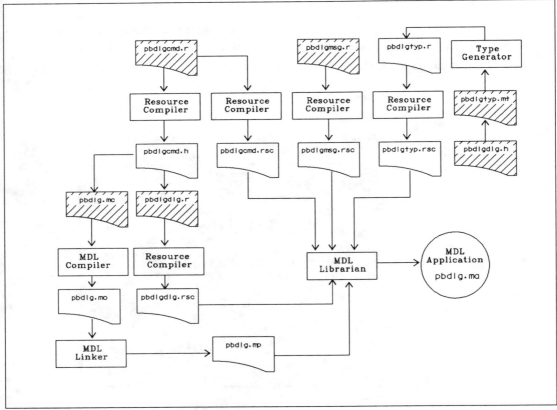

Figure 3.2 The PBDLG Development Stages

The files used in the PBDLG are:

pbdlgcmd.r	Command syntax.
pbdlgmsg.r	Screen messages.
pbdlgdlg.r	Dialog Resource source file.
pbdlgdlg.h	Include file containing dialog types.
pbdlgtyp.mt	Data structure to publish.
pbdlg.mc	MDL Source file.
pbdlg.mke	Makefile for the application.

We have broken down the resource files into dialog, messages, command syntax and published data type. In *pbdlg.mke*, the inference rules will take care of compiling the resources in the right sequence.

TIP

Don't re-invent the wheel. When starting a new application, make a copy of an existing program, and modify it to suit. This sort of prototyping shortens the development cycle. We will use a stripped down version of the PBDLG files as the seed file for our SEEDDLG.

The first step in creating a dialog interface, for an application, is to determine what goes into the dialog box. From here we can create the data structure. The data structure matches the dialog box very closely. Once we have the dialog box data sorted out, we are half-way there.

We will create a structure to hold the cell name, the string that goes in the box, the group mode (how we group the elements together), and whether we have a leader line. The structure is shown here:

```
typedef struct placeboxinfo
  {
  char    cellName[8];
  char    String[127];
  int     groupMode;
  int     leaderLine;
  }
  PlaceBoxInfo;
```

The Dialog Manager

The Dialog Manager controls the operation of the resizable MicroStation Windows that appear on the screen. There are two types of windows, **view windows** and **dialog box windows**. View windows are used to display and change MicroStation design files. They are covered in the chapter 'Advanced Dialog Box'. In this chapter we will discuss the design and creation of the dialog box window. A dialog box window contains **dialog items**, which are user interface controls.

Designing Dialog Boxes

In a dialog box, we can have dialog items. These are:

ColorPicker	select a color from a palette of 255 choices.
Generic	customizable item. No default behavior.
GroupBox	draw a rectangle, with a 3D appearance, around a group of dialog items.
Label	draw a text string in dialog box.
LevelMap	select or change the state of the file levels.
List Box	allow the display of multiple text strings.
MenuBar	used to create a strip of pulldown menus.
OptionButton	select an option from a set of choices.
OptionPulldown	a pulldown menu with a list of options. It can be text or icons
PushButton	activates a command with a push of a button.
TextPulldown	a menu that contains a series of text strings.
ScrollBar	a sliding bar that can change a value of a variable, between a maximum and minimum range.
Text	accept an input string.
ToggleButton	turns a variable's state on or off.

In our example we will use **Text, OptionButton, ToggleButton** and **PushButton**. The **Text** part of the Dialog box will prompt for the PLBOX cellname. We will initialize this box with the string "PLBOX" and then allow the user to change this if he wishes. We will use an **OptionButton** for the grouping method; whether it will be a cell, graphic group, or none at all. The **ToggleButton** is good for turning an option on or off. In our example, we will use a ToggleButton to select whether we draw the box with or without a leader line. The OK **PushButton** will launch the program.

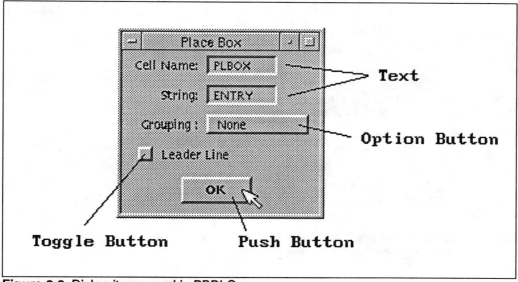

Figure 3.3 Dialog items used in PBDLG

Dialog Box Resolution

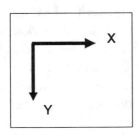

Dialog boxes are defined in local coordinates. The origin of a dialog box is the top left corner, with positive Y going down and positive X going to the right. The coordinate units in a dialog box are either **pixel** or **dialog coordinates**. Pixel units are actual screen pixels. The dialog coordinates are defined as 1/12 of the current dialog box's current font height.

To position our dialog information and items, we will use dialog coordinates. This will guarantee consistency with different dialog fonts, or when the dialog box is moved from one screen to another.

In the include file < dlogbox.h > there are three constants that reflect the points we've discussed.

```
#define DCOORD_RESOLUTION 12
#define XC (DCOORD_RESOLUTION / 2)
#define YC DCOORD_RESOLUTION
```

The constant DCOORD_RESOLUTION is defined to contain 12 pixels. XC is the width of one character font, which is half the font height. YC is the height of one character font. To define the size of our dialog box, we will put the following constants in our dialog resource file.

```
#define OVERALLWIDTH  25 * XC
#define OVERALLHEIGHT 11 * YC
```

To put it simply, our dialog box will be 25 characters wide and 11 characters high. In < dlogbox.h > there is a macro that aids in dialog box construction. The macro calculates the vertical position from the row number. The use of this macro will position properly the dialog items, with the appropriate gap between them. The macro is shown below.

```
#define GAP 3
#define GENY(row)  ((row-1)*(YC+GAP) + YC/2)
```

The following constants define the positions of the information in our dialog box.

```
#define  OVERALLWIDTH      25 * XC
#define  OVERALLHEIGHT     11 * YC
#define  NEWLINE           2 * YC

#define  X1 11 * XC        /* cell Name */
#define  X2 11 * XC        /* Leader Line */
#define  X3 2 * XC         /* group Mode */
#define  X4 (OVERALLWIDTH/2) - (5 * XC)  /* middle of OKAY button */

#define  Y1 GENY(1)        /* cell Name */
#define  Y2 Y1 + NEWLINE   /* input string */
#define  Y3 Y2 + NEWLINE   /* group Mode */
#define  Y4 Y3 + NEWLINE   /* leader Line */
#define  Y5 Y4 + NEWLINE   /* Okay button */
#define  BW XC * 9         /* box width */
```

Figure 3.4 shows the layout of the PBDLG dialog items. Notice that the coordinates of the Text and Option Button items define the position of the item, and not the start of the string label.

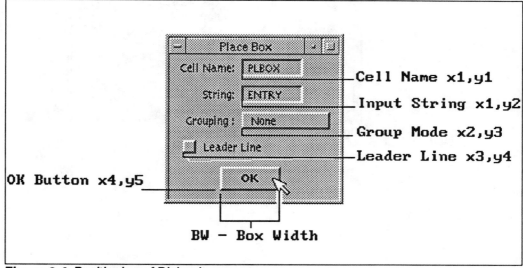

Figure 3.4 Positioning of Dialog Items

Notice how we have added 2 * YC (NEWLINE) to the GENY macros. This
is required to make sure that the items are not too close to each other. If we
used GENY to define the rows, as shown here:

```
#define  Y1 GENY(1)          /* cell Name */
#define  Y2 GENY(2)          /* input string */
#define  Y3 GENY(3)          /* group Mode */
#define  Y4 GENY(4)          /* leader Line */
#define  Y5 GENY(5)          /* Okay button  */
```

The resulting dialog box would have the lines too close together.

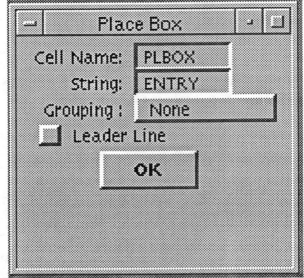

Figure 3.5 Use of GENY macro

Creating a Dialog Box Resource

The dialog manager uses resource files to separate the user defined dialog box from the application program. Therefore, any changes to the dialog only require the dialog resource to be modified, and not the application.

The dialog box is defined by the structure *DialogBoxRsc*, shown below.

```
typedef struct dialogboxrsc
   {
   ULong   attributes;        /* dialog attributes */
   int     width;             /* dialog coords */
   int     height;            /* dialog coords */
   ULong   helpInfo;          /* help for dialog */
   ULong   helpSource;        /* help task ID */
   long    dialogHookId;      /* dialog hook ID */
   long    parentDialogId;    /* inform when destroyed */
#if defined (resource)
   char    label[];               /* dialog title */
   DialogItemRsc itemList[];  /* array of dialog items */
#else
   long    labelLength;       /* dialog title string length */
   char    label[1];          /* dialog title */
#endif
} DialogBoxRsc;
```

The *attributes* field specifies the characteristics of the dialog box. Constants are used in this field. We will use the default attribute, DIALOGATTR_DEFAULT. The possible attributes are:

DIALOGATTR_DEFAULT	Default, no attributes set.
DIALOGATTR_MODAL	Specify Modal dialog box. See Chapter 7 for more detail on Modal dialog boxes.
DIALOGATTR_GROWABLE	Dialog box is resizable.
DIALOGATTR_SINKABLE	Dialog box can be sent behind view windows.
DIALOGATTR_UNCLOSEABLE	Cannot close dialog box.
DIALOGATTR_NOAUTOSWITCH	Keyboard focus will not automatically switch to another window.
DIALOGATTR_CLOSEONNEW	Close dialog box if opening a new design file.
DIALOGATTR_ALWAYSSETSTATE	Set item's state when user interacts with item.

width and *height* define the size of our dialog box. We will use our constants OVERALLWIDTH and OVERALLHEIGHT.

Fields *helpInfo* and *helpSource* are a user defined help facility for the application. Since no help exists, we will set the fields to NOHELP and MHELP respectively.

Dialog hooks are discussed later in this chapter. For now we will not use dialog hooks, therefore we will use the constant NOHOOK for this field.

In designing our dialog, we can have one dialog launching another. The *parentDialogId* designates the parent dialog, to inform when a child dialog is destroyed. In our example, we have no parent dialog, therefore we will assign the field with NOPARENTID.

The *label* field contains the string to display in the menu bar of the dialog box. The dialog *itemlist* are discussed in the next section. Our resource DIALOGID_PlaceBox is shown here.

```
DialogBoxRsc DIALOGID_PlaceBox =
{
  DIALOGATTR DEFAULT,
  OVERALLWIDTH, OVERALLHEIGHT,
  NOHELP, MHELP, NOHOOK, NOPARENTID,
  "Place Box",
          .
          .
          .
```

Dialog Items

Looking back to the start of this chapter, we can see that our dialog box has several items, namely Text, Option Button, PushButton and a ToggleButton. The dialog box manager breaks the dialog items into the **dialog item resource** and the **dialog item list** specifications. The dialog item list is defined with the structure *dialogitemrsc*. The sequence in which we define these items is important, because this is the sequence in which the Dialog Box manager displays and prompts. The dialog item resource structure is listed here:

```
typedef struct dialogitemrsc
{
  Sextent extent;    /* sensitive area, origin (in dialog coords), if width*/
                     /* height is zero use dimensions specified in item */
  long    type;      /* item type */
  long    id;
  byte    attributes;
  long    itemArg;
#if defined (resource)
  char    label[];
  char    auxInfo[];
#else
  long    labelLength;
  char    label[1];
#endif
} DialogItemRsc;
```

The definition of *Sextent* is shown here:

```
typedef struct spoint2d
    {
    short       x;
    short       y;
    } Spoint2d, SPoint2d;

typedef struct extent
    {
    SPoint2d    origin;         /* upper left */
    short       width;
    short       height;
    } Sextent;
```

The extent field defines the area that the dialog item will cover in the dialog box. The first two extent fields specify the start of the item from the origin of the dialog box (upper left corner). The next two extent fields specify the width and height of our item. If we specify 0 for width and height, then defaults will be used. In the example below, the first dialog item will start 11 characters to the right and 1 row down. It will be 9 characters long.

```
{ /* dialog item list */
{{X1, Y1, BW, 0},   Text,   TEXTID_cellName, ON, 0, "", ""},
{{X1, Y2, BW, 0},   Text,   TEXTID_String, ON, 0, "", ""},
{{X2, Y3, 0, 0},    OptionButton, OPTIONBUTTONID_groupMode, ON, 0,"", ""},
{{X3, Y4, 0, 0},    ToggleButton, TOGGLEID_leaderLine,  ON, 0, "", ""},
{{X4, Y5, BW, 0},   PushButton, PUSHBUTTONID_ok, ON, 0, "", ""}
}
```

Common Item Resource Fields

There are many fields that are the same for each of the dialog items. These fields are, in order:

commandNumber, contains the command number to be placed at the end of the MicroStation input queue. This is useful in executing MicroStation commands. For example, we could design a dialog box to set the active level. The command number we would use is CMD_ACTIVE_LEVEL. For a complete list of the command numbers, please refer to the include file < cmdlist.h >. If we do not wish to send a command, then we use NOCMD.

commandSource , specifies the source that executes the *commandNumber*. Use MCMD to specify that MicroStation will be executing the command. Otherwise, use LCMD, which indicates that the task owning the dialog should execute the command. If we have specified NOCMD, then we use LCMD for this field.

unparsed, passes the string with the *commandNumber* into the input queue. If we do not wish to place a string with the *commandNumber* then we use two double quotes "" to specify a null string.

helpInfo, specifies the help ID. If no help exists then use NOHELP for this field.

helpSource, specifies the task that will handle the help. If no help is available then use MHELP for this field.

itemHookId, defines the ID of the hook function. If no hooks are used then we specify NOHOOK for this field. Hooks allow us to modify the default actions of dialog boxes and items. Hooks are covered in detail, in the chapter 'Advanced Dialog Box'.

itemHookArg, specifies the argument for the hook function. If no arguments are required then we use NOARG for this field.

label, is the user supplied string that will be shown in the dialog box.

accessStr, is the variable that the dialog item will control. For example, we want any changes in the dialog item to reflect in the following variable, *plBoxInfo->String*. Thus, *accessStr* will be "plBoxInfo->String". The dialog box knows about this variable, because it has been informed. More about this when we discuss the MDL source, *pbdlg.mc* program.

synonymsId , defines the corresponding dialog item to change when this dialog item is modified. The best example is the ColorPicker dialog item, which has the *synonymsId* as the Text Item. Whenever the ColorPicker changes, the Text Item reflects the corresponding color number. We have an example of this in the chapter Advanced Dialog Box.

Text Dialog Item

A Text Dialog Item is used to prompt the user for text input. In our example, we prompt for the cell name and the string to place in the design file. The following lines are the item list specification for our Text Dialog Item.

```
{{X1, Y1, BW, 0},   Text,   TEXTID_cellName, ON, 0, "", ""},
{{X1, Y2, BW, 0},   Text,   TEXTID_String, ON, 0, "", ""},
```

The structure of the text resource dialog item is defined by *ditem_textrsc*.

```
typedef struct ditem_textrsc
  {
  ULong   commandNumber;
  ULong   commandSource;
  long    synonymsId;
  ULong   helpInfo;
  ULong   helpSource;
  long    itemHookId;
  long    itemHookArg;

  byte    maxSize;                /* max # of chars in field */
  char    formatToDisplay[16];    /* format str to convert from internal */
  char    formatToInternal[16];   /* convert to internal from display str */
  char    minimum[16];            /* minimum value */
  char    maximum[16];            /* maximum value */
  ULong   mask;                   /* only used with integer types */
  UShort  attributes;             /* other attributes */
#if defined (resource)
  char    label[];
  char    accessStr[];
#else
  long    labelLength;
  char    label[1];
#endif
  } DItem_TextRsc;
```

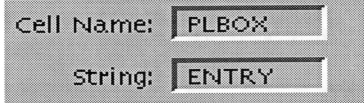

Figure 3.6 Text Item for PBDLG

In our dialog resource file, *pbdlgdlg.r* we define the text item resource as:

```
DItem_TextRsc TEXTID_cellName =
{
  NOCMD, LCMD, NOSYNONYM, NOHELP, MHELP, NOHOOK, NOARG,
  8, "%s", "%s", "", "", NOMASK, NOCONCAT,
  "Cell Name:",
  "plBoxInfo->cellName"
};

DItem_TextRsc TEXTID_String =
{
  NOCMD, LCMD, NOSYNONYM, NOHELP, MHELP, NOHOOK, NOARG,
  127, "%s", "%s", "", "", NOMASK, NOCONCAT,
  "String:",
  "plBoxInfo->string"
};
```

Most of the fields are discussed in the previous section on Common Item Resource Fields. The *maxSize* field specifies the maximum number of characters that this text item can edit. Notice that the *maxSize* in TEXTID_String is 127, even though we are displaying only 9 characters in the dialog box. This is possible because the text item allows horizontal scrolling. It can edit text characters that otherwise would not fit in the allowable space.

Keyboard Focus

The dialog item that is currently processing user keystrokes is said to be in **focus**. When a dialog is ready to accept keystrokes, it will darken (as shown in Figure 3.7). The Text Dialog Item and the Scroll Bar are two examples of a focusable dialog item.   Not all dialog items are focusable, therefore MicroStation will apply keyboard **focus auto-switching**. This moves the focus to the Command Window.

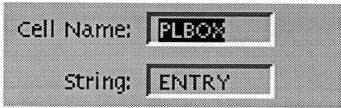

Figure 3.7 The Cell Name dialog is in focus

Option Button Item

An Option Button allows the user to select an option, from a set of choices. When we select the button, the list of available choices will appear. Dragging the cursor highlights the choices. Releasing it makes the highlighted item the current selection (Figure 3.8).

```
typedef struct optionbutton_iteminfo
    {
    int     subItemIndex;

    char    *labelP;
    ULong   *iconTypeP;
    long    *iconIdP;
    int     *commandSourceP;
    ULong   *valueP;
    ULong   *maskP;
    int     *enabledP;
    void    *userDataP;
    } OptionButton_ItemInfo;
```

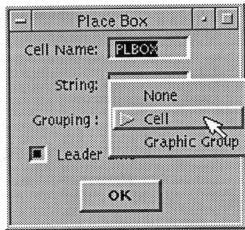

Figure 3.8 Using the Option Button

In our dialog resource file, *pbdlgdlg.r* we define the Option Button Item resource as:

```
DItem_OptionButtonRsc    OPTIONBUTTONID_groupMode =
{
  NOSYNONYM, NOHELP, MHELP, NOHOOK, NOARG,
  "Grouping :",
  "plBoxInfo->groupMode",
  {
  {NOTYPE, NOICON, NOCMD, LCMD, 0, NOMASK, ON, "None"},
  {NOTYPE, NOICON, NOCMD, LCMD, 1, NOMASK, ON, "Cell"},
  {NOTYPE, NOICON, NOCMD, LCMD, 2, NOMASK, ON, "Graphic Group"},
  }
};
```

Push Button Item

A Push Button is used to activate a command. It is often used in launching another dialog box, or as an acknowledgement. In our example we use the push button to execute the PLACE BOX program. We also supply user hooks in our program. This allows the dialog box to be present at all times, but we can access other commands. When the user hits the OK push button, the user hook will activate the PLACE BOX program. The Push Button resource item is defined by *ditem_pushbuttonrsc*.

```
typedef struct ditem_pushbuttonrsc
  {
  char    isDefault;              /* TRUE if this is default button */
  ULong   helpInfo;
  ULong   helpSource;
  long    itemHookId;
  long    itemHookArg;
  ULong   commandNumber;
  ULong   commandSource;
#if defined (resource)
  char    unparsed[];
  char    label[];
#else
  long    unparsedLength;
  char    unparsed[1];
#endif
  } DItem_PushButtonRsc;
```

If the field *isDefault* is set to TRUE, then it defines that this is the default button. Therefore, hitting the Enter key has the same effect as selecting the button with a mouse. The Push Button Item for our application is listed here:

```
DItem_PushButtonRsc PUSHBUTTONID_ok =
{
  NOT_DEFAULT_BUTTON, NOHELP, MHELP,
  HOOKITEMID_Button_Place, 0, NOCMD, MCMD, "",
  "  OK  "
};
```

Toggle Button Item

A Toggle Button acts and looks like a toggle. It has only two states, on or off (1 or 0). A feature of the toggle button is its ability to make direct changes to the variable, without any explicit programming. Figure 3.9 shows the toggle dialog item turned "on". The toggle button is defined by the structure *ditem_togglebuttonrsc*, as shown below. Most of the fields have been discussed previously.

```
typedef struct ditem_togglebuttonrsc
  {
  ULong   commandNumber;
  ULong   commandSource;
  long    synonymsId;
  ULong   helpInfo;
  ULong   helpSource;
  long    itemHookId;
  long    itemHookArg;
  ULong   mask;
  char    invertFlag;

#if defined (resource)
  char    label[];
  char    accessStr[];
#else
  long    labelLength;
  char    label[1];
#endif
  } DItem_ToggleButtonRsc;
```

Figure 3.9 Toggle Button set on

mask and *invertFlag* are used together with *accessStr* to change the value of *accessStr*, making it a very powerful feature.

For example, a search for elements is based on a search mask. If we were to define a toggle button for each element, then depressing the button indicates that this is the element to locate. We can set *invertFlag* to NOINVERT and supply a mask for the element type. For example a line is a Type 3 element, therefore our toggle button would look something like the following:

```
DItem_ToggleButtonRsc TOGGLEID_Line =
{
  NOCMD, MCMD, NOSYNONYM, NOHELP, MCMD, NOHOOK, NOARG,
  0x4, NOINVERT, "Line", "typmask[0]"
};
```

In the above example, *typmask[0]* will be ORed with 0x4, thereby setting the third bit ON. This feature does not require any explicit programming and yet it provides all the power of a large program.

```
DItem_ToggleButtonRsc TOGGLEID_leaderLine =
{
  NOCMD, MCMD, NOSYNONYM, NOHELP, MCMD, NOHOOK, NOARG,
  NOMASK, NOINVERT,
  "Leader Line",
  "plBoxInfo->leaderLine"
};
```

Dialog Box General Functions

Before we can go through our *pbdlg.mc* program, we must look at the general dialog functions. These function operate on the dialog box as a whole.

mdlDialog_closeCommandQueue queues a command to close the dialog box.

mdlDialog_cmdNumberQueue   queue a command onto the input queue.

mdlDialog_find   return the dialog box specified by a resource ID.

mdlDialog_hookDialogSendUserMsg send a user message to a dialog hook function.

mdlDialog_hookItemSendUserMsg send a user message to an item hook function.

mdlDialog_hookPublish   publish hook function ID numbers with hook function addresses.

mdlDialog_lastActionTypeSet   used to indicate why the dialog box was closed.

mdlDialog_open   open a modeless dialog box. That is, a dialog box which allows interaction with other dialog boxes.

mdlDialog_openAlert   open an alert dialog box.

mdlDialog_openModal   open a modal dialog box. This dialog box will force all operations inside the modal dialog box.

mdlDialog_openPalette   open a modeless dialog box, which contains a single icon command palette item.

mdlDialog_parentIdGet   get the parent ID of a dialog box.

mdlDialog_parentIdSet   set the parent ID of a dialog box.

mdlDialog_publishBasicPtr   publish a pointer for a basic C data type.

mdlDialog_publishBasicVariable	publish a basic C data type variable for use in C expression strings.
mdlDialog_publishComplexPtr	publish a pointer to a structure type variable.
mdlDialog_publishComplexVariable	publish a structure type variable.
mdlDialog_publishStructure	publish a structure declaration.
mdlDialog_synonymsSynch	forces the appearance of all items to match their external state.
mdlDialog_userDataPtrGet	get a user pointer associated with a dialog box.
mdlDialog_userDataPtrSet	set a user pointer associated with a dialog box.

Dialog Hook Functions

The dialog manager has three sub-systems that handle dialog boxes. These are **dialog box functions**, **item handler functions** and **user hooks**. The sub-systems communicates by sending a **message** data structure to each other. The **dialog item handler** defines the default functionality and appearance of dialog items.

Since all dialog items have default behaviours, it is often desirable to modify the default action. Dialog hooks allow the programmer to attach user functions to either dialog boxes (known as **dialog hook functions**), or dialog items (known as **item hook functions**). In our PBDLG example we will look at a simple implementation of the item hook function. In the chapter Advanced Dialog Box, we will discuss the advanced features of the item hook function.

Dialog Box Communications

Dialog Box's sub-system communicates by sending various messages (see Figure 3.10). Each message is a data structure containing a message type and a corresponding union. The Dialog Manager communicates with the dialog hook functions via the *DialogMessage* structure (defined in < dlogitem.h >). Some common dialog hook message types are:

DIALOG_MESSAGE_CREATE	sent before item hooks are sent create messages.
DIALOG_MESSAGE_INIT	sent after all item hooks are sent create messages.
DIALOG_MESSAGE_DESTROY	sent when dialog box is about to be destroyed.
DIALOG_MESSAGE_UPDATE	sent after dialog manager updates dialog box.
DIALOG_MESSAGE_BUTTON	sent when a mouse button event occurs in dialog box.

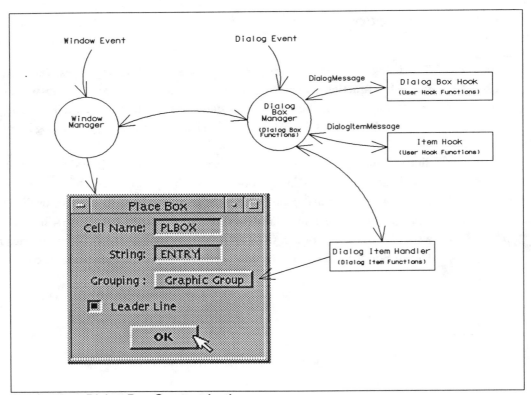

Figure 3.10 Dialog Box Communications

When the dialog item hook is called. It receives the message structure *DialogItemMessage* (defined in <dlogitem.h>). Some common message types are:

DITEM_MESSAGE_CREATE	sent after the item is created.
DITEM_MESSAGE_DESTROY	sent when the item is about to be destroyed.
DITEM_MESSAGE_BUTTON	sent when a mouse button event occurs in a mouse sensative item.
DITEM_MESSAGE_INIT	sent after item is created.
DITEM_MESSAGE_SETSTATE	sent when an item handler needz to set an item's state.
DITEM_MESSAGE_GETSTATE	sent when an item handler needz to determine an item's state.

Debugging Dialog Messages

The Dialog Manager provides a message tracking facility through the command DMSG. The following key-ins opens a dialog box and print all messages between the dialog hook functions, item hook functions, or item handlers.

Key-in	Description
DMSG ITEMDEBUG [ON/OFF]	turn on/off the display of messages sent to dialog item hook function.
DMSG HANDLERDEBUG [ON/OFF]	turn on/off the display of messages that have been sent to item handlers.
DMSG DIALOGDEBUG [ON/OFF]	turn on/off the display of messages sent to a dialog hook function.
DMSG VERBOSEDEBUG [ON/OFF]	toggle between brief and detailed debugging information for the above messages.
DMSG CLEARDEBUG	clear dialog debug message screen.

Hook Function IDs

The **hook function ID** is a positive long integer ID which we allocate. The ID is required to allow the dialog manager to find the appropriate hook function given by the ID. By passing the hook function ID, and the function address, to *mdlDialog_hookPublish*, we make the hook function known to the dialog manager.

```
/* publish dialog item hooks */
mdlDialog_hookPublish(sizeof(uHooks)/sizeof(DialogHookInfo), uHooks);
```

When we execute the PLACE BOX command it brings the dialog box up on the screen, through the function *mdlDialog_open*.

```
/* Display the dialog box if it it not already displayed.   */
if (! mdlDialog_find (DIALOGID_PlaceBox, NULL))
    mdlDialog_open (NULL, DIALOGID_PlaceBox);
```

We can change the default settings by manipulating the appropriate dialog items. However, the boxed text will not be placed until we push the "OK" button. In the dialog resource file *pbdlgdlg.r*, we have defined our push button dialog item to have a hook id HOOKITEMID_Button_Place.

```
DItem_PushButtonRsc PUSHBUTTONID_ok =
{
  NOT_DEFAULT_BUTTON, NOHELP, MHELP,
  HOOKITEMID_Button_Place, 0, NOCMD, MCMD, "",
  " OK "
};
```

At the start of our program *pbdlg.mc* we have defined the hook id, HOOKITEMID_Button_Place, to point to our function plButtonHook. When the "OK" button is pushed, it activates the function plButtonHook.

```
static   DialogHookInfo uHooks[]=
    {
        {HOOKITEMID_Button_Place, plButtonHook }
    };
```

The argument to the plButtonHook function is a pointer to a *DialogItemMessage* structure. This is the message structure to which we referred earlier. Different items support different dialog item messages. Referring to the MDL Manual we find that the Push Button Item supports the message type DITEM_MESSAGE_BUTTON. This indicates that the user has pressed the "OK" button.

If we set to TRUE, the variable *msgUnderstood*, in the structure *DialogItemMessage*, our hook function processes the message. If set to FALSE, we leave it to the item handler to do the default processing.

```
Private int  plButtonHook (DialogItemMessage *dimP)
{
  dimP->msgUnderstood = TRUE;
  switch (dimP->messageType)
  {
  case DITEM_MESSAGE_BUTTON:
    {
    mdlState_startPrimitive (placeBox_firstPoint, placeBox_done, 1, 2);
    break;
    }
  default:
    {
    /* tell the dialog manager that we don't handle this message */
    dimP->msgUnderstood = FALSE;
    break;
    }
  }
}
```

Resource Management

Dialog Boxes use resource files to save, among other things, the position of the dialog box on the screen. The user resources are saved in the file *userpref.rsc*, in the directory specified by the environment variable MS_RSRCPATH. The default directory for MS_RSRCPATH is *\ustation\data* (for DOS).

User Preference is an example of a dynamic resource which is created, modified and deleted. In developing and testing dynamic resources it is safer to delete the *userpref.rsc* and let our application recreate it. We have found that accessing the old resource file format causes irregular behavior in the MDL program.

 In the development cycle, delete the old userpref.rsc, and let the application recreate it.

Below is a summary of the resource management functions.

mdlResource_add	add a new resource to the resource file.
mdlResource_changeAlias	assign a new alias name to the resource.
mdlResource_closeFile	close a resource file.
mdlResource_createFile	create a new resource file from the current file.
mdlResource_delete	delete a resource from the resource file.
mdlResource_directAdd	add a new resource using *fwrite*.
mdlResource_directAddComplete	tells the resource manager that the direct add is complete.
mdlResource_directLoad	load a resource using *fread*.
mdlResource_free	remove a loaded resource.
mdlResource_getRscIdByAlias	get resource ID number from alias.
mdlResource_load	load resource into memory.
mdlResource_loadFromStringList	load a string from *StringList* resource.

mdlResource_openFile	open a resource file.
mdlResource_query	query information on a resource.
mdlResource_queryClass	query information on a resource class.
mdlResource_queryFile	query information on a resource file.
mdlResource_resize	adjust the size of the resource.
mdlResource_write	write an updated resource back to the resource file.

User Preference Resource

The function *mdlResource_openFile* opens a user resource file. If the dialog manager cannot find the specified resource file then it opens the default resource file *userpref.rsc*.

If we were running our MDL application for the first time, we would not have any preferences in the resource file. If no resource occurrences are found for our application then we start with an initialized set of values. Otherwise we use the preferences from the last session.

```
if (!boxRscP)
{
    /* No resource was found */
    plBoxInfo->groupMode = 0;
    plBoxInfo->leaderLine = 0;
    strcpy(plBoxInfo->cellName,"PLBOX");
    plBoxInfo->String[0]= '\0';
} else {
    /* Copy resource into internal structure */
    *plBoxInfo = *boxRscP;
    mdlResource_free (boxRscP);
}
```

Saving resources

If we terminate our application, then we need to save the parameters for the next session. We can establish a state function that executes when we unload our application. The parameter SYSTEM_UNLOAD_PROGRAM, passed to *mdlSystem_setFunction*, with the function name, makes sure that our cleanup function is called at unload time.

```
mdlSystem_setFunction (SYSTEM_UNLOAD_PROGRAM, unloadFunction);
```

The unload function opens the user preference file from disk. It will try to locate the resource for this particular application. If it doesn't exist, then it will create it. If it does exist, it will take the resource information that is currently in memory and write it to disk. The unload function is a standard function, and we will include it in our *seeddlg* application.

```
Private int unloadFunction ()
{
  RscFileHandle    userPrefsH;
  PlaceBoxInfo     *boxRscP;

  /* Open userpref.rsc to hold our small pref resource */
  mdlDialog_userPrefFileOpen (&userPrefsH);
  boxRscP = (PlaceBoxInfo *)mdlResource_load (NULL, RTYPE_plBox,
          RSCID_plBoxPrefs);

  if (!boxRscP)
  {
  /* Our pref resource does not exist, so add it */
  mdlResource_add (userPrefsH, RTYPE_plBox, RSCID_plBoxPrefs,
      plBoxInfo, sizeof(PlaceBoxInfo), NULL);
  }
  else
  {
      *boxRscP = *plBoxInfo;
      /* Write out and free the updated resource */
      mdlResource_write (boxRscP);
      mdlResource_free (boxRscP);
  }
  /* Clean up */
  mdlResource_closeFile (userPrefsH);
  free(plBoxInfo);
  return (FALSE);
}
```

C Expression

MDL provides the facilities to evaluate C expressions at run-time. The dialog manager uses C expressions to handle access strings. The C expression may contain references to fields contained in structures or unions, which must be defined in a resource file.

Access Strings

Early in this chapter, we briefly mentioned Access Strings. In the example below, the access string is *plBoxInfo->cellName*.

```
DItem_TextRsc TEXTID_cellName =
{
  NOCMD, LCMD, NOSYNONYM, NOHELP, MHELP, NOHOOK, NOARG,
  8, "%s", "%s", "", "", NOMASK, NOCONCAT,
  "Cell Name:",
  "plBoxInfo->cellName"
};
```

Access strings defines variables, structures or pointers to structures, for the dialog item to inspect and modify. We must give the dialog item permission to manipulate our data, by publishing the variable, structure or pointer.

In our application we have defined the structure and union declarations in the file *pbdlgtyp.mt*. This file contains the include file and the publishStructures statement. The publishStructures statement identifies the structure to be defined in the resource source file. The structure may not contain dynamic declarations (those that allocate space), or executable statements.

pbdlgtyp.mt

```
#include    "pbdlgdlg.h"

publishStructures (placeboxinfo);
```

Passing the file *pbdlgtyp.mt* through the **type generator** will generate a resource source file *pbdlgtyp.r*. This we can use as input to the resource compiler, to generate the resource file.

The header file *pbdlgdlg.h*, contains the desired structure and union definitions. *pbdlgdlg.h* is listed here. Notice that all the IDs are positive numbers, as the negative numbers are used by MicroStation.

pbdlgdlg.h

```
/*------------------------------------------------------------------------+
|    Dialog Box IDs                                                       |
+----------------------------------------------------------------------*/
#define DIALOGID_PlaceBox            1
/*------------------------------------------------------------------------+
|    PopupMenu Item IDs                                                   |
+----------------------------------------------------------------------*/
#define OPTIONBUTTONID_groupMode 1
/*------------------------------------------------------------------------+
|    PushButton Item IDs                                                  |
+----------------------------------------------------------------------*/
#define PUSHBUTTONID_ok              1
/*------------------------------------------------------------------------+
|    Resource Type and ID for Prefs                                       |
+----------------------------------------------------------------------*/
#define RTYPE_plBox                 'pLBt'
#define RSCID_plBoxPrefs            1
/*------------------------------------------------------------------------+
|    Text Item IDs                                                        |
+----------------------------------------------------------------------*/
#define TEXTID_cellName             1
#define TEXTID_String               2
/*------------------------------------------------------------------------+
|    Toggle Button IDs                                                    |
+----------------------------------------------------------------------*/
#define TOGGLEID_leaderLine         1
/*------------------------------------------------------------------------+
|    Hook Id's                                                            |
+----------------------------------------------------------------------*/
#define HOOKITEMID_Button_Place       1
/*------------------------------------------------------------------------+
|    Local Structure Definitions                                          |
+----------------------------------------------------------------------*/
typedef struct placeboxinfo
{
  char      cellName[8];
  char      String[127];
  int       groupMode;
  int       leaderLine;
}
  PlaceBoxInfo;
```

Type Generator

The type generator, **rsctype**, compiles a structure and union declaration, and generates a definition.

Command line syntax for the type generator is as follows:

```
rsctype  [-flag, -flag, ...]  input-file
```

where `input-file` is our source code. If no extension is specified then the type generator will append ".mt" to the filename.

where **-flag** is optional. Valid flags are:-

-d*name* = *value*
  Used to define *name* with a *value*. The *name* is found in the preprocessor *#define* statement.

-i*dir*   add extra directories to search for the include files. The compiler can support up to 40 include directories.

-o*filename*
  resource source output filename. If not specified, then the output file will have the extension ".r" appended to the input filename prefix.

-p   display preprocessor output.

-v   verbose, show compiler progress.

C Expression Functions

MDL provides several functions to publish and manage a symbol set. These symbol sets can contain a C variable name, or a C function name. Below is a summary of these functions.

mdlCExpression_freeSet   free a symbol set.

mdlCExpression_generateMessage generate an error message.

mdlCExpression_getValue   evaluate an expression and return the value.

mdlCExpression_initializeSet   initialize symbol set for use with dialog boxes and/or calculator/preprocessor.

mdlCExpression_isArray   determine whether type definition is an array.

mdlCExpression_isCharPointer   determine whether type definition is a character pointer.

mdlCExpression_isStructUnion   determine whether type definition is a structure or union.

mdlCExpression_symbolPublish publish symbols for the dialog manager.

mdlCExpression_setValue   evaluate an expression and set the value.

mdlCExpression_typeArray   make an array type definition.

mdlCExpression_typeFromRsc   create memory resident definition of a structure or union, based on the definition in the resource file.

mdlCExpression_typePointer   make a pointer type definition.

Symbol Sets

The Symbol Set is a pointer to a region in memory, where the dialog item can find the application's variables, structures and pointers. To set up and publish our structure *plBoxInfo* for access, we use the following commands.

```
setP = mdlCExpression_initializeSet (VISIBILITY_DIALOG_BOX, 0, TRUE);

boxTypeP = mdlCExpression_typeFromRsc (setP, "placeboxinfo", NULL);
boxTypeP = mdlCExpression_typePointer (setP, boxTypeP );
mdlCExpression_symbolPublish(setP, "plBoxInfo", SYMBOL_CLASS_VAR,
          boxTypeP, &plBoxInfo);
```

In the first line, the function *mdlCExpression_initializeSet* initializes the *setP* symbol set. The visibility flag is allocated to each symbol. During a search, the visibility flag is examined to determine if the symbol set is included in the search.

We specify VISIBILITY_DIALOG_BOX as we use these symbols for dialog boxes. If the symbols are used for the calculator/preprocessor then we specify VISIBILITY_CALCULATOR. If the symbols are used for both then specify (VISIBILITY_DIALOG_BOX | VISIBILITY_CALCULATOR). If the symbols are used with the debugger then we specify VISIBILITY_DEBUGGER.

In the next line we create an in-memory definition of structure *placeboxinfo* with a call to *mdlCExpression_typeFromRsc*. The function *mdlCExpression_typePointer* defines this symbol as a pointer.

Finally we publish the symbol for use with the function *mdlCExpression_symbolPublish*. The symbol class is one of the following:

SYMBOL_CLASS_FUNCTION	an MDL function.
SYMBOL_CLASS_SCOPE	Used only by the debugger.
SYMBOL_CLASS_SOURCE	Used only by the debugger.
SYMBOL_CLASS_STRUCT	Structures and unions.
SYMBOL_CLASS_VAR	Variables.

Graphic Group

In our first example we showed how to create orphan cells as a method of grouping elements together. In this instance we will use the graphic group. The methodology used is straightforward. The contents of TCB variable *tcb->cugraf* are used to give the element its graphic group number. If this number is zero then the element does not belong to any group.

The TCB variable, *tcb->graphic* contains the next free graphic group number. If we assign this number to *tcb->cugraf* then every element we place, from here on, will belong to this group number.

```
int size=1, offset=GRAPHIC;

if (plBoxInfo->groupMode == 2)
{
    tcb->cugraf=tcb->graphic;
    tcb->graphic++;
}
generateImage(pt , view, NORMALDRAW);

if (plBoxInfo->groupMode == 2)
{
    mdlParams_storeType9Variable(&tcb->graphic, size, offset);
    tcb->cugraf=0;
}
```

The bulk of the PBDLG program is taken from PLBOX. Exceptions are the graphic group, placing the arrow head and the hook function. We will leave the discussion on how to place the arrow head until the chapter on Mathematics and Geometry. It is introduced in this chapter only to make the PBDLG application complete.

pbdlg.mc

Here is the complete code for our dialog box application. To load the application enter *mdl l pbdlg*. To execute the application, enter PLACE BOX. Since the command is identical to the previous application PLBOX, you must unload the previous application.

```
/*-------------------------------------------------------------------+
|  Copyright (c) 1991 Mach Dinh-Vu, All Rights Reserved              |
|                                                                    |
|  pbdlg.mc -   place a text string and a box enclosing the string.  |
|               This MDL program shows how to use the dialog box in  |
|               a working application.                               |
|                                                                    |
|               PLACE BOX                                            |
+-------------------------------------------------------------------*/
#include     <tcb.h>
#include     <mselems.h>
#include     <global.h>
#include     <scanner.h>
#include     <msinputq.h>
#include     <userfnc.h>
#include     <mdl.h>
#include     <cexpr.h>
#include     <rscdefs.h>
#include     <dlogitem.h>

#include     "pbdlgcmd.h"     /*  Generated by resource compiler (rcomp) */
#include     "pbdlgdlg.h"     /*  Need to know dialog id to open */

/*-------------------------------------------------------------------+
|    Private Function declaration                                    |
+-------------------------------------------------------------------*/
Private int plButtonHook();

/*-------------------------------------------------------------------+
|    Private Global variables                                        |
+-------------------------------------------------------------------*/
static   DialogHookInfo uHooks[]=
    {
        {HOOKITEMID_Button_Place, plButtonHook }
    };


Dpoint3d      pntP[2];
static PlaceBoxInfo        *plBoxInfo;

#define GRAPHIC 1160
```

```
/*------------------------------------------------------------------+
|   name    unloadFunction                                          |
+------------------------------------------------------------------*/
Private int unloadFunction ()
{
  RscFileHandle    userPrefsH;
  PlaceBoxInfo    *boxRscP;

  /* Open userpref.rsc to hold our small pref resource */
  mdlDialog_userPrefFileOpen (&userPrefsH);
  boxRscP = (PlaceBoxInfo *)mdlResource_load (NULL, RTYPE_plBox,
            RSCID_plBoxPrefs);

  if (!boxRscP)
  {
      /* Our pref resource does not exist, so add it */
      mdlResource_add (userPrefsH, RTYPE_plBox, RSCID_plBoxPrefs,
                            plBoxInfo, sizeof(PlaceBoxInfo), NULL);
  }
  else
  {
      *boxRscP = *plBoxInfo;
      /* Write out and free the updated resource */
      mdlResource_write (boxRscP);
      mdlResource_free (boxRscP);
  }

  /* Clean up */
  mdlResource_closeFile (userPrefsH);
  free(plBoxInfo);
  return (FALSE);
}

/*------------------------------------------------------------------+
| name       main                                                   |
+------------------------------------------------------------------*/
main()
  {
  RscFileHandle rfHandle, userPrefsH;
  PlaceBoxInfo    *boxRscP;
  char            *setP, *boxTypeP;

  /* publish dialog item hooks */
  mdlDialog_hookPublish(sizeof(uHooks)/sizeof(DialogHookInfo), uHooks);

  /* Open our file for access to command table and dialog */
  mdlResource_openFile (&rfHandle, NULL, FALSE);

  /* setup plBoxInfo */
  plBoxInfo = malloc(sizeof(PlaceBoxInfo));
```

```
    /* Prepare to read resource. The resource file was used to save
    information the last time place box was used. */
    boxRscP = NULL;
    userPrefsH = NULL;
    mdlDialog_userPrefFileOpen(&userPrefsH);
    if (userPrefsH)
        boxRscP = (PlaceBoxInfo *)mdlResource_load (NULL, RTYPE_plBox,
            RSCID_plBoxPrefs);

    if (!boxRscP)
    {
        /* No resource was found */
        plBoxInfo->groupMode = 0;
        plBoxInfo->leaderLine = 0;
        strcpy(plBoxInfo->cellName,"PLBOX");
        plBoxInfo->String[0]= '\0';
    } else {
        /* Copy resource into internal structure */
        *plBoxInfo = *boxRscP;

        /* This is unnecessary because the closeFile will free all resources,
        * but it is recommended practice */
        mdlResource_free (boxRscP);
    }

    if (userPrefsH)
        mdlResource_closeFile (userPrefsH);

    /* Set up and Publish plBoxInfo for access by the dialog manager */
    setP = mdlCExpression_initializeSet (VISIBILITY_DIALOG_BOX, 0, TRUE);

    boxTypeP = mdlCExpression_typeFromRsc (setP, "placeboxinfo", NULL);
    boxTypeP = mdlCExpression_typePointer (setP, boxTypeP );
    mdlCExpression_symbolPublish(setP, "plBoxInfo", SYMBOL_CLASS_VAR,
            boxTypeP, &plBoxInfo);

    /* Make sure our function gets called at unload time */
    mdlSystem_setFunction (SYSTEM_UNLOAD_PROGRAM, unloadFunction);

    /* Load the command table */
    if (mdlParse_loadCommandTable (NULL) == NULL)
        mdlOutput_error ("Unable to load command table.");
    else
        mdlOutput_error ("Key-in PLACE BOX to execute.");
}

/*----------------------------------------------------------------------+
| name generateImage - dynamic function for complex case.               |
+----------------------------------------------------------------------*/
```

```
Private int        generateImage
(
Dpoint3d *pt,
int          view,
int          drawMode
)
{
 MSElementUnion el;
 Dpoint3d      tPts[3];
 Dpoint3d      origin;
 Dpoint3d      shapep[5];
 double        zangle;
 long          cellFilePos;
 unsigned long arrowsize;

 arrowsize =  tcb->chheight / 2;
 pntP[1] = *pt;

 mdlCurrTrans_begin();
 mdlCurrTrans_identity();
 mdlCurrTrans_translateOrigin(&pntP[0]);
 mdlCurrTrans_invtransPointArray( tPts, pntP, 2 );
 origin = tPts[1];      /* origin of text */

 /* Create Text in dgnBuf for MicroStation Dynamics to display */
 mdlText_create (&el, NULL, plBoxInfo->String, &tPts[1],
                 NULL, NULL, NULL, NULL);
 mdlElement_display (&el, drawMode);
 if (drawMode == NORMALDRAW)
 {
    if (plBoxInfo->groupMode == 1)
        cellFilePos=mdlCell_begin(plBoxInfo->cellName, NULL, NULL, 0);
    mdlElement_add(&el);
 }

 mdlText_extractShape(shapep, NULL, &el, TRUE, view);
 if (tPts[0].x <  origin.x)
 {
 if (tPts[0].y < origin.y)
    {
        tPts[1].x=shapep[0].x;
        tPts[1].y=shapep[0].y;
    } else {
        tPts[1].x=shapep[3].x;
        tPts[1].y=shapep[3].y;
    }
 } else {
    if (tPts[0].y < origin.y)
    {
        tPts[1].x=shapep[1].x;
```

```
            tPts[1].y=shapep[1].y;
        } else {
            tPts[1].x=shapep[2].x;
            tPts[1].y=shapep[2].y;
        }
    }

    mdlShape_create(&el, NULL, shapep, 5, -1);
    mdlElement_display (&el, drawMode);
    if (drawMode == NORMALDRAW)
        mdlElement_add(&el);

    /* Create shape in dgnBuf for MicroStation Dynamics to display */
    if (plBoxInfo->leaderLine)
    {
        mdlLine_create (&el, NULL, tPts);
        mdlElement_display (&el, drawMode);
        if (drawMode == NORMALDRAW)
            mdlElement_add(&el);

        /* calculate angle of line */
        zangle = atan2 ((tPts[0].y-tPts[1].y),(tPts[0].x-tPts[1].x));
        mdlCurrTrans_rotateByAngles( 0.0, 0.0, zangle);

        /* Create arrowhead */
        tPts[1]   = tPts[0];
        tPts[2].x = tPts[0].x - arrowsize;
        tPts[2].y = tPts[0].y - (arrowsize/2);
        tPts[0].x -= arrowsize;
        tPts[0].y += arrowsize/2;

        mdlLineString_create (&el, NULL, tPts, 3);
        mdlElement_display (&el, drawMode);
        if (drawMode == NORMALDRAW)
            mdlElement_add(&el);
    }

    if (drawMode == NORMALDRAW  && plBoxInfo->groupMode == 1)
    {
        mdlElement_add(&el);
        mdlCell_end(cellFilePos);
    }
    mdlCurrTrans_end();
    return  SUCCESS;
}

/*------------------------------------------------------------------+
| name          placeBox_done                                       |
+------------------------------------------------------------------*/
Private void    placeBox_done
```

```
(
)
{
  mdlState_clear();
  mdlOutput_rscPrintf (MSG_PROMPT, NULL, 0, 4);
}

/*------------------------------------------------------------------+
| name            placeBox_secondPoint                              |
+------------------------------------------------------------------*/
Private void     placeBox_secondPoint
(
Dpoint3d *pt,
int        view
)
{
  int size=1, offset=GRAPHIC;

  if (plBoxInfo->groupMode == 2)
  {
      tcb->cugraf=tcb->graphic;
      tcb->graphic++;
  }
  generateImage(pt , view, NORMALDRAW);

  if (plBoxInfo->groupMode == 2)
  {
      mdlParams_storeType9Variable(&tcb->graphic, size, offset);
      tcb->cugraf=0;
  }
  placeBox_done();
}

/*------------------------------------------------------------------+
| name            placeBox_firstPoint                               |
+------------------------------------------------------------------*/
Private void     placeBox_firstPoint
(
Dpoint3d     *pt,
int          view
)
{
  /* save first point */
  pntP[0] = *pt;

  /* Set the datapoint state function for the second point. */
  mdlState_setFunction (STATE_DATAPOINT, placeBox_secondPoint);
  mdlState_setFunction (STATE_RESET, placeBox_done);
  mdlOutput_rscPrintf (MSG_PROMPT, NULL, 0, 3);
  mdlState_setFunction (STATE_COMPLEX_DYNAMICS, generateImage);
```

```
}
/*--------------------------------------------------------------------+
| name          placeBox_start                                        |
+--------------------------------------------------------------------*/
cmdName  placeBox_start
(
void
)
cmdNumber    CMD_PLACE_BOX
{
  /* Display the dialog box if it it not already displayed.   */
  if (! mdlDialog_find (DIALOGID_PlaceBox, NULL))
     mdlDialog_open (NULL, DIALOGID_PlaceBox);
}


/*--------------------------------------------------------------------+
| name              plButtonHook                                      |
+--------------------------------------------------------------------*/
Private int   plButtonHook
(
DialogItemMessage *dimP
)
{
  dimP->msgUnderstood = TRUE;
  switch (dimP->messageType)
  {
  case DITEM_MESSAGE_BUTTON:
     {
     mdlState_startPrimitive (placeBox_firstPoint, placeBox_done, 1, 2);
     break;
     }
  default:
        {
     /* tell the dialog manager that we don't handle this message */
     dimP->msgUnderstood = FALSE;
     break;
     }
  }
}
```

pbdlgdlg.r

pbdlgdlg.r contains the resource source, which defines the dialog box.

```
/*----------------------------------------------------------------+
|      PBDLG Place Box Dialog Resources                           |
+----------------------------------------------------------------*/
#include <rscdefs.h>
#include <dlogbox.h>
#include <dlogids.h>
#include "pbdlgdlg.h"
#include "pbdlgcmd.h"
/*----------------------------------------------------------------+
|   Dialog Box                                                    |
+----------------------------------------------------------------*/
#define  OVERALLWIDTH        25 * XC
#define  OVERALLHEIGHT       11 * YC
#define  NEWLINE             2 * YC

#define  X1 11 * XC          /* cell Name */
#define  X2 11 * XC          /* Leader Line */
#define  X3 2 * XC           /* group Mode */
#define  X4 (OVERALLWIDTH/2) - (5 * XC)  /* middle of OKAY button */

#define  Y1 GENY(1)          /* cell Name */
#define  Y2 Y1 + NEWLINE     /* input string */
#define  Y3 Y2 + NEWLINE     /* group Mode */
#define  Y4 Y3 + NEWLINE     /* leader Line */
#define  Y5 Y4 + NEWLINE     /* Okay button  */
#define  BW XC * 9           /* box width */

DialogBoxRsc DIALOGID_PlaceBox =
{
  DIALOGATTR_DEFAULT,
  OVERALLWIDTH, OVERALLHEIGHT,
  NOHELP, MHELP, NOHOOK, NOPARENTID,
  "Place Box",
  {
  {{X1, Y1, BW, 0},   Text,   TEXTID_cellName, ON, 0, "", ""},
  {{X1, Y2, BW, 0},   Text,   TEXTID_String, ON, 0, "", ""},
  {{X2, Y3, 0, 0},    OptionButton, OPTIONBUTTONID_groupMode, ON, 0,"", ""},
  {{X3, Y4, 0, 0},    ToggleButton, TOGGLEID_leaderLine,   ON, 0, "", ""},
  {{X4, Y5, BW, 0},   PushButton, PUSHBUTTONID_ok, ON, 0, "", ""}
  }
};

/*----------------------------------------------------------------+
```

```
|      Option Items                                                             |
+------------------------------------------------------------------------------*/
DItem_OptionButtonRsc    OPTIONBUTTONID_groupMode =
{
  NOSYNONYM, NOHELP, MHELP, NOHOOK, NOARG,
  "Grouping :",
  "plBoxInfo->groupMode",
  {
  {NOTYPE, NOICON, NOCMD, LCMD, 0, NOMASK, ON, "None"},
  {NOTYPE, NOICON, NOCMD, LCMD, 1, NOMASK, ON, "Cell"},
  {NOTYPE, NOICON, NOCMD, LCMD, 2, NOMASK, ON, "Graphic Group"},
  }
};
/*-----------------------------------------------------------------------------+
|      Text Items                                                              |
+------------------------------------------------------------------------------*/
DItem_TextRsc TEXTID_cellName =
{
  NOCMD, LCMD, NOSYNONYM, NOHELP, MHELP, NOHOOK, NOARG,
  8, "%s", "%s", "", "", NOMASK, CONCAT,
  "Cell Name:",
  "plBoxInfo->cellName"
};

DItem_TextRsc TEXTID_String =
{
  NOCMD, LCMD, NOSYNONYM, NOHELP, MHELP, NOHOOK, NOARG,
  127, "%s", "%s", "", "", NOMASK, CONCAT,
  "String:",
  "plBoxInfo->String"
};
/*-----------------------------------------------------------------------------+
|   Toggle Buttons                                                             |
+------------------------------------------------------------------------------*/
DItem_ToggleButtonRsc TOGGLEID_leaderLine =
{
  NOCMD, MCMD, NOSYNONYM, NOHELP, MCMD, NOHOOK, NOARG,
  NOMASK, NOINVERT,
  "Leader Line",
  "plBoxInfo->leaderLine"
};
/*-----------------------------------------------------------------------------+
|      Push Button Items                                                       |
+------------------------------------------------------------------------------*/
DItem_PushButtonRsc PUSHBUTTONID_ok =
{
  NOT_DEFAULT_BUTTON, NOHELP, MHELP,
  HOOKITEMID_Button_Place, 0, NOCMD, MCMD, "",
  "  OK  "
};
```

pbdlgmsg.r

In the last chapter, the message and command file were one. In this example, we have separated them into *pbdlgmsg.r* and *pbdlgcmd.r* respectively.

```
/*-----------------------------------------------------------------+
|        PBDLGMSG.R                                                |
+-----------------------------------------------------------------*/
#include "rscdefs.h"
#include "cmdclass.h"

MessageList 0 =
{
    {
    { 0, "" },
    { 1, "MDL Place Box 2" },
    { 2, "Define Start Point" },
    { 3, "Define Box Position" },
    { 4, "PlBox Done" },
    }
};
```

pbdlgcmd.r

This command table is identical to the one used for the PLBOX application. Therefore, you can have only one application with the command PLACE BOX. You must unload the PLBOX application if you wish to use the PBDLG application.

```
/*-----------------------------------------------------------------+
|  pbdlgcmd.r - command table for pbdlg.mc                         |
+-----------------------------------------------------------------*/
#include "rscdefs.h"
#include "cmdclass.h"

#define    CT_NONE          0
#define    CT_PLACE         1
#define    CT_BOX           2

Table   CT_PLACE =
{
    { 1,  CT_BOX,      PLACEMENT,      REQ,      "PLACE" },
};
Table   CT_BOX =
{
    { 1,  CT_NONE,     INHERIT,        DEF,      "BOX" },
};
```

To build the PBDLG application, enter *bmake -a pbdlg*.

pbdlg.mke

```
#--------------------------------------------------------------------
#          PBDLG   MDL Make File
#--------------------------------------------------------------------
%include $(MS)/mdl/include/mdl.mki


#--------------------------------------------------------------------
#          Define constants specific to this example
#--------------------------------------------------------------------
progmdl       = d:/progmdl/disk/
baseDir       = $(progmdl)pbdlg/
objectDir     = $(mdlexample)objects/
privateInc    = $(baseDir)

pbdlgObjs     = $(objectDir)pbdlg.mo

pbdlgRscs     =    $(objectDir)pbdlgcmd.rsc \
                   $(objectDir)pbdlgdlg.rsc \
                   $(objectDir)pbdlgtyp.rsc \
                   $(objectDir)pbdlgmsg.rsc \
                   $(objectDir)pbdlg.mp


#--------------------------------------------------------------------
#          Generate Command Tables
#--------------------------------------------------------------------
$(PrivateInc)pbdlgcmd.h      : $(baseDir)pbdlgcmd.r

$(objectDir)pbdlgcmd.rsc     : $(baseDir)pbdlgcmd.r


#--------------------------------------------------------------------
#          Compile Dialog Resources
#--------------------------------------------------------------------
$(objectDir)pbdlgdlg.rsc     : $(baseDir)pbdlgdlg.r $(PrivateInc)pbdlgcmd.h


#--------------------------------------------------------------------
#          Prompts and command numbers
#--------------------------------------------------------------------
#   Don't generate an include file for the prompts and command numbers
$(objectDir)pbdlgmsg.rsc     : $(baseDir)pbdlgmsg.r


#--------------------------------------------------------------------
#          Make resource to publish structure(s)
#--------------------------------------------------------------------
$(objectDir)pbdlgtyp.r       : $(baseDir)pbdlgtyp.mt $(privateInc)pbdlgdlg.h
```

```
$(objectDir)pbdlgtyp.rsc   : $(objectDir)pbdlgtyp.r


#------------------------------------------------------------
#        Compile and link MDL Application
#------------------------------------------------------------
$(objectDir)pbdlg.mo          : $(baseDir)pbdlg.mc $(PrivateInc)pbdlgcmd.h

$(objectDir)pbdlg.mp          : $(objectDir)pbdlg.mo
  $(msg)
  >$(objectDir)temp.cmd
  -a$@
  -s8000
  $(linkOpts)
  $(pbdlgObjs)
  $(mdlLibs)ditemlib.ml
  <
  $(linkCmd) @$(objectDir)temp.cmd
  ~time


#------------------------------------------------------------
#        Merge Objects into one file
#------------------------------------------------------------
$(mdlapps)pbdlg.ma             : $(pbdlgRscs)
  $(msg)
  >$(objectDir)temp.cmd
  -o$@
  $(pbdlgRscs)
  <
  $(rscLibCmd) @$(objectDir)temp.cmd
  ~time
```

4 : Element Search & Manipulation

In the first three chapters we looked at adding elements to the design file. In this chapter we will discuss the steps involved with manipulating existing elements. We need to locate the required element, make the changes and write the modified element back into the file. Development tools like UCMs and MicroCSL require us to handle all stages, from making sure the words to follow are correct on complex elements, to deleting the old element if the new element does not fit into the previous position. This requires a comprehensive understanding of the design file, element format and file pointers. A simple mistake can result in file corruption.

Element Manipulation is one of the most common operations in developing an MDL application. To make our task easier, MDL provides a series of functions which take care of the low level manipulation of elements. For example, the function *mdlModify_elementSingle* reads one element from the design file, and calls a function for each component of that element. We can pass the argument MODIFY_ORIG, which makes the modification to the original element. If the new element does not fit into the old position, the function deletes the old element and adds the new element to the end of file. These features make MDL a powerful language, leaving the programmer more time to write the application, rather than working on the mundane tasks.

Let's start with a program that will prompt for an element and then change it's level to the active level.

Locating an element

Elements are located in one of three possible ways.
- By nominating the element.
- Searching the entire file for the element.
- Searching the fence for the element.

MDL provides several functions to locate elements and we will discuss each method. None of these methods is necessarily better than the others, but some are better suited for certain applications.

Element Location Functions

Below is a summary of Element Location Functions. For a detailed description of the arguments, please consult your MDL Manual.

mdlLocate_allowLocked   sets the search mask to locate all displayable elements from the master and attached files.

mdlLocate_clearElemSearchMask turns off search for specified element types.

mdlLocate_findElement   search for an element in the active file and all of its reference files.

mdlLocate_getProjectedPoint   returns a point on the located element, closest to the selection point.

mdlLocate_identifyElement   locate the next element.

mdlLocate_init   start the search from the beginning of the design file.

mdlLocate_noElemAllowLocked   set the search mask to locate all elements from all files. It then clears the search type mask.

mdlLocate_noElemNoLocked   set the search mask for unlocked elements. It then clears the search type mask.

mdlLocate_normal locate only displayable and unlocked elements in the current file.

mdlLocate_clearElemSearchMask clear all bits in the search mask for element types.

mdlLocate_setElemSearchMask set search mask for specified element types.

mdlLocate_setFunction specify function to use in processing located elements.

Establishing a search criteria

Our first step is to tell MicroStation which elements we wish to locate. This is done by establishing a search mask, from an array of element types. The function `setSearchType` below, establishes a search for all elements. The element types are found in the include file < mselems.h > (refer to Appendix A).

```
Private void    setSearchType()
  {
  static int searchType[]={CELL_HEADER_ELM, LINE_ELM,
        LINE_STRING_ELM, SHAPE_ELM, TEXT_NODE_ELM,
        CURVE_ELM, CMPLX_STRING_ELM, CONIC_ELM,
        CMPLX_SHAPE_ELM, ELLIPSE_ELM, ARC_ELM,
        TEXT_ELM, SURFACE_ELM, SOLID_ELM}

  /* initialize search criteria to find nothing */
  mdlLocate_noElemNoLocked():

  /* add elements to search to list */
  mdlLocate_setElemSearchMask(sizeof(searchType)/sizeof(int), searchType);
  }
```

The function *mdlLocate_noElemNoLocked* sets the search mask for unlocked elements in the master file and clears search bits for all element types. Therefore, we need to call *mdlLocate_setElemSearchMask* to establish the elements to search.

We could use *mdlLocate_normal*. This is the same as *mdlLocate_noElemNoLocked*, but it sets the search mask to find all displayable elements. Using *mdlLocate_normal* saves the trouble of listing the elements to search, as we did with the array `searchType`. The advantage of using *mdlLocate_setElemSearchMask* is that we could use the function `setSearchType` as a seed for future routines.

Element Modification Functions

Element modification is done through three separate functions. Each of these functions operates on the three different modification methods. These are, single element modification, modification on a group of elements (either a selection set or graphic group), and modification to an element descriptor (discussed later in this book). The last function, *mdlModify_freeGGMap* is a support routine for the element modification functions.

mdlModify_elementSingle   a user defined function is used to modify a single element (or a complex element).

mdlModify_elementMulti   similar to the single modification function, but will work on selection set or graphic group (if graphic group lock is on).

mdlModify_elementDescr   modifies the element descriptor currently in memory.

mdlModify_freeGGMap   in an element copy, memory is allocated to map the original graphic group number to the new number. This function frees the allocated memory.

The function *mdlState_startModifyCommand* will set the stage for a locate and modify command. Because it is a state function, we set up a function to execute depending on subsequent events. When the `change_single` function executes, it displays "Identify Element" in the prompt field, and displays string 1, from *MessageList*, in the command field. A data point on an element displays string 2, from *MessageList*, in the prompt field. A second data point validates the element selection, and executes the function `mod_accept`.

```
Private void change_single()
  {
  setSearchType();
  mdlState_startModifyCommand (
          change_single, /* function to call on RESET */
          mod_accept,    /* function to call on DATA */
          NULL,          /* function to call for DYNAMIC */
          NULL,          /* function to call on SHOW */
          NULL,          /* function to call on CLEAN */
          1,             /* index into MESSAGE LIST */
          2,             /* index into PROMPT LIST */
          TRUE,          /* Modify SELECTION SET ? */
          FALSE);        /* additional data points required */

  /* start element search from the beginning of file */
  mdlLocate_init ();
  }
```

Selection Set Functions

Selection sets are a new way to manipulate elements. In previous versions of MicroStation we selected the operator (for example the copy command) and then specified the elements on which to operate. Selection sets reverse this thinking, requiring the user to specify first the elements and then the operator. This is very much like the English noun-verb as against the French verb-noun. A summary of the Selection Set Functions are listed here.

mdlSelect_addElement	add an element to the current selection set.
mdlSelect_allElements	add all displayable elements to the selection set.
mdlSelect_freeAll	free the memory used to store the selection set and remove elements from the set.
mdlSelect_isActive	true if selection set is active. Use this function to process selection set and not graphic groups.
mdlSelect_removeElement	remove a specified element from the selection set.
mdlSelect_returnPositions	returns the file positions of elements in the selection set.

4-6 Programming with MDL

Modifying a Selection Set

Previously, we defined function mod_accept to be activated by a selection set
or by a data point on an element. The function mod_accept is shown here.

```
Private void    mod_accept ()
  {
  ULong  filePos, compOffset;
  int    currFile=0;

  filePos = mdlElement_getFilePos (FILEPOS_CURRENT, &currFile);
  if (mdlSelect_isActive())
  {
  mdlModify_elementMulti (currFile,    /* file to process */
        filePos,      /* file position for element */
        MODIFY_REQUEST_HEADERS, /* process complex headers */
        MODIFY_ORIG, /* modify original element */
        editelem,     /* modify routine for each element */
        NULL,         /* parameters for editelem */
        TRUE);        /* process graphic group */
  } else {
  mdlModify_elementSingle (currFile,
        filePos,      /* file position for element */
        MODIFY_REQUEST_HEADERS, /* process complex headers */
        MODIFY_ORIG, /* modify original element */
        editelem,     /* modify routine for each element */
        NULL,         /* parameters for editelem */
        FALSE);       /* offset for component elements */
  }

  /* restart the element location process */
  mdlLocate_restart (FALSE);
}
```

The function *mdlElement_getFilePos* returns a file position, depending on the
first argument. Specifying FILEPOS_CURRENT, indicates that we want it to
return the file position of the current element.

If the selection set is active, the function *mdlSelect_isActive* will return true.
mdlModify_elementMulti goes through each element in the selection set (or
graphic group) and calls editelem for the modifications.
mdlModify_elementMulti is one of those set-and-forget functions. We just
supply the appropriate arguments, and we are guaranteed the work. The
advantage with such a function is a consistency in command behaviour.

The argument MODIFY_REQUEST_HEADERS means that editelem will be called for complex headers, and all component elements. But, if we were changing the elements levels and we located a cell, we wouldn't want to change the level of the cell header, because it is always zero. Therefore, in the editelem function we must check for cell headers. The possible arguments are:

MODIFY_REQUEST_NOHEADERS	do not call modify routine for complex headers.
MODIFY_REQUEST_HEADERS	call modify routine for all elements.
MODIFY_REQUEST_ONLYONE	call modify routine only once for the component elements.

The argument MODIFY_ORIG tells *mdlModify_elementMulti* to call editelem and modify the original element. If the modification changes the size of the element, then the old element is deleted and the new one added to the end of the file. The possible values for the modify flag are:

MODIFY_ORIG	modify original element.
MODIFY_COPY	add a copy of the element to the file and make modifications to this element.
MODIFY_DONTERASEORIG	do not erase original element from screen.
MODIFY_DONTDRAWNEW	do not draw newly created element.
MODIFY_DRAWINHILITE	draw the new element in the hilite color.

The function editelem is the user defined function, which does the modification to the element. We will discuss this later.

Modifying a single element

Modifications to a single element are done with the function *mdlModify_elementSingle*. Most of the arguments are the same as for *mdlModify_elementMulti*. For complex elements we have to do several things to ensure that our function editelem is not called for complex headers. This is not to say that the complex headers are not changed. In fact, the family of *mdlModify_* functions guarantees to look after the words in description, number of components and so on.

Once we locate the element we reset the search window pointers with the function *mdlLocate_restart(FALSE)*. This function allows us to use the second data point as the accept button, and also highlight another element to modify. Thus our application looks and feels like a MicroStation primitive.

The function that actually makes the modification is straightforward. The element to modify is passed as an argument to `editelem` and we assign it a new level. The return value MODIFY_STATUS_REPLACE tells the *mdlModify_* routines to replace the original element with the new element. This is very important, as the assignment in `editelem` makes the change in memory. It is the return value that changes the element in the file. There are several return values. A brief summary is shown here:

MODIFY_STATUS_ABORT	stop processing component elements.
MODIFY_STATUS_DELETE	delete current element.
MODIFY_STATUS_ERROR	combination of MODIFY_STATUS_ABORT and MODIFY_STATUS_FAIL.
MODIFY_STATUS_FAIL	error has occurred, abandon all changes.
MODIFY_STATUS_NOCHANGE	do not change original element.
MODIFY_STATUS_REPLACE	replace original element with new element.
MODIFY_STATUS_REPLACEDSCR	replace original element descriptor with a new descriptor.

When we receive a cell header, we do not want to change its level because it is always zero. By using MODIFY_STATUS_NOCHANGE, we can skip the cell header.

```
Private int editelem
(
MSElementUnion *el
)
{
  int  actlevel;

  if (el->ehdr.type == CELL_HEADER_ELM)
      return (MODIFY_STATUS_NOCHANGE);
  mdlParams_getActive(&actlevel, ACTIVEPARAM_LEVEL);
  el->ehdr.level = actlevel;
  return (MODIFY_STATUS_REPLACE);
}
```

Active Settings

A series of functions is available to query and change active settings. We use these functions to protect our code from changes in element formats. The other advantage is that we do not have to look up the built-in variables for the correct format. For example, the active color is defined in the TCB variable as *tcb->symbology.color*.   The   equivalent   function   call   is *mdlParams_getActive(&color,* ACTIVEPARAM_COLOR*).*

mdlParams_getActive	get active setting.
mdlParams_setActive	change active setting.
mdlParams_storeType9Variable	same as a FILE DESIGN but only changes the specified variable. Equivalent to the UCM command STO.
mdlParams_saveMasterLevelSymbology	rewrite symbology element (Type 10) with current symbology information.

The available active parameters are:

Active Parameter	description	key in
ACTIVEPARAM_ANGLE	active angle	AA =
ACTIVEPARAM_AREAMODE	active area (solid/hole)	ACTIVE AREA
ACTIVEPARAM_AXISANGLE	axis increment	ACTIVE AXIS
ACTIVEPARAM_AXISORIGIN	axis origin	AXIS ORIGIN
ACTIVEPARAM_CAPMODE	surface or solid cap	ACTIVE CAPMODE
ACTIVEPARAM_CELLNAME	active cell	AC =
ACTIVEPARAM_CLASS	active class	ACTIVE CLASS
ACTIVEPARAM_COLOR	active color	CO =
ACTIVEPARAM_COLOR_BY_NAME	active color	CO =
ACTIVEPARAM_DIMCOMPAT	dimension compatibility	
ACTIVEPARAM_FILLMODE	active fill	ACTIVE FILL
ACTIVEPARAM_FONT	active font	FT =
ACTIVEPARAM_GRIDMODE	orthogonal or iso grid	ACTIVE GRIDMODE
ACTIVEPARAM_GRIDRATIO	grid aspect ratio	ACTIVE GRIDRATIO
ACTIVEPARAM_GRIDREF	reference grid	GR =
ACTIVEPARAM_GRIDUNITS	master grid	GU =
ACTIVEPARAM_KEYPOINT	snap divisor	KY =
ACTIVEPARAM_LEVEL	active level	LV =
ACTIVEPARAM_LINELENGTH	active line length	LL =
ACTIVEPARAM_LINESPACING	active line spacing	LS =

ACTIVEPARAM_LINESTYLE	active line style	LC =
ACTIVEPARAM_LINEWEIGHT	active line weight	WT =
ACTIVEPARAM_MLINECOMPAT	multiline compatibility	
ACTIVEPARAM_NODEJUST	active text node justification	ACTIVE TNJ
ACTIVEPARAM_PATTERNDELTA	active pattern delta	PD =
ACTIVEPARAM_PATTERNANGLE	active pattern angle	PA =
ACTIVEPARAM_PATTERNSCALE	active pattern scale	PS =
ACTIVEPARAM_PATTERNCELL	active pattern cell	AP =
ACTIVEPARAM_POINT	active point	ACTIVE POINT
ACTIVEPARAM_SCALE	active scale	AS =
ACTIVEPARAM_STREAMDELTA	active stream delta	SD =
ACTIVEPARAM_STREAMTOLERANCE	active stream tolerance	ST =
ACTIVEPARAM_STREAMANGLE	active stream angle	ACTIVE STREAM ANGLE
ACTIVEPARAM_STREAMAREA	active stream area	ACTIVE STREAM AREA
ACTIVEPARAM_TAB	special char for each tab	none
ACTIVEPARAM_TAGINCREMENT	tag increment	TI =
ACTIVEPARAM_TERMINATOR	active line terminator	LT =
ACTIVEPARAM_TERMINATORSCALE	terminator scale	TS =
ACTIVEPARAM_TEXTHEIGHT	active text height	TH =
ACTIVEPARAM_TEXTWIDTH	active text width	TW =
ACTIVEPARAM_TEXTJUST	active text justification	ACTIVE TXJ
ACTIVEPARAM_UNITROUNDOFF	active unit round	UR =

We will make our code truly portable by changing the line *el->ehdr.level = actlevel* to use the MDL function *mdlElement_setProperties*. The modified `editelem` function now looks like:

```
Private int editelem
(
MSElement    *el
)
  {
  int   actlevel;

  if (mdlElement_getType(el) == CELL_HEADER_ELM)
      return (MODIFY_STATUS_NOCHANGE);

  mdlParams_getActive(&actlevel, ACTIVEPARAM_LEVEL);
  mdlElement_setProperties (el,  /* element to change */
              &actlevel, /* level */
              NULL,     /* graphic group number */
              NULL,     /* class */
              NULL,     /* locked */
              NULL,     /* new */
              NULL,     /* modified */
              NULL,     /* view independent */
              NULL      /* solid hole */
              );
  return (MODIFY_STATUS_REPLACE);
  }
```

The complete listing for the program *modsing.mc* is given below. To load the application, enter *mdl l modsing*. To execute the application, enter MODIFY SINGLE. You can abbreviate this to MOD SING.

modsing.mc

```
/*-------------------------------------------------------------------+
|   Copyright (c) 1991 Mach Dinh-Vu, All Rights Reserved             |
|                                                                    |
|   modsing.mc - modify the element's level using the                |
|                active level. Will operate on a selection           |
|                set and a graphic group. This program               |
|                supports the command                                |
|                                                                    |
|                MODIFY SINGLE                                        |
+-------------------------------------------------------------------*/
#include <mdl.h>
#include <mselems.h>
#include <rscdefs.h>
#include <tcb.h>
#include <global.h>
#include <scanner.h>
#include "modsing.h"

/*-------------------------------------------------------------------+
|   name        main                                                 |
+-------------------------------------------------------------------*/
main ()
  {
  RscFileHandle    rfHandle;

  /* --- load our command table --- */
  if (mdlParse_loadCommandTable (NULL) == NULL)
     mdlOutput_error ("Unable to load command table.");
  mdlOutput_prompt ("to execute, key-in MODIFY SINGLE");
  mdlResource_openFile (&rfHandle, NULL, FALSE);
  }

/*-------------------------------------------------------------------+
|   name        setSearchType                                        |
+-------------------------------------------------------------------*/
Private void setSearchType()
  {
  static int searchType[]={CELL_HEADER_ELM, LINE_ELM, LINE_STRING_ELM,
        SHAPE_ELM, TEXT_NODE_ELM, CURVE_ELM, CMPLX_STRING_ELM,
        CONIC_ELM, CMPLX_SHAPE_ELM, ELLIPSE_ELM, ARC_ELM,
        TEXT_ELM, SURFACE_ELM, SOLID_ELM};

  /* initialize search criteria to find nothing */
```

```
    mdlLocate_noElemNoLocked();

    /* add elements to search to list */
    mdlLocate_setElemSearchMask(sizeof(searchType)/sizeof(int),searchType);
    }
/*----------------------------------------------------------------------------+
| name        editelem                                                         |
+----------------------------------------------------------------------------*/
Private int editelem
(
MSElement   *el
)
    {
    int   actlevel;

    if (mdlElement_getType(el) == CELL_HEADER_ELM)
        return (MODIFY_STATUS_NOCHANGE);

    mdlParams_getActive(&actlevel, ACTIVEPARAM_LEVEL);
    mdlElement_setProperties (el,  /* element to change */
                    &actlevel, /* level */
                    NULL,      /* graphic group number */
                    NULL,      /* class */
                    NULL,      /* locked */
                    NULL,      /* new */
                    NULL,      /* modified */
                    NULL,      /* view independent */
                    NULL       /* solid hole */
                    );
    return (MODIFY_STATUS_REPLACE);
    }
/*----------------------------------------------------------------------------+
| name        mod_accept                                                       |
+----------------------------------------------------------------------------*/
Private void    mod_accept ()
    {
    ULong  filePos, compOffset;
    int    currFile=0;

    filePos = mdlElement_getFilePos (FILEPOS_CURRENT, &currFile);
    if (mdlSelect_isActive())
    {
    mdlModify_elementMulti (currFile,    /* file to process */
        filePos,       /* file position for element */
        MODIFY_REQUEST_HEADERS, /* process complex headers */
        MODIFY_ORIG, /* modify original element */
        editelem,    /* modify routine for each element */
        NULL,        /* parameters for editelem */
        TRUE);       /* process graphic group */
    } else {
```

```
   mdlModify_elementSingle (currFile,
         filePos,       /* file position for element */
         MODIFY_REQUEST_HEADERS, /* process complex headers */
         MODIFY_ORIG, /* modify original element */
         editelem,      /* modify routine for each element */
         NULL,          /* parameters for editelem */
         FALSE); /* offset for component elements */
   }

   /* restart the element location process */
   mdlLocate_restart (FALSE);
}
/*---------------------------------------------------------------------------+
| name        change_sing                                                    |
+---------------------------------------------------------------------------*/
Private void change_sing()
  {
  setSearchType();
  mdlState_startModifyCommand (
            change_sing, /* function to call on RESET */
            mod_accept,    /* function to call on DATA */
            NULL,          /* function to call for DYNAMIC */
            NULL,          /* function to call on SHOW */
            NULL,          /* function to call on CLEAN */
            1,             /* index into MESSAGE LIST */
            2,             /* index into PROMPT LIST */
            TRUE,          /* Modify SELECTION SET ? */
            FALSE);        /* additional data points required */

   /* start element search from the beginning of file */
   mdlLocate_init ();
   }
/*---------------------------------------------------------------------------+
| name        modsing                                                        |
+---------------------------------------------------------------------------*/
cmdName       modsing ()
cmdNumber     CMD_MODIFY_SINGLE
  {
  change_sing();
  }
```

modsing.r

The file *modsing.r* contains both the command table and prompt messages.

```
/*─────────────────────────────────────────────────────────────────+
| name        modsing.r                                             |
+──────────────────────────────────────────────────────────────────*/

#include "rscdefs.h"
#include "cmdclass.h"

#define      CT_NONE          0
#define      CT_MODIFY        1
#define      CT_SING          2

Table   CT_MODIFY =
{
    { 1,  CT_SING,        PLACEMENT,        REQ,            "MODIFY" },
};
Table   CT_SING =
{
    { 1,  CT_NONE,        INHERIT,        DEF,            "SINGLE" },
};

MessageList 0 =
{
    {
    { 1, "Modify Element Level" },
    { 2, "Accept/Reject element" },
    }
};
```

To build the MODSING application, enter *bmake -a modsing*.

modsing.mke

```
#--------------------------------------------------------------------
#          MODSING MDL Make File
#--------------------------------------------------------------------
%include $(MS)/mdl/include/mdl.mki

#--------------------------------------------------------------------
#          Define constants specific to this modsing application
#--------------------------------------------------------------------
progmdl             = d:/progmdl/disk/
baseDir             = $(progmdl)scanfile/
objectDir           = $(mdlexample)objects/
privateInc          = $(baseDir)

modallObjs          = $(objectDir)modall.mo
modallRscs          = $(objectDir)modall.rsc \
                        $(objectDir)modall.mp

$(privateInc)modall.h        : $(baseDir)modall.r

$(objectDir)modall.rsc       : $(baseDir)modall.r

$(objectDir)modall.mo        : $(baseDir)modall.mc

$(objectDir)modall.mp            : $(modallObjs)
        $(msg)
        > $(objectDir)temp.cmd
        -a$@
        -s6000
        $(linkOpts)
        $(modallObjs)
        <
        $(linkCmd) @$(objectDir)temp.cmd
        ~time

$(mdlapps)modall.ma              : $(modallRscs)
        $(msg)
        > $(objectDir)temp.cmd
        -o$@
        $(modallRscs)
        <
        $(rscLibCmd) @$(objectDir)temp.cmd
        ~time
```

Locating Elements

In this section we will locate a series of elements by scanning the entire file. The bulk of this program is similar to the single element modification program discussed earlier.

Scan Functions

The following functions are used to establish search criteria.

mdlScan_initScanList	initialize a *scanList*.
mdlScan_initialize	loads the *scanList* into the MicroStation design file scanner.
mdlScan_setDrawnElements	sets the *scanList* so it will return displayable elements.
mdlScan_noRangeCheck	sets the *scanList* so that all elements are located in the entire file. This way, no elements are rejected on range.
mdlScan_singleViewClass	returns only elements that are currently displayed in a particular view.
mdlScan_viewRange	find only elements in a particular view.
mdlScan_file	scan the file according to the established criteria.

The function change_all does the job of locating the desired elements. The first step is to establish the scan list with the elements that we want to locate and work with.

Scan Criteria

We will define a variable *scanList* which is of type *ExtScanlist*, a structure defined in < scanner.h >. Using *scanList* we can specify a search criteria for the scanner to quickly locate elements. The following constants specify the *scantype*.

ELEMDATA	if true, store data
NESTCELL	if true, cell is treated as one element
PICKCELL	if true, compare cell name
PROPCLAS	if true, compare on properties and class
GRPHGRP	if true, compare on graphics group
MULTI	if true, there are multiple scan ranges
SKEW	if true, do a skew scan
BOTH	if true, get both pointers and data
ONEELEM	if true, get only one element
ATTRENT	if true, compare on attribute linkage entity
ATTROCC	if true, compare on attribute occurrence #
STOPSECT	if true, check stop sector
LEVELS	if true, compare on levels
ELEMTYPE	if true, compare on element type

The following constants are used in *extendedType*

RETURN3D	if true, return 3D elements from 2D file
FILEPOS	if true, return file pos, not block/byte
MEMPTRS	if true, return mem pointers or elements
EXTATTR	if true, do extended attribute scan

The following constants are the properties indicators.

ELELOCKED	set if locked
ELENEW	set if new
ELEMOD	set if modified
ELEATTR	attribute data present
ELERELTVE	set if relative to database
ELEPLANR	set if planar
ELESNAP	set if element is snappable
ELEHOLE	set if element is a hole

Our first step is to establish the *scantype*. We want the scanner to compare on element type and return one element at a time.

```
scanList.scantype        = ELEMTYPE | ONEELEM;
scanList.extendedType    = FILEPOS;
```

Next, we establish a type mask, telling the scanner which element type to locate. The *typmask* variable is a 16 bit mask, where each bit is an element type. For example, if bit 0 of *typmask[0]* is set, then we will be locating element type 1. If bit 0 of *typmask[1]* is set, then we are locating element type 17, a text element. The *typmask* array is eight words long, therefore we can have up to 128 (8 * 16) possible element types. Most of the displayable element types are in the range 0 to 32. (Note: The new MicroStation elements, i.e., multi-lines, dimensions and shared cells, are element types greater than 32). Knowing this, we can set all bits in the first two words of *typmask*, as shown here:

```
scanList.typmask[0] = 0xffff;        /* set all bits using HEX */
scanList.typmask[1] = 0xffff;
```

We won't be doing this, because it takes a lot of work to calculate the Hex value to scan for lines and circles. In the include file < mselems.h > there is a series of *#defines* for element type masks. For example, the mask TMSK0_LINE must be 'OR'ed with *typmask[0]*. The same applies to TMSK1_TEXT, which must be 'OR'ed with *typmask[1]*. Our program now looks like this:

```
scanList.typmask[0]  = TMSK0_LINE|TMSK0_LINE_STRING|TMSK0_SHAPE;
scanList.typmask[0] |= TMSK0_TEXT_NODE|TMSK0_CURVE ;
scanList.typmask[0] |= TMSK0_CONIC| TMSK0_CMPLX_SHAPE ;
scanList.typmask[0] |= TMSK0_ARC|TMSK0_CMPLX_STRING|TMSK0_ELLIPSE;
scanList.typmask[1]  = TMSK1_TEXT|TMSK1_SURFACE|TMSK1_SOLID;
```

In the debugger, if we enter *scanList.typmask[0]* at the mdb > prompt, we can see the decimal value of *scanList.typmask[0]* with the appropriate bits set. Imagine calculating this long-hand.

NOTE: *The scanner will locate all elements in the file that satisfy the search criteria. Elements that are not displayed (i.e., elements that are on a level that is off in the current view) will be searched and modified. This applies as well, to non-displayable elements like complex headers, group data elements, file header elements and type 66 elements. Be careful when scanning the entire file.*

Now, we are ready to start the scan. We initialize *scanList* with *mdlScan_initScanList*. We must make sure that the scanner does not check the element range. If we are scanning all elements in the design file, then we use *mdlScan_noRangeCheck* to stop the scanner excluding elements on range. We initialize the scanner with the function *mdlScan_initialize* and call *mdlScan_file* to scan the file.

```
mdlScan_initScanlist (&scanList);
mdlScan_noRangeCheck (&scanList);
mdlOutput_message ("Scanning file ....");

scanList.scantype          = ELEMTYPE | ONEELEM;
scanList.extendedType      = FILEPOS;
scanList.typmask[0]  = TMSK0_LINE|TMSK0_LINE_STRING|TMSK0_SHAPE;
scanList.typmask[0] |= TMSK0_TEXT_NODE|TMSK0_CURVE ;
scanList.typmask[0] |= TMSK0_CONIC| TMSK0_CMPLX_SHAPE ;
scanList.typmask[0] |= TMSK0_ARC|TMSK0_CMPLX_STRING|TMSK0_ELLIPSE;
scanList.typmask[1]        = TMSK1_TEXT|TMSK1_SURFACE|TMSK1_SOLID;
eofPos  = mdlElement_getFilePos (FILEPOS_EOF, NULL);
filePos = 0L;      /* start seacrh from top of file */

mdlScan_initialize (0, &scanList);
do {
    scanWords = sizeof(elemAddr)/sizeof(short);
    status    = mdlScan_file (elemAddr, &scanWords,
                    sizeof(elemAddr),&filePos);
    numAddr   = scanWords / sizeof(short);

    for (i=0; i < numAddr; i++)
    {
        if (elemAddr[i] >= eofPos)  break;
        mdlModify_elementSingle (0, elemAddr[i],
            MODIFY_REQUEST_NOHEADERS, MODIFY_ORIG, editelem,
            &numchanged, 0L);
    }
} while (status == BUFF_FULL);
```

The complete listing for the program *modall.mc* is given below. To load the application enter   *mdl l modall*. To execute the application, enter MOD LEVEL ALL.

modall.mc

```
/*---------------------------------------------------------------+
| Copyright (c) 1991 Mach Dinh-Vu, All Rights Reserved          |
|                                                                |
| modall.mc -   modify the element's level using the            |
|               active level. This program will scan the        |
|               entire DGN file for the elements.               |
|                                                                |
|               MODIFY LEVEL ALL                                 |
+--------------------------------------------------------------*/
#include <mdl.h>
#include <mselems.h>
#include <rscdefs.h>
#include <tcb.h>
#include <global.h>
#include <scanner.h>
#include "modall.h"

/*---------------------------------------------------------------+
| name        main                                               |
+--------------------------------------------------------------*/
main ()
  {
  RscFileHandle   rfHandle;

  /* --- load our command table --- */
  if (mdlParse_loadCommandTable (NULL) == NULL)
      mdlOutput_error ("Unable to load command table.");
  mdlOutput_prompt ("to execute, key-in MODIFY LEVEL ALL");
  mdlResource_openFile (&rfHandle, NULL, FALSE);
  }

/*---------------------------------------------------------------+
| name        editelem                                           |
+--------------------------------------------------------------*/
Private int editelem
(
MSElement    *el,
int          *numchanged
)

  {
  int  actlevel;
```

```
    if (mdlElement_getType(el) == CELL_HEADER_ELM)
        return (MODIFY_STATUS_NOCHANGE);

mdlParams_getActive(&actlevel, ACTIVEPARAM_LEVEL);
mdlElement_setProperties (el,  /* element to change */
                &actlevel,  /* level */
                NULL,       /* graphic group number */
                NULL,       /* class */
                NULL,       /* locked */
                NULL,       /* new */
                NULL,       /* modified */
                NULL,       /* view independent */
                NULL        /* solid hole */
                );
(*numchanged)++;
mdlOutput_rscPrintf(MSG_MESSAGE, NULL, 0, 2, (*numchanged));
return (MODIFY_STATUS_REPLACE);
}
/*-----------------------------------------------------------------+
| name        change_all                                          |
+----------------------------------------------------------------*/
Private void change_all()
    {
    ULong         elemAddr[50], eofPos, filePos;
    int           scanWords, numchanged=0, status, i, numAddr;
    ExtScanlist   scanList;
    char          buffer[50];

    mdlScan_initScanlist (&scanList);
    mdlScan_noRangeCheck (&scanList);
    mdlOutput_message("Scanning file ....");

    scanList.scantype        = ELEMTYPE | ONEELEM;
    scanList.extendedType    = FILEPOS;
    scanList.typmask[0]  = TMSK0_LINE|TMSK0_LINE_STRING|TMSK0_SHAPE;
    scanList.typmask[0] |= TMSK0_TEXT_NODE|TMSK0_CURVE ;
    scanList.typmask[0] |= TMSK0_CONIC| TMSK0_CMPLX_SHAPE ;
    scanList.typmask[0] |= TMSK0_ARC|TMSK0_CMPLX_STRING|TMSK0_ELLIPSE;
    scanList.typmask[1]      = TMSK1_TEXT|TMSK1_SURFACE|TMSK1_SOLID;

    eofPos = mdlElement_getFilePos (FILEPOS_EOF, NULL);
    filePos = 0L;      /* start seacrh from top of file */

    mdlScan_initialize (0, &scanList);
    /* loop through all text elements in file */
    do {
        scanWords = sizeof(elemAddr)/sizeof(short);
        status   = mdlScan_file(elemAddr, &scanWords,
                        sizeof(elemAddr),&filePos);
        numAddr   = scanWords / sizeof(short);
```

```
      for (i=0; i < numAddr; i++)
      {
          if (elemAddr[i] >= eofPos)  break;
          mdlModify_elementSingle (0, elemAddr[i],
               MODIFY_REQUEST_HEADERS, MODIFY_ORIG, editelem,
               &numchanged, 0L);
      }
   } while (status == BUFF_FULL);

  mdlOutput_prompt(" ");
}
/*----------------------------------------------------------------------+
| name       modall                                                     |
+----------------------------------------------------------------------*/
cmdName      modall ()
cmdNumber    CMD_MODIFY_LEVEL_ALL
  {
  change_all();
  }
```

The file *modall.r* contains both the command table and prompt messages.

modall.r

```
/*----------------------------------------------------------------------+
| modall.r - command table and messages for modall.mc                   |
+----------------------------------------------------------------------*/
#include "rscdefs.h"
#include "cmdclass.h"

#define        CT_NONE        0
#define        CT_MODIFY      1
#define        CT_LEVEL       2
#define        CT_ALL         3

Table   CT_MODIFY =
{
    { 1,  CT_LEVEL,     MANIPULATION,      REQ,         "MODIFY"},
};

Table   CT_LEVEL =
{
    { 1,  CT_ALL,       INHERIT,      REQ,              "LEVEL"},
}

Table   CT_ALL =
{
```

```
    { 1,  CT_NONE,        INHERIT,     NONE,           "ALL"},
};

MessageList 0 =
{
    {
    { 1, "Modify All Element Level" },
    { 2, "Element(s) modified %d" },
    }
};
```

     To build the MODALL application enter *bmake -a modall*.

modall.mke

```
#---------------------------------------------------------------------
#           MODALL MDL Make File
#---------------------------------------------------------------------
%include $(MS)/mdl/include/mdl.mki


#---------------------------------------------------------------------
#          Define constants specific to this modall application
#---------------------------------------------------------------------
progmdl           = d:/progmdl/disk/
baseDir           = $(progmdl)scanfile/
objectDir         = $(mdlexample)objects/
privateInc        = $(baseDir)

modallObjs        = $(objectDir)modall.mo
modallRscs        = $(objectDir)modall.rsc \
                    $(objectDir)modall.mp

$(privateInc)modall.h        : $(baseDir)modall.r

$(objectDir)modall.rsc       : $(baseDir)modall.r

$(objectDir)modall.mo        : $(baseDir)modall.mc

$(objectDir)modall.mp            : $(modallObjs)
        $(msg)
        > $(objectDir)temp.cmd
        -a$@
        -s6000
        $(linkOpts)
        $(modallObjs)
        <
        $(linkCmd) @$(objectDir)temp.cmd
        ~time
```

```
$(mdlapps)modall.ma              : $(modallRscs)
       $(msg)
       > $(objectDir)temp.cmd
       -o$@
       $(modallRscs)
       <
       $(rscLibCmd) @$(objectDir)temp.cmd
       ~time
```

Fence Search

In the application MODSYMB, we use all search methods, namely:- single elements, the entire file and those enclosed by a fence. We introduce also, a wider range of element manipulation. Our application can make changes to the element's level, color, weight and style.

We use, as well, the *mode* variable, which tells the application what we are modifying. For example, when we enter the command MODIFY WEIGHT SINGLE, *mode* will be set to 5. *Mode* is used to index into the *MessageList*, and display the appropriate prompts. It is used also, in *editelem* to modify the level or symbology.

```
cmdName        modfence_weight()
cmdNumber      CMD_FENCE_MODIFY_WEIGHT
 {
 setSearchType();
 mode = WEIGHT;
 mdlState_startFenceCommand(changeFenceContents,
      NULL,              /* function to define fence outline */
      NULL,              /* function for DATA point */
      modfence_weight,   /* function for RESET */
      6,                 /* message for command name */
      mode);             /* prompt for fence */
 }
```

The bulk of this program is derived from our earlier examples, with the exception of the fence search. The function *mdlState_startFenceCommand* calls the user function changeFenceContents for the elements that meet the fence search criteria.

The function `changeFenceContents` then calls *mdlModify_elementSingle* for each element returned by the fence. If the fence finds a complex element, then it passes the complex element header, and all of its component elements to *mdlModify_elementSingle*. From here the user function `editelem` is called for each component element, and its header, as specified by MODIFY_REQUEST_HEADERS.

```
Private int       changeFenceContents()
  {
  ULong   filePos;
  int     currFile=0;

  filePos = mdlElement_getFilePos (FILEPOS_CURRENT, &currFile);
  mdlModify_elementSingle (currFile,
      filePos,                      /* file position for element */
      MODIFY_REQUEST_HEADERS,       /* process complex headers */
      MODIFY_ORIG,                  /* modify original element */
      editelem,                     /* modify routine for each element */
      &numchanged,                  /* parameters for editelem */
      FALSE);                       /* offset for component elements */
  return SUCCESS;
}
```

The function `editelem` is only slightly different from previous versions. We have put a test on the modification *mode* and used *mdlElement_setSymbology* to make the changes.

```
switch (mode)
  {
  case LEVEL:
      if (mdlElement_getType(el) == CELL_HEADER_ELM)
          return (MODIFY_STATUS_NOCHANGE);
      mdlElement_setProperties (el, &actlevel, NULL, NULL, NULL,
                  NULL, NULL, NULL, NULL);
      break;
  case COLOR:
      mdlElement_setSymbology(el, &actcolor, NULL, NULL);
      break;
  case WEIGHT:
      mdlElement_setSymbology(el, NULL, &actweight, NULL);
      break;
  case STYLE:
      mdlElement_setSymbology(el, NULL, NULL, &actstyle);
      break;
  }
```

The complete listing for the program *modsymb.mc* is given below. To load
the application enter *mdl l modsymb*. To execute the application enter any
one of the commands shown below.

modsymb.mc

```
/*-------------------------------------------------------------------------+
 Copyright (c) 1991 Mach Dinh-Vu, All Rights Reserved

 modsymb.mc -  modify the element's level, color, weight and style using
               using the active settings. The location method is a user
               identification, a fence or the entire file.

       MODIFY LEVEL SINGLE      FENCE MODIFY ALL       MODIFY LEVEL ALL
       MODIFY COLOR SINGLE      FENCE MODIFY COLOR     MODIFY COLOR ALL
       MODIFY WEIGHT SINGLE     FENCE MODIFY WEIGHT    MODIFY WEIGHT ALL
       MODIFY STYLE SINGLE      FENCE MODIFY STYLE     MODIFY STYLE ALL
+-------------------------------------------------------------------------*/
#include <mdl.h>
#include <mselems.h>
#include <rscdefs.h>
#include <tcb.h>
#include <global.h>
#include <scanner.h>
#include "modsymb.h"


/*-------------------------------------------------------------------------+
 | These numbers are significant, as they match the message                |
 | number in the resource file.                                            |
+-------------------------------------------------------------------------*/
#define  LEVEL    2
#define  STYLE    3
#define  COLOR    4
#define  WEIGHT   5

int     mode, numchanged;
/*-------------------------------------------------------------------------+
| name       main                                                          |
+-------------------------------------------------------------------------*/
main ()
 {
 RscFileHandle   rfHandle;

 /* --- load our command table --- */
 if (mdlParse_loadCommandTable (NULL) == NULL)
  mdlOutput_error ("Unable to load command table.");
 mdlResource_openFile (&rfHandle, NULL, FALSE);
 }
/*-------------------------------------------------------------------------+
```

```
|  name         editelem                                                    |
+---------------------------------------------------------------------------*/
Private int editelem
(
MSElement    *el,
int          *numchanged
)
 {
 int  actlevel, actweight, actcolor, actstyle;

 mdlParams_getActive(&actlevel, ACTIVEPARAM_LEVEL);
 mdlParams_getActive(&actcolor, ACTIVEPARAM_COLOR);
 mdlParams_getActive(&actweight, ACTIVEPARAM_LINEWEIGHT);
 mdlParams_getActive(&actstyle, ACTIVEPARAM_LINESTYLE);

 switch (mode)
  {
  case LEVEL:
     if (mdlElement_getType(el) == CELL_HEADER_ELM)
         return (MODIFY_STATUS_NOCHANGE);
     mdlElement_setProperties (el, &actlevel, NULL, NULL, NULL,
                  NULL, NULL, NULL, NULL);
     break;
  case COLOR:
     mdlElement_setSymbology(el, &actcolor, NULL, NULL);
     break;
  case WEIGHT:
     mdlElement_setSymbology(el, NULL, &actweight, NULL);
     break;
  case STYLE:
     mdlElement_setSymbology(el, NULL, NULL, &actstyle);
     break;
  }

 (*numchanged)++;
 mdlOutput_rscPrintf(MSG_MESSAGE, NULL, 0, 7, (*numchanged));
 return (MODIFY_STATUS_REPLACE);
 }
/*--------------------------------------------------------------------------+
|  name        change_all                                                    |
+---------------------------------------------------------------------------*/
Private void change_all()
 {
 ULong         elemAddr[50], eofPos, filePos;
 int           scanWords, status, i, numAddr;
 ExtScanlist   scanList;
 char          buffer[50];

 numchanged = 0;
 mdlScan_initScanlist (&scanList);
```

```
mdlScan_noRangeCheck (&scanList);
mdlOutput_rscPrintf(MSG_COMMAND, NULL, 0, 1, NULL);

scanList.scantype        = ELEMTYPE | ONEELEM;
scanList.extendedType    = FILEPOS;
scanList.typmask[0]  = TMSK0_LINE|TMSK0_LINE_STRING|TMSK0_SHAPE;
scanList.typmask[0]  |= TMSK0_TEXT_NODE|TMSK0_CURVE ;
scanList.typmask[0]  |= TMSK0_CONIC| TMSK0_CMPLX_SHAPE ;
scanList.typmask[0]  |= TMSK0_ARC|TMSK0_CMPLX_STRING|TMSK0_ELLIPSE;
scanList.typmask[1]      = TMSK1_TEXT|TMSK1_SURFACE|TMSK1_SOLID;

eofPos  = mdlElement_getFilePos (FILEPOS_EOF, NULL);
filePos = 0L;            /* start seacrh from top of file */

mdlScan_initialize (0, &scanList);
/* loop through all text elements in file */
do {
 scanWords = sizeof(elemAddr)/sizeof(short);
 status    = mdlScan_file (elemAddr, &scanWords, sizeof(elemAddr),&filePos);
 numAddr   = scanWords / sizeof(short);

 for (i=0; i < numAddr; i++)
 {
    if (elemAddr[i] = eofPos)  break;
        mdlModify_elementSingle (0, elemAddr[i],
            MODIFY_REQUEST_NOHEADERS, MODIFY_ORIG, editelem,
            &numchanged, 0L);

 }
} while (status == BUFF_FULL);

 mdlOutput_command(" ");
}
/*-----------------------------------------------------------------------+
| name        setSearchType                                              |
+-----------------------------------------------------------------------*/
Private void setSearchType()
 {
 static int searchType[]={CELL_HEADER_ELM, LINE_ELM, LINE_STRING_ELM,
        SHAPE_ELM, TEXT_NODE_ELM, CURVE_ELM, CMPLX_STRING_ELM,
        CONIC_ELM, CMPLX_SHAPE_ELM, ELLIPSE_ELM, ARC_ELM,
        TEXT_ELM, SURFACE_ELM, SOLID_ELM};

 numchanged = 0;
 /* initialize search criteria to find nothing */
 mdlLocate_noElemNoLocked();

 /* add elements to search to list */
 mdlLocate_setElemSearchMask(sizeof(searchType)/sizeof(int),searchType);
 }
```

```
/*------------------------------------------------------------------+
| name        mod_accept                                            |
+------------------------------------------------------------------*/
Private void    mod_accept ()
 {
 ULong       filePos, compOffset;
 int         currFile=0;

 filePos = mdlElement_getFilePos (FILEPOS_CURRENT, &currFile);
 if (mdlSelect_isActive())
 {
 mdlModify_elementMulti (currFile,    /* file to process */
     filePos,                         /* file position for element */
     MODIFY_REQUEST_NOHEADERS,        /* do not process complex headers */
     MODIFY_ORIG,                     /* modify original element */
     editelem,                        /* modify routine for each element */
     &numchanged,                     /* parameters for editelem */
     TRUE);                           /* process graphic group */
 } else {
 mdlModify_elementSingle (currFile,
     filePos,                         /* file position for element */
     MODIFY_REQUEST_HEADERS,          /* process complex headers */
     MODIFY_ORIG,                     /* modify original element */
     editelem,                        /* modify routine for each element */
     &numchanged,                     /* parameters for editelem */
     FALSE);                          /* offset for component elements */
 }
 /* restart the element location process */
 mdlLocate_restart (FALSE);
 }


/*------------------------------------------------------------------+
| name    changeFenceContents                                       |
+------------------------------------------------------------------*/
Private int    changeFenceContents()
 {
 ULong  filePos;
 int    currFile=0;

 filePos = mdlElement_getFilePos (FILEPOS_CURRENT, &currFile);
 mdlModify_elementSingle (currFile,
     filePos,                         /* file position for element */
     MODIFY_REQUEST_HEADERS,          /* process complex headers */
     MODIFY_ORIG,                     /* modify original element */
     editelem,                        /* modify routine for each element */
     &numchanged,                     /* parameters for editelem */
     FALSE);                          /* offset for component elements */
 return SUCCESS;
 }
```

```
/*--------------------------------------------------------------------+
| name        change_single                                          |
+---------------------------------------------------------------------*/
Private void change_single()
  {
  setSearchType();
  mdlState_startModifyCommand (
      change_single, /* function to call on RESET */
      mod_accept,    /* function to call on DATA */
      NULL,          /* function to call for DYNAMIC */
      NULL,          /* function to call on SHOW */
      NULL,          /* function to call on CLEAN */
      0,             /* index into MESSAGE LIST */
      mode,          /* index into PROMPT LIST */
      TRUE,          /* Modify SELECTION SET ? */
      FALSE);        /* additional data points required */

  /* start element search from the beginning of file */
  mdlLocate_init ();
  }
/*--------------------------------------------------------------------+
| name        modsing_level                                          |
+---------------------------------------------------------------------*/
cmdName  modsing_level()
cmdNumber   CMD_MODIFY_LEVEL_SINGLE
  {
  mode = LEVEL;
  change_single();
  }

/*--------------------------------------------------------------------+
| name        modsing_color                                          |
+---------------------------------------------------------------------*/
cmdName     modsing_color()
cmdNumber   CMD_MODIFY_COLOR_SINGLE
  {
  mode = COLOR;
  change_single();
  }

/*--------------------------------------------------------------------+
| name        modsing_weight                                         |
+---------------------------------------------------------------------*/
cmdName     modsing_weight()
cmdNumber   CMD_MODIFY_WEIGHT_SINGLE
  {
  mode = WEIGHT;
  change_single();
  }
```

```
/*-----------------------------------------------------------------------+
| name          modsing_style                                            |
+-----------------------------------------------------------------------*/
cmdName        modsing_style()
cmdNumber      CMD_MODIFY_STYLE_SINGLE
 {
 mode = STYLE;
 change_single();
 }
/*-----------------------------------------------------------------------+
| name          modall_level                                             |
+-----------------------------------------------------------------------*/
cmdName        modall_level ()
cmdNumber      CMD_MODIFY_LEVEL_ALL
 {
 mode = LEVEL;
 change_all();
 }
/*-----------------------------------------------------------------------+
| name          modall_color                                             |
+-----------------------------------------------------------------------*/
cmdName        modall_color ()
cmdNumber      CMD_MODIFY_COLOR_ALL
 {
 mode = COLOR;
 change_all();
 }
/*-----------------------------------------------------------------------+
| name          modall_weight                                            |
+-----------------------------------------------------------------------*/
cmdName        modall_weight()
cmdNumber      CMD_MODIFY_WEIGHT_ALL
 {
 mode = WEIGHT;
 change_all();
 }
/*-----------------------------------------------------------------------+
| name          modall_style                                             |
+-----------------------------------------------------------------------*/
cmdName        modall_style()
cmdNumber      CMD_MODIFY_STYLE_ALL
 {
 mode = STYLE;
 change_all();
 }
/*-----------------------------------------------------------------------+
| name          modfence_level                                           |
+-----------------------------------------------------------------------*/
cmdName        modfence_level ()
cmdNumber      CMD_FENCE_MODIFY_LEVEL
```

```
    {
    setSearchType();
    mode = LEVEL;
    mdlState_startFenceCommand(changeFenceContents,
        NULL,                   /* function to define fence outline */
        NULL,                   /* function for DATA point */
        modfence_level,         /* function for RESET */
        6,                      /* message for command name */
        mode);                  /* prompt for fence */
    }
/*--------------------------------------------------------------------+
| name        modfence_color                                          |
+--------------------------------------------------------------------*/
cmdName      modfence_color()
cmdNumber    CMD_FENCE_MODIFY_COLOR
    {
    setSearchType();
    mode = COLOR;
    mdlState_startFenceCommand(changeFenceContents,
        NULL,                   /* function to define fence outline */
        NULL,                   /* function for DATA point */
        modfence_color,         /* function for RESET */
        6,                      /* message for command name */
        mode);                  /* prompt for fence */
    }
/*--------------------------------------------------------------------+
| name        modfence_weight                                         |
+--------------------------------------------------------------------*/
cmdName      modfence_weight()
cmdNumber    CMD_FENCE_MODIFY_WEIGHT
    {
    setSearchType();
    mode = WEIGHT;
    mdlState_startFenceCommand(changeFenceContents,
        NULL,                   /* function to define fence outline */
        NULL,                   /* function for DATA point */
        modfence_weight,        /* function for RESET */
        6,                      /* message for command name */
        mode);                  /* prompt for fence */
    }
/*--------------------------------------------------------------------+
| name        modfence_style                                          |
+--------------------------------------------------------------------*/
cmdName      modfence_style()
cmdNumber    CMD_FENCE_MODIFY_STYLE
    {
    setSearchType();
    mode = STYLE;
    mdlState_startFenceCommand(changeFenceContents,
        NULL,                   /* function to define fence outline */
```

```
        NULL,                    /* function for DATA point */
        modfence_style,          /* function for RESET */
        6,                       /* message for command name */
        mode);                   /* prompt for fence */
    }
```

The file *modsymb.r* contains both the command table and prompt messages.

modsymb.r

```
/*-----------------------------------------------------------------------+
 | modsymb.r - command table and messages for modsymb.mc                 |
 +-----------------------------------------------------------------------*/
#include "rscdefs.h"
#include "cmdclass.h"

#define     CT_NONE         0
#define     CT_MODIFY       1
#define     CT_MODOPT       2
#define     CT_FENCE        3
#define     CT_ALL          4
#define     CT_OPTION       5

Table   CT_MODIFY =
{
    { 1,  CT_MODOPT,      MANIPULATION,       REQ,        "MODIFY" },
    { 2,  CT_FENCE,       FENCE,              REQ,        "FENCE" },
};

Table   CT_MODOPT =
{
    { 1,  CT_ALL,    INHERIT,     NONE,        "LEVEL" },
    { 2,  CT_ALL,    INHERIT,     NONE,        "STYLE" },
    { 3,  CT_ALL,    INHERIT,     NONE,        "WEIGHT" },
    { 4,  CT_ALL,    INHERIT,     NONE,        "COLOR" },
};

Table   CT_FENCE =
{
    { 1,  CT_OPTION,   INHERIT,         REQ,        "MODIFY" },
};

Table   CT_ALL =
{
    { 1,  CT_NONE,    INHERIT,     DEF,         "SINGLE" },
    { 2,  CT_NONE,    INHERIT,     NONE,          "ALL" },
};
```

```
Table    CT_OPTION =
{
    { 1,    CT_NONE,    INHERIT,        REQ,        "LEVEL" },
    { 2,    CT_NONE,    INHERIT,        REQ,        "STYLE" },
    { 3,    CT_NONE,    INHERIT,        REQ,        "WEIGHT" },
    { 4,    CT_NONE,    INHERIT,        REQ,        "COLOR" },
};

MessageList 0 =
{
    {
    { 0, "Modify Element" },
    { 1, "Modify All Elements" },
    { 2, "Accept/Reject to change Level" },
    { 3, "Accept/Reject to change Style" },
    { 4, "Accept/Reject to change Color" },
    { 5, "Accept/Reject to change Weight" },
    { 6, "Fence Modify Elements" },
    { 7, "Element(s) modified %d" },
    }
};
```

   To build the MODSYMB application, enter *bmake -a modsymb*.

modsymb.mke

```
#---------------------------------------------------------------------
#         MODSYMB MDL Make File
#---------------------------------------------------------------------
%include $(MS)/mdl/include/mdl.mki

#---------------------------------------------------------------------
#         Define constants specific to this modsymb application
#---------------------------------------------------------------------
progmdl           = d:/progmdl/disk/
baseDir           = $(progmdl)scanfile/
objectDir         = $(mdlexample)objects/
privateInc        = $(baseDir)

modsymbObjs = $(objectDir)modsymb.mo
modsymbRscs         = $(objectDir)modsymb.rsc \
                     $(objectDir)modsymb.mp

$(privateInc)modsymb.h      : $(baseDir)modsymb.r

$(objectDir)modsymb.rsc     : $(baseDir)modsymb.r
```

```
$(objectDir)modsymb.mo        : $(baseDir)modsymb.mc

$(objectDir)modsymb.mp         : $(modsymbObjs)
        $(msg)
        > $(objectDir)temp.cmd
        -a$@
        -s6000
        $(linkOpts)
        $(modsymbObjs)
        <
        $(linkCmd) @$(objectDir)temp.cmd
        ~time

$(mdlapps)modsymb.ma          : $(modsymbRscs)
        $(msg)
        > $(objectDir)temp.cmd
        -o$@
        $(modsymbRscs)
        <
        $(rscLibCmd) @$(objectDir)temp.cmd
        ~time
```

5 : Element Descriptors

Manipulating elements from within a program has always been a chore. It requires a detailed knowledge of how a design file works. For example, in a UCM we need to read the element into DGNBUF, make the changes and write it back into the design file. Since this operation bypasses the display processor, the changes do not show until the screen is updated. Reading and writing the element at this level requires that we maintain the file pointers, and a miscalculation can corrupt the file.

This problem is further complicated with complex elements, because the DGNBUF can hold only one element at a time. This means that the complex header, and its component elements, need to be read into DGNBUF one at a time, and treated appropriately. Consider the problem of moving a cell from one level to another. First, we need to calculate the position of the component elements, from the cell header. We then scan and change the levels of the component elements. Finally, we go back to the cell header and modify the cell level bit mask, to reflect the new levels.

MDL provides a series of functions, known as element descriptors. These allow us to manipulate component elements, without the need to maintain the header. Element descriptors are not restricted to complex elements, they can be used on simple elements, or a list of simple elements. The underlying feature is that they are manipulated in memory, and MDL can guarantee the integrity of the data through functions like *mdlElmdscr_validate*. The programmer calls MDL functions that allocates the memory, and therefore must release it with the function *mdlElmdscr_freeAll*.

Element Descriptor Functions

A summary of the Element Descriptor functions are listed here.

mdlElmdscr_add	add element in the descriptor to the file.
mdlElmdscr_addToChain	append descriptor to another element descriptor.
mdlElmdscr_append	append element in the descriptor to the file.
mdlElmdscr_appendDscr	append descriptor to another element descriptor (use on a single complex element).
mdlElmdscr_appendElement	append the element to the descriptor.
mdlElmdscr_convertTo2D	convert 3D descriptor to 2D descriptor.
mdlElmdscr_convertTo3D	convert 2D descriptor to 3D descriptor.
mdlElmdscr_display	display descriptor in all views.
mdlElmdscr_displayFromFile	display an element in all views.
mdlElmdscr_duplicate	copy an element descriptor.
mdlElmdscr_freeAll	free memory used in element descriptor chain.
mdlElmdscr_markElement	mark element in descriptor for latter processing.
mdlElmdscr_new	create a new descriptor from an existing element.
mdlElmdscr_igdsSize	return the descriptor's size.
mdlElmdscr_insertElement	insert an existing element into the descriptor chain.
mdlElmdscr_operation	call a user function for each element in the descriptor.
mdlElmdscr_read	read the element from the design file and create a new descriptor.
mdlElmdscr_removeElement	remove element from descriptor.
mdlElmdscr_replaceElement	replace element in descriptor.
mdlElmdscr_rewrite	rewrite over an existing element.

mdlElmdscr_stroke	stroke element descriptor into vectors.
mdlElmdscr_transform	transform descriptor by a transformation matrix.
mdlElmdscr_undoableDelete	delete an element in the descriptor from the file. UNDO can undelete the element.
mdlElmdscr_validate	update complex header from descriptor.

Element Descriptor Structure

The element descriptor is defined by the structure *MSElementDescr* , found in < mselems.h >.

```
typedef struct msElementDescr MSElementDescr;
struct msElementDescr
    {
    struct
        {
        MSElementDescr  *next;       /* ptr to first entry in list */
        MSElementDescr  *previous; /* ptr to last entry in list */
        MSElementDescr  *myHeader; /* ptr to my hdr (NULL = not cmplx) */
        MSElementDescr  *firstElem;/* ptr to first element if header */
        int             isHeader; /* is this a complex header */
        int             isValid;  /* INTERNAL USE ONLY */
        long            userData1; /* available for user */
        long            userData2; /* available for user */
        } h;
    MSElement           el;        /* elem data (hdr only if complex) */
    };
```

To access the linked list of elements in the descriptor, we use the recursive routine *elemDscr_show* . This routine is useful in debugging the content of the element descriptor.

```
Public int        elemDscr_show
(
MSElementDescr   *elemDescr,
char              *currentIndent
)
    {
    char      indent[128];
    int       color, weight, style, level, ggNum, class, locked, new,
              modified, viewIndepend, solidHole;

    if (elemDescr == NULL)
        return SUCCESS;

    strcpy (indent, currentIndent);
    strcat (indent, "|    ");

    do
        {
        mdlElement_getSymbology (&color, &style, &weight, &elemDescr-el);
        mdlElement_getProperties (&level, &ggNum, &class, &locked, &new,
                  &modified, &viewIndepend, &solidHole, &elemDescr->el);
        printf ("%shdr=%d, typ=%d, cmplx=%d", currentIndent,
                  elemDescr->h.isHeader, elemDescr- >el.hdr.ehdr.type,
                  elemDescr->el.hdr.ehdr.complex);
        printf (",c=%d,w=%d,s=%d,l=%d,gg=%d,cl=%d\n",
                  color, weight, style, level, ggNum, class);

        if (elemDescr->h.isHeader)
            {
            elemDscr_show (elemDescr->h.firstElem, indent);
            printf ("%send of chain\n", currentIndent);
            }

        elemDescr = elemDescr->h.next;
        } while (elemDescr);
    }
```

Creating Element Descriptors

Now, we will now rewrite the PLBOX application using element descriptors to place complex elements. The bulk of the program is the same as PLBOX, except for the function generateImage.

The first step is to begin a new descriptor, with a call to *mdlElmdscr_new*. Then, using *mdlElmdscr_appendElement,* we gradually build the complex element.

```
/* create new descriptor using cell header */
mdlCell_create(&el, "pbdscr", &origin, FALSE);
mdlElmdscr_new(&elmDP, NULL, &el);

mdlText_create (&el, NULL, textin, &pntP[1], NULL, NULL, NULL, NULL);
mdlElmdscr_appendElement(elmDP, &el);

mdlText_extractShape(shapep, NULL, &el, TRUE, view);
mdlShape_create(&el, NULL, shapep, 5, -1);
mdlElmdscr_appendElement(elmDP, &el);
```

Finally, using *mdlElmdscr_add*, we write the element descriptor from memory into the design file.

```
if (drawMode == NORMALDRAW)
    mdlElmdscr_add(elmDP);
```

Remember to clear the allocated memory with *mdlElmdscr_freeAll*.

```
mdlElmdscr_freeAll(&elmDP);
```

The revised PLBOX is shown here as the PBDSCR application. To load the application enter *mdl l pbdscr*. To run the application, enter PLACE DBOX.

pbdscr.mc

```
/*-------------------------------------------------------------------+
| Copyright (C) 1991 Mach N. Dinh-Vu, All Rights Reserved           |
| Program   : pbdscr.mc                                             |
| Revision  : 1.0.a                                                 |
+-------------------------------------------------------------------+
| Example MDL function to place a box around a text string with a leader |
| line using element descriptors.                                   |
+-------------------------------------------------------------------*/
/*-------------------------------------------------------------------+
|    Include Files                                                  |
+-------------------------------------------------------------------*/
#include <mdl.h>/* system include files */
#include <global.h>
#include <mselems.h>
#include <userfnc.h>
#include <rscdefs.h>
#include <tcb.h>
#include "pbdscr.h"
/*-------------------------------------------------------------------+
|    Private Global variables                                       |
+-------------------------------------------------------------------*/
static char textin[128];
Dpoint3d pntP[2];

/*-------------------------------------------------------------------+
| name        main                                                 |
+-------------------------------------------------------------------*/
main()
{
  RscFileHandle   rfHandle;

  /* load our command table */
  if (mdlParse_loadCommandTable (NULL) == NULL)
     mdlOutput_error ("Unable to load command table.");
  mdlResource_openFile (&rfHandle, NULL, FALSE);
  mdlOutput_prompt("Key-in PLACE DBOX to execute");
}
/*-------------------------------------------------------------------+
| name            generateImage - dynamic function for box.        |
+-------------------------------------------------------------------*/
Private int      generateImage
(
Dpoint3d      *pt,
```

```
int           view,
int           drawMode
)
{
MSElementDescr  *elmDP;
MSElementUnion  el;
Dpoint3d        origin;
Dpoint3d        shapep[5];
long            cellFilePos;

pntP[1] = origin = *pt;

/* create new descriptor using cell header */
mdlCell_create(&el, "pbdscr", &origin, FALSE);
mdlElmdscr_new(&elmDP, NULL, &el);

mdlText_create (&el, NULL, textin, &pntP[1], NULL, NULL, NULL, NULL);
mdlElmdscr_appendElement(elmDP, &el);

mdlText_extractShape(shapep, NULL, &el, TRUE, view);
mdlShape_create(&el, NULL, shapep, 5, -1);
mdlElmdscr_appendElement(elmDP, &el);

if (pntP[0].x < origin.x)
{
        if (pntP[0].y  < origin.y)
        {
            pntP[1].x=shapep[0].x;
            pntP[1].y=shapep[0].y;
        } else {
            pntP[1].x=shapep[3].x;
            pntP[1].y=shapep[3].y;
        }
} else {
        if (pntP[0].y < origin.y)
        {
            pntP[1].x=shapep[1].x;
            pntP[1].y=shapep[1].y;
        } else {
            pntP[1].x=shapep[2].x;
            pntP[1].y=shapep[2].y;
        }
}
/* Place the modified leader line */
mdlLine_create (&el, NULL, pntP);
mdlElmdscr_appendElement(elmDP, &el);
mdlElmdscr_display(elmDP, 0, drawMode);

if (drawMode == NORMALDRAW)
   mdlElmdscr_add(elmDP);
```

```
 mdlElmdscr_freeAll(&elmDP);
 return  SUCCESS;
}
/*----------------------------------------------------------------+
| name       keyinText                                            |
+-------------------------------------------------------------*/
Private void    keyinText ()
{
  if (!*statedata.cmdstring)
     return;
  strncpy(textin, statedata.cmdstring, sizeof(textin));
}
/*----------------------------------------------------------------+
| name       placeBox_done                                        |
+-------------------------------------------------------------*/
Private void    placeBox_done()
{
 mdlOutput_rscPrintf (MSG_PROMPT, NULL, 0, 4);
 mdlState_restartCurrentCommand();
}
/*----------------------------------------------------------------+
| name       placeBox_secondPoint                                 |
+-------------------------------------------------------------*/
Private void     placeBox_secondPoint
(
Dpoint3d    *pt,
int         view
)
{
 generateImage(pt , view, NORMALDRAW);
}
/*----------------------------------------------------------------+
| name       placeBox_firstPoint                                  |
+-------------------------------------------------------------*/
Private void     placeBox_firstPoint
(
Dpoint3d    *pt,
int         view
)
{
 /* save first point */
 pntP[0] = *pt;

 /* Set the datapoint state function for the second point. */
 mdlState_setFunction (STATE_KEYIN,keyinText);
 mdlState_setFunction (STATE_DATAPOINT, placeBox_secondPoint);
 mdlState_setFunction (STATE_RESET, placeBox_done);
 mdlOutput_rscPrintf (MSG_PROMPT, NULL, 0, 3);
```

```
/* Setup Rubber Banding function */
mdlState_setFunction (STATE_COMPLEX_DYNAMICS, generateImage);
}
/*-------------------------------------------------------------------+
| name           placeBox_start                                      |
+-------------------------------------------------------------------*/
cmdName  placeBox_start ()
cmdNumber    CMD_PLACE_DBOX
{
  mdlState_startPrimitive (placeBox_firstPoint, placeBox_start, 1, 2);
}
```

The file *pbdscr.r* contains both the command table and prompts.

pbdscr.r

```
/*-------------------------------------------------------------------+
|   PBDSCR.R command table and messages for PBDSCR.MC                |
/*-------------------------------------------------------------------*/
#include "rscdefs.h"
#include "cmdclass.h"

#define     CT_NONE          0
#define     CT_PLACE         2

Table   1 =
{
   { 1,  CT_PLACE,      PLACEMENT,      REQ,                      "PLACE" },
};

Table   CT_PLACE =
{
   { 1,  CT_NONE,       INHERIT,       NONE | CMDSTR (1),     "DBOX" },
};


MessageList 0 =
{
   {
   { 0, "" },
   { 1, "MDL Place Box (descriptors)" },
   { 2, "Define start point" },
   { 3, "Define Box position" },
   { 4, "PlBox complete" },
   }
};
```

To build the PBDSCR application, enter *bmake -a pbdscr.*

pbdscr.mke

```
#-----------------------------------------------------------------------
#          PBDSCR MDL Make File
#-----------------------------------------------------------------------
%include $(MS)/mdl/include/mdl.mki

#-----------------------------------------------------------------------
#          Define constants specific to this PBDSCR application
#-----------------------------------------------------------------------
progmdl            = d:/progmdl/disk/
baseDir            = $(progmdl)plbox/
objectDir          = $(mdlexample)objects/
privateInc         = $(baseDir)

pbdscrObjs = $(objectDir)pbdscr.mo
pbdscrRscs         = $(objectDir)pbdscr.rsc \
                          $(objectDir)pbdscr.mp

$(privateInc)pbdscr.h        : $(baseDir)pbdscr.r

$(objectDir)pbdscr.rsc       : $(baseDir)pbdscr.r

$(objectDir)pbdscr.mo        : $(baseDir)pbdscr.mc

$(objectDir)pbdscr.mp            : $(pbdscrObjs)
        $(msg)
        > $(objectDir)temp.cmd
        -a$@
        -s6000
        $(linkOpts)
        $(pbdscrObjs)
        <
        $(linkCmd) @$(objectDir)temp.cmd
        ~time

$(mdlapps)pbdscr.ma              : $(pbdscrRscs)
        $(msg)
        > $(objectDir)temp.cmd
        -o$@
        $(pbdscrRscs)
        <
        $(rscLibCmd) @$(objectDir)temp.cmd
        ~time
```

Manipulating Complex Elements

Our PBDSCR application adds elements to the design file using element descriptors. However, the real power of element descriptors is manipulating existing complex elements. In the application STRTEXT, we will scan the entire file for text and text nodes, then stroke the text string and export it to a specified file. By converting text into line-work, we can use conversion software (e.g. DXFOUT) to export text strings to other CAD systems.

Text strings are no problem, but when the scanner reads a text node, it will load the entire complex element into memory. If we manipulate the descriptor as a whole, then we cannot get access to the component elements. The function *mdlElmdscr_operation* solves this problem, by calling a user function according to an operation flag.

The valid flags are:

ELMD_ELEMENT   call user function for each component element.

ELMD_PRE_HDR   call user function for the outermost header element
                        before calling it for each component element.

ELMD_PRE_NESTEDHDR   call user function for each nested header element
                        before calling it for each component element.

ELMD_POST_HDR   call user function for each component element,
                        then call it for the outermost header element.

ELMD_POST_NESTEDHDR   call user function for each component element,
                        then call it for the nested header element.

ELMD_ALL_ONCE   call user function once for each component element.
                        Same as (ELMD_ELEMENT | ELMD_PRE_HDR |
                              ELMD_PRE_NESTEDHDR)

ELMD_HDRS_ONCE   call user function once for each header element.
                        Same as (ELMD_PRE_HDR | ELMD_PRE_NESTEDHDR)

In our application, we will call `stroke_elm` for each component element.

```
mdlElmdscr_operation(edP, stroke_elm, NULL, ELMD_ELEMENT);
```

In `stroke_elm` we will check if the element passed from *mdlElmdscr_operation* is a text string. This may sound redundant, as the only complex elements to be processed are text nodes. We must assume then, that the components must be text strings. While this is true, our defensive programming will make it robust against future changes in the element format. `stroke_elm` must return SUCCESS to *mdlElmdscr_operation*, otherwise it will abort.

```
if (mdlElement_getType(el) != TEXT_ELM)
    return SUCCESS;
```

Passing the text string to *mdlElement_stroke* will return an array of points, defining the text. Then we will create a line string from these points. Since a line string can have a maximum of 101 points, we will verify that the number of points is within these limits.

```
if (mdlElement_stroke(&points, &numpnts, el, TOLERANCE) == SUCCESS)
    {
    if (numpnts > MAX_VERTICES)
        numpnts = MAX_VERTICES;
```

We then build a new descriptor, from the line string, using the symbologies and properties of the text string.

```
/* get element display symbology of current element */
mdlElement_getSymbology(&color, &style, &weight, el);
/* get properties of current element */
mdlElement_getProperties(&level, &ggNum, NULL, NULL,
                        NULL, NULL, NULL, NULL, el);

mdlLineString_create(&elm, NULL, points, numpnts);

/* set element display symbology of line string */
mdlElement_setSymbology(&elm, &color, &style, &weight);
/* set properties of line string */
mdlElement_setProperties(&elm, &level, &ggNum, NULL, NULL,
                        NULL, NULL, NULL, NULL);
```

Using *mdlWorkDgn_write* we can export the line string to another DGN file. The *mdlWorkDgn_* functions are discussed in the next section.

Finally we will highlight the exported text string, and then release the memory held by the line string element descriptor.

```
mdlElmdscr_new(&elmDP, NULL, &elm);
workPos = mdlWorkDgn_write(elmDP, workPos, fp, NULL, 0);

/* Display text written */
mdlElement_display (el, HILITE);

/* Free temporary descriptor */
mdlElmdscr_freeAll (&elmDP);
```

Work File

MDL provides a series of functions to manipulate a temporary work file, while keeping the current design file open. The temporary work file can be a design file, or cell library.

The work file is opened with *fopen*, but manipulated using the *mdlWorkDgn_* functions. These functions are elementary routines that read and write formatted data from the element descriptor.

mdlWork_delete	delete the element descriptor from the work file.
mdlWork_findEOF	returns the end-of-file position for the work file.
mdlWork_igdsSize	return the size of the element contained in the element descriptor.
mdlWork_read	read an element descriptor from the work file.
mdlWork_write	write an element descriptor to the work file.
mdlWork_validate	update the header of the complex element in the element descriptor.

The work file is opened with the standard *fopen* command. We must be sure that the file was opened correctly with the following test. When we finish with the work file, we must close it with the *fclose* command.

```
if ((fp=fopen(filename,"w")) == NULL)
{
    mdlOutput_rscPrintf(MSG_MESSAGE, NULL, 0, 3, filename);
    mdlUtil_beep(1);
    return;
}
```

The only work file function we will use is *mdlWorkDgn_write*. We will pass it the file pointer *fp*, so that it knows to which file to write. The position to write the element descriptor to the work file is defined by *workPos*. The first time we write to the work file we set *workPos* to -1L, which tells it to append the element to the end of file. Since the *mdlWorkDgn_write* function returns the next free position, we will assign this to *workPos* and use it for the next write.

```
workPos = mdlWorkDgn_write(elmDP, workPos, fp, NULL, 0);
```

The *mdlWorkDgn_write* function will write MicroStation elements. It is not aware of the previous, or the following elements. If we are starting a new design file, we need to write the element headers (type 9, 8, 10) from the current file, to the work file. This will create the work file as a design file.

```
else if ((edP->el.ehdr.type == DGNFIL_HEADER_ELM) ||
         (edP->el.ehdr.type == DIG_SETDATA_ELM) ||
         (edP->el.ehdr.type == LEV_SYM_ELM))
         {
         workPos = mdlWorkDgn_write(edP, workPos, fp, NULL, 0);
         }
```

To load the application enter *mdl l strtext*. To run the application enter STRTEXT at the uSTN> prompt.

strtext.mc

```
/*------------------------------------------------------------------+
|  Copyright (C) 1991 Mach N. Dinh-Vu, All Rights Reserved          |
|  Program   : strtext.mc                                           |
|  Revision  : 1.0.a                                                |
+------------------------------------------------------------------+
|      Scan the entire DGN file and located all text string.       |
|      Stroke the text into linestrings and the export to another DGN |
|      file.                                                        |
+-----------------------------------------------------------------*/
/*------------------------------------------------------------------+
|   Include Files                                                   |
+-----------------------------------------------------------------*/
#include <mdl.h>                    /* system include files */
#include <global.h>
#include <mselems.h>
#include <userfnc.h>
#include <rscdefs.h>
#include <tcb.h>
#include <stdio.h>

#include "strtext.h"

#define      NEWELEMENT   -1
#define      TOLERANCE    1000

FILE    *fp;
ULong   workPos = -1L;
int     number_exported = 0;

/*------------------------------------------------------------------+
| name            main                                              |
+-----------------------------------------------------------------*/
main()
{
 RscFileHandle    rfHandle;

 /* load our command table */
 if (mdlParse_loadCommandTable (NULL) == NULL)
        mdlOutput_error ("Unable to load command table.");
 mdlResource_openFile (&rfHandle, NULL, FALSE);
 mdlOutput_prompt("Key-in STRTEXT [filename] to execute");
}
```

```
/*----------------------------------------------------------------------+
| name              stroke_elm                                          |
+---------------------------------------------------------------------*/
stroke_elm
(
MSElement          *el,
void               *params,
int                operation,
ULong              offset,
MSElementDescr     *edP
)
{
    Dpoint3d           *points;
    MSElementDescr     *elmDP;
    MSElement          elm;
    int                numpnts;
    int                color, weight, style, level, ggNum, class;
    int                locked, new, modified, viewI, solHole;


    if (mdlElement_getType(el) != TEXT_ELM)
        return SUCCESS;

    if (mdlElement_stroke(&points, &numpnts, el, TOLERANCE) == SUCCESS)
        {
        if (numpnts > MAX_VERTICES)
            numpnts = MAX_VERTICES;

    mdlOutput_rscPrintf(MSG_MESSAGE, NULL, 0, 2, ++number_exported);

        /* get element display symbology of current element */
        mdlElement_getSymbology(&color, &style, &weight, el);
        /* get properties of current element */
        mdlElement_getProperties(&level, &ggNum, NULL, NULL,
                            NULL, NULL, NULL, NULL, el);

        mdlLineString_create(&elm, NULL, points, numpnts);

        /* set element display symbology of line string */
        mdlElement_setSymbology(&elm, &color, &style, &weight);
        /* set properties of line string */
        mdlElement_setProperties(&elm, &level, &ggNum, NULL, NULL,
                            NULL, NULL, NULL, NULL);

        mdlElmdscr_new(&elmDP, NULL, &elm);
        workPos = mdlWorkDgn_write(elmDP, workPos, fp, NULL, 0);

        /* Display text written */
        mdlElement_display (el, HILITE);
```

```
        /* Free temporary descriptor */
        mdlElmdscr_freeAll (&elmDP);
        }
    return SUCCESS;
}
/*------------------------------------------------------------------+
|   name       writeFile                                            |
+------------------------------------------------------------------*/
Private void writeFile
(
char *filename
)
{
    ULong           position = 0L;
    MSElementDescr  *edP, *elmDP;

    if ((fp=fopen(filename,"w")) == NULL)
    {
        mdlOutput_rscPrintf(MSG_MESSAGE, NULL, 0, 3, filename);
        mdlUtil_beep(1);
        return;
    }
    mdlOutput_rscPrintf(MSG_PROMPT, NULL, 0, 1, filename);

    while ((position = mdlElmdscr_read (&edP, position, 0, FALSE,
                       NULL)) != 0L)
        {
        if ((edP->el.ehdr.type == TEXT_ELM ) ||
            (edP->el.ehdr.type == TEXT_NODE_ELM ))
        {
            mdlElmdscr_operation(edP, stroke_elm, NULL, ELMD_ELEMENT);
        }
        else if ((edP->el.ehdr.type == DGNFIL_HEADER_ELM) ||
                 (edP->el.ehdr.type == DIG_SETDATA_ELM) ||
                 (edP->el.ehdr.type == LEV_SYM_ELM))
                {
                workPos = mdlWorkDgn_write(edP, workPos, fp, NULL, 0);
                }

        mdlElmdscr_freeAll (&edP);
        } /* end-while */

    /* cleanup */
    mdlOutput_prompt(" ");
    mdlOutput_command(" ");
    fclose(fp);
}
```

```
/*-----------------------------------------------------------------+
| name          keyinText                                          |
+-----------------------------------------------------------------*/
Private void keyinText ()
    {
    char      filename[128];

    /* do nothing on <CR> only */
    if (!*statedata.cmdstring)
        return;

    /* save DGN filename */
    strncpy (filename, statedata.cmdstring, sizeof(filename));
    writeFile(filename);
    }

/*-----------------------------------------------------------------+
| name          setTextState                                       |
+-----------------------------------------------------------------*/
Private void setTextState()
{
    mdlState_setFunction(STATE_KEYIN, keyinText);
    mdlOutput_prompt("Enter DGN filename");
}
/*-----------------------------------------------------------------+
| name          strfile                                            |
+-----------------------------------------------------------------*/
cmd_name strfile (pStrings) cmd_number CMD_STRTEXT
char *pStrings;
{
    char      filename[128];

    mdlOutput_rscPrintf(MSG_COMMAND, NULL, 0, 0);
    if (*pStrings)
        {
        strcpy(filename, pStrings);
        writeFile(filename);
        }
    else
        setTextState();
}
```

The file *strtext.r* contains the command table and messages for the STRTEXT application.

strtext.r

```
/*-------------------------------------------------------------------+
|    strtext.r command table and messages for strtext.mc            |
/*-------------------------------------------------------------------*/
#include "rscdefs.h"
#include "cmdclass.h"

#define      CT_NONE           0
#define      CT_STRTEXT        1

Table   CT_STRTEXT =
{
    { 1, CT_NONE,        MANIPULATION,        NONE | TRY,      "STRTEXT" },
};


MessageList 0 =
{
    {
    { 0, "Stroke TEXT to FILE" },
    { 1, "Output to File (%s)" },
    { 2, "TEXT written to file = %d" },
    { 3, "Unable to open file = %s" },
    }
};
```

To build the STRTEXT application, enter *bmake -a strtext*.

strtext.mke

```
#-------------------------------------------------------------------
#           STRTEXT MDL Make File
#-------------------------------------------------------------------
debug = 1
%include $(MS)/mdl/include/mdl.mki
#-------------------------------------------------------------------
#           Define constants specific to this STRTEXT application
#-------------------------------------------------------------------
progmdl            = d:/progmdl/disk/
baseDir            = $(progmdl)strtext/
objectDir          = $(mdlexample)objects/
```

```
privateInc        = $(baseDir)

strtextObjs = $(objectDir)strtext.mo
strtextRscs         = $(objectDir)strtext.rsc \
                        $(objectDir)strtext.mp


$(privateInc)strtext.h        : $(baseDir)strtext.r

$(objectDir)strtext.rsc       : $(baseDir)strtext.r

$(objectDir)strtext.mo        : $(baseDir)strtext.mc

$(objectDir)strtext.mp            : $(strtextObjs)
        $(msg)
        > $(objectDir)temp.cmd
        -a$@
        -s6000
        $(linkOpts)
        $(strtextObjs)
        <
        $(linkCmd) @$(objectDir)temp.cmd
        ~time

$(mdlapps)strtext.ma          : $(strtextRscs)
        $(msg)
        > $(objectDir)temp.cmd
        -o$@
        $(strtextRscs)
        <
        $(rscLibCmd) @$(objectDir)temp.cmd
        ~time
```

Orphan Cells

Orphan cells are cells that do not originate from a cell library, but are created by a program. We have seen the use of orphan cells in the PLACE BOX application. These cells were easy to create, as we were adding elements to the file. In the next example, we will create orphan cells from existing elements in the design file.

The first step is to set the search criteria. The function *mdlLocate_normal* will locate only displayable and unlocked elements in the file.

```
mdlLocate_noElemNoLocked();
mdlLocate_normal();
```

We will use a fence to define the elements for our cell. The function *mdlState_startFenceCommand* will establish cellFenceContents as the function to be called to process the fence elements. When the user defines the origin of the cell, a call to startCell will create the cell header, and build the element descriptor.

```
mdlState_startFenceCommand
        (cellFenceContents, /* routine for fence content */
         NULL,              /* function to define fence outline */
         startCell,         /* function for DATA point */
         modfence,          /* function for RESET */
         1,                 /* message for command name */
         2);                /* prompt for fence */
```

The function startCell will take the data point from *statedata.pointstack* as the origin of the cell. It will create the cell header with a call to *mdlCell_create*. We will call our cell "ORPHAN" to indicate that it is an orphan cell.

```
/* convert cell origin to Dpoint3d */
mdlCnv_IPointToDPoint(&origin, &statedata.pointstack[0]);

/* create orphan cell header */
mdlCell_create(&el, CELLNAME, &origin, FALSE);
mdlElmdscr_new(&elmDP, NULL, &el);
```

```
mdlFence_process(NULL);

mdlElmdscr_display(elmDP, 0, NORMALDRAW);
```

The function *mdlFence_process* will call the function `cellFenceContents` for each accepted element in the fence. Once we have built the cell in the element descriptor *elmDP*, we will add it to the design file. Adding the element to the file is straightforward with a call to *mdlElmdscr_add*.

We have to update the cell header with the component element information such as level bit mask, words in description, and the class bit mask. A call to *mdlCell_end* will do the hard work for us, but we did not start the cell with *mdlCell_begin*. To overcome this problem we will retrieve the end of file position before we add the element descriptor to the file. The variable *filePos* will then become the file position of the cell header. A call *mdlCell_end* will finish our orphan cell.

```
filePos = mdlElement_getFilePos (FILEPOS_EOF, &currFile);
mdlElmdscr_add(elmDP);

mdlCell_end(filePos);
mdlElmdscr_freeAll(&elmDP);
```

The function `cellFenceContents` does two things. First, it will read the elements in the fence, into the element descriptor. The function *mdlElmdscr_read* can read a single non-complex element, or a complex header and all its component elements. This is an extremely powerful feature, as it allows us to create orphan cells that have nested cells. Finally, we will delete the original element in the file with *mdlElmdscr_undoableDelete*.

```
filePos = mdlElement_getFilePos (FILEPOS_CURRENT, &currFile);
mdlElmdscr_read(&cellDP, filePos, MASTERFILE, FALSE, NULL);
mdlElmdscr_addToChain(elmDP, cellDP);
mdlElmdscr_undoableDelete(cellDP, filePos, TRUE);
```

Putting the code fragments together, we have the source to the ORCELL application. To load the application enter *mdl l orcell*. To run the application enter CELL ORPHAN at the uSTN> prompt.

orcell.mc

```
/*----------------------------------------------------------------------+
|          Copyright (c) 1991 Mach Dinh-Vu, All Rights Reserved         |
|                                                                       |
|      Create an ORPHAN cell from existing elements in the design file. |
|                                                                       |
|          CELL ORPHAN                                                  |
+----------------------------------------------------------------------*/
#include <mdl.h>
#include <mselems.h>
#include <rscdefs.h>
#include <tcb.h>
#include <global.h>
#include <scanner.h>
#include <userfnc.h>
#include "orcell.h"

#define   CELLNAME "ORPHAN"

MSElementDescr  *elmDP;
MSElementUnion  el;
int             currFile=0;
ULong           filePos;
/*----------------------------------------------------------------------+
| name           main                                                   |
+----------------------------------------------------------------------*/
main ()
 {
 RscFileHandle   rfHandle;

 /* --- load our command table --- */
 if (mdlParse_loadCommandTable (NULL) == NULL)
        mdlOutput_error ("Unable to load command table.");
 mdlOutput_error ("to execute, key-in CELL ORPHAN");
 mdlResource_openFile (&rfHandle, NULL, FALSE);
 }
/*----------------------------------------------------------------------+
| name           setSearchType                                          |
+----------------------------------------------------------------------*/
Private void setSearchType()
 {
 /* initialize search criteria to find nothing */
 mdlLocate_noElemNoLocked();
```

```
mdlLocate_normal();
}
/*-------------------------------------------------------------------+
| name          startCell                                           |
+-------------------------------------------------------------------*/
Private int     startCell()
{
Dpoint3d  origin;

/* convert cell origin to Dpoint3d */
mdlCnv_IPointToDPoint(&origin, &statedata.pointstack[0]);
/* create orphan cell header */
mdlCell_create(&el, CELLNAME, &origin, FALSE);
mdlElmdscr_new(&elmDP, NULL, &el);
mdlFence_process(NULL);
mdlElmdscr_display(elmDP, 0, NORMALDRAW);
filePos = mdlElement_getFilePos (FILEPOS_EOF, &currFile);
mdlElmdscr_add(elmDP);

mdlCell_end(filePos);
mdlElmdscr_freeAll(&elmDP);
}
/*-------------------------------------------------------------------+
| name          cellFenceContents                                   |
+-------------------------------------------------------------------*/
Private int     cellFenceContents()
{
MSElementDescr  *cellDP;

filePos = mdlElement_getFilePos (FILEPOS_CURRENT, &currFile);
mdlElmdscr_read(&cellDP, filePos, MASTERFILE, FALSE, NULL);
mdlElmdscr_addToChain(elmDP, cellDP);
mdlElmdscr_undoableDelete(cellDP, filePos, TRUE);
return SUCCESS;
}
/*-------------------------------------------------------------------+
| name          modfence                                            |
+-------------------------------------------------------------------*/
cmdName      modfence ()
cmdNumber    CMD_CELL_ORPHAN
{
setSearchType();
mdlState_startFenceCommand
            (cellFenceContents, /* routine for fence content */
             NULL,              /* function to define fence outline */
             startCell,         /* function for DATA point */
             modfence,          /* function for RESET */
             1,                 /* message for command name */
             2);                /* prompt for fence */
}
```

orcell.r

The file *orcell.r* contains the command table and messages for the ORCELL application.

```
/*---------------------------------------------------------------------+
|   orcell.r command table and messages for orcell.mc                  |
*--------------------------------------------------------------------*/
#include "rscdefs.h"
#include "cmdclass.h"

#define     CT_NONE          0
#define     CT_CELL          1
#define     CT_ORPHAN        2

 Table   CT_CELL =
 {
    { 1,  CT_ORPHAN,    MANIPULATION,        REQ,         "CELL" },
 };

 Table   CT_ORPHAN =
 {
    { 1,  CT_NONE,      INHERIT,             REQ,         "ORPHAN" },
 };

 MessageList 0 =
 {
     {
     { 1, "Create Orphan Cell" },
     { 2, "Define Cell Origin" },
     }
 };
```

orcell.mke

To build the ORCELL application, enter *bmake -a orcell*.

```
#----------------------------------------------------------------
#          orcell MDL Make File
#----------------------------------------------------------------
%include $(MS)/mdl/include/mdl.mki


#----------------------------------------------------------------
#          Define constants specific to this orcell application
#----------------------------------------------------------------
progmdl          = d:/progmdl/disk/
baseDir          = $(progmdl)orcell/
objectDir        = $(mdlexample)objects/
privateInc       = $(baseDir)

orcellObjs = $(objectDir)orcell.mo
orcellRscs         = $(objectDir)orcell.rsc \
                         $(objectDir)orcell.mp

$(privateInc)orcell.h      : $(baseDir)orcell.r

$(objectDir)orcell.rsc     : $(baseDir)orcell.r

$(objectDir)orcell.mo      : $(baseDir)orcell.mc

$(objectDir)orcell.mp          : $(orcellObjs)
        $(msg)
        > $(objectDir)temp.cmd
        -a$@
        -s6000
        $(linkOpts)
        $(orcellObjs)
        <
        $(linkCmd) @$(objectDir)temp.cmd
        ~time

$(mdlapps)orcell.ma            : $(orcellRscs)
        $(msg)
        > $(objectDir)temp.cmd
        -o$@
        $(orcellRscs)
        <
        $(rscLibCmd) @$(objectDir)temp.cmd
        ~time
```

6 : Mathematics and Geometry

In this chapter we will cover Vector Geometry, Current Transformation, View Transformation, Transformation and Rotation Matrices. The last four topics fall under the general heading of Geometric Transformations, which is an integral part of all graphics applications. If the thought of doing matrix calculation frightens you, don't despair - let the MDL functions do the hard work for you. We will only concern ourselves with which function to call, to provide the desired result.

Floating Point Constants

MDL provides pre-defined floating point constants for use in our programs. These constants are actual variables and therefore will change if assigned a new value. Use of these variables will vary, depending on our program. It may not seem logical to use *fc_1* in place of 1.0, but we should use the calculated constants, like *fc_piover180*, as they will make our program readable.

Floating Point Constant	Value
fc_onehalf	0.5
fc_zero	0.0
fc_1	1.0
fc_m1	-1.0
fc_2	2.0
fc_3	3.0
fc_4	4.0
fc_5	5.0
fc_10	10.0
fc_100	100.0
fc_p1	0.1
fc_p01	0.01
fc_p001	0.001
fc_p0001	0.0001
fc_pi	π
fc_180overpi	$180.0/\pi$
fc_piover180	$\pi/180.0$
fc_piover2	$\pi/2.0$
fc_piover3	$\pi/3.0$
fc_piover4	$\pi/4.0$
fc_piover6	$\pi/6.0$
fc_30	30.0
fc_60	60.0
fc_90	90.0
fc_180	180.0
fc_270	270.0
fc_360	360.0
fc_750	750.0
fc_1000	1000.0
fc_10000	10000.0
fc_100000	100000.0
fc_2pi	$2.0 * \pi$
fc_epsilon	0.00001
fc_mm_per_in	25.40
fc_360000	360000.0
fc_iang_to_rad	$(\pi/180.0)/360000.0$
fc_rad_to_iang	$(180.0*360000.)/\pi$
fc_miang_to_rad	$-1.0*(\pi/180.0)/360000.0$
fc_rmaxi4	RMAXI4
fc_rmini4	RMINI4
fc_rmaxui4	RMAXUI4
fc_tan30	0.5773502692

Table of floating point constants.

Vector Geometry

Vectors are a way to represent distance and direction. A vector can be thought of as an arrow starting from the origin. The components of this vector define the tip of the arrow. Each vector has three components, namely x, y, and z. The length of a vector is represented in some unit, and is known as the magnitude.

Scaling makes a vector longer or shorter. For example, to scale a vector, we write $A = sB$, where s is the scale factor. The length or magnitude of a vector A, is computed as the square root of the sum of the squares of its components. The magnitude of a vector A is denoted by $|A|$.

Dot product and cross product are two other vector operations that are useful in computer graphics.

Dot Product

The dot product of vectors A and B is defined by the equation:

$$A . B = |A| \, |B| \, \cos \theta$$

Where θ measures the smallest angle determined by A and B. The vector that we get by projecting B onto the line through A is denoted by $proj_A B$ (see figure 6.1).

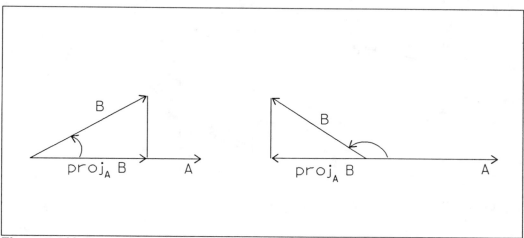

Figure 6.1 Vector projection of B onto A

Dot product is a convenient way to calculate the component of **B** in the direction of **A**. Therefore, the component of **B** in the direction of **A** is :

$$\frac{A.B}{|A|}$$

The sign is plus if proj$_A$**B** has the same direction as +**A**, and is minus if it has the same direction as -**A**.

Cross Product

The cross product of two vectors will return a unit vector perpendicular to the plane defined by A and B. In the first example in Figure 6.2, we can see that A x B and B x A are not commutative (the results are not the same). By reversing the order of the factors, we change the direction of the unit vector perpendicular to plane. The direction is determined by the Right-Hand Rule, with rotation from the first vector to the second.

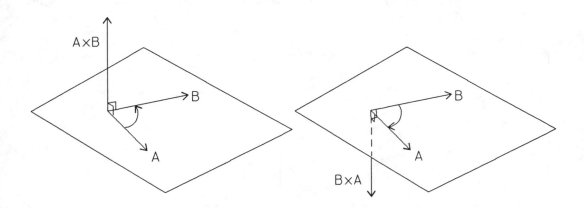

Figure 6.2 Cross Product of A x B and B x A

Vector Manipulation Functions

MDL provides several vector manipulation functions that make Vector geometry easy for the programmer. They are summarized below.

mdlVec_addPoint	add two direction vectors and return a direction vector.
mdlVec_addPointArray	same as above, but works on a point array.
mdlVec_areParrallel	determines if two vectors are parallel.
mdlVec_arePerpendicular	determines if two vectors are perpendicular.
mdlVec_colinear	determines if three points are colinear.
mdlVec_computeNormal	calculate a normal vector from 2 points
mdlVec_crossProduct	return the cross product of two vectors.
mdlVec_distance	return the magnitude of a vector from two points.
mdlVec_dotProduct	return the dot product of two vectors.
mdlVec_forcePlanarity	project a point to the closest point on a plane.
mdlVec_intersect	calculate the intersection point from two lines.
mdlVec_magnitude	return the magnitude of a vector.
mdlVec_normalize	normalize the direction vector, so its magnitude is 1.
mdlVec_pointEqual	check if two points are the same
mdlVec_pointEqualUOR	check if two points are the same, within one UOR.
mdlVec_projectPoint	project a point, by a distance, along a vector.
mdlVec_scale	scale a vector.
mdlVec_subtractPoint	subtract two direction vectors.
mdlVec_subtractPointArray	same as above, but operates on an array of points.

To better understand vector geometry, we will discuss the PLCIRC program. This program is based on the PLBOX program we discussed earlier. Here, instead of a box, we will place a circle around the text, and an arrowhead on the leader line.

Our leader line will run from the edge of the circle, to the tip of the arrowhead. We need to calculate this, given the origin of the circle and the point of the arrowhead. Using vectors, we can easily calculate the intersection between the circle and the line.

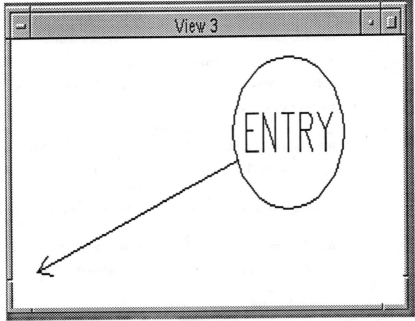

Figure 6.3 Result of the PLCIRC program

We are given two points. The first is the center of the circle, and the second is where we want the arrowhead to be. Subtracting the two points with *mdlVec_substractPoint* we obtain the directional vector, *dirVector*. By normalizing *dirVector*, we force its magnitude to be 1.0. Scaling *dirVector* by the radius of the circle will give us a direction vector with a magnitude of the radius of the circle. Adding this vector to the center of the circle, we return the intersection point on the circle (see Figure 6.4).

The MDL function is listed here.

```
/*-----------------------------------------------------------------+
| name          constIntersectionPoint                             |
+----------------------------------------------------------------*/
Private void constIntersectionPoint
(
Dpoint3d       *intersectionPt,      /* intersection point on circle */
double         *radius,              /* radius of circle */
Dpoint3d       *centerPt,            /* center of circle */
Dpoint3d       *directionPt          /* end point of arrowhead */
)
  {
  Dpoint3d     dirVector;

  mdlVec_subtractPoint (&dirVector, directionPt, centerPt);
  mdlVec_normalize (&dirVector);
  mdlVec_scale (&dirVector, &dirVector, *radius);
  mdlVec_addPoint (intersectionPt, centerPt, &dirVector);
  }
```

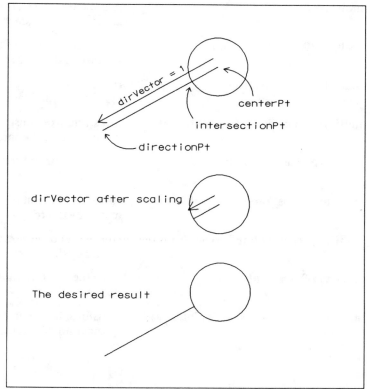

Figure 6.4 Calculating the leader line

Current Transformation

Current Transformation provides a very powerful feature for placing elements. A point, or set of points, passed through the current transformation matrix may be translated, rotated and/or scaled. A common use of Current Transformation is having all coordinates in Working Units. This makes the application transparent between design files that use different Positional Unit to Working Unit combinations.

Below is a summary of the Current Transformation functions.

mdlCurrTrans_begin	push a copy of the current transformation matrix onto a stack.
mdlCurrTrans_clear	pop all transformation matrix off the stack.
mdlCurrTrans_end	pop the transformation matrix at the top of the stack.
mdlCurrTrans_getAddress	return the address of the current forward and inverse transformation.
mdlCurrTrans_identity	replace the current transformation matrix with the identity matrix.
mdlCurrTrans_invTransPointArray	transform from design file coordinates into the current coordinate system.
mdlCurrTrans_rotateByAngles	rotate the current transformation matrix by the angle.
mdlCurrTrans_rotateByRMatrix	rotate the current transformation matrix by the rotation matrix.
mdlCurrTrans_rotateByView	rotate the current transformation matrix by the view.
mdlCurrTrans_scale	scale the current transformation matrix.
mdlCurrTrans_transformPointArray	transform from current coordinate system into design file coordinate system.

mdlCurrTrans_translateOrigin	set the new origin for the current transformation matrix.
mdlCurrTrans_translateOriginWorld	set the new origin for the current transformation matrix, using UORs.
mdlCurrTrans_masterUnitsIdentity	replace the current transformation matrix with the identity matrix, using UORs per master units.

We will now place an arrowhead at the tip of the leader line in our application **PLCIRC** (imagine writing this application without the aid of the Current Transformation matrix). First we need to calculate the angle of the line. Next, we place the arrowhead, then rotate and move it to the correct position.

A call to *mdlCurrTrans_begin* will push a copy of the current transformation onto a stack. The function *mdlCurrTrans_identity* will let us create the transformation from a known point. *mdlCurrTrans_translateOrigin* will move the origin of the current transformation to be the tip of the arrowhead. *mdlCurrTrans_invtransPointArray* will map all points from positional units into the current coordinate system (i.e the current Working Unit).

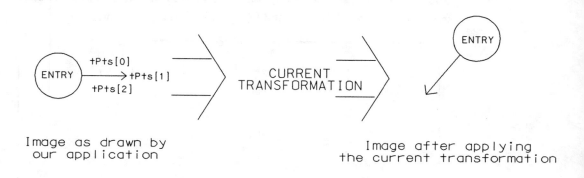

Figure 6.5 The result of a transformation

```
mdlCurrTrans_begin();
mdlCurrTrans_identity();
mdlCurrTrans_translateOrigin(&pntP[0]);
mdlCurrTrans_invtransPointArray( tPts, pntP, 2 );
```

Using current transformation, we will assume that the arrowhead is placed horizontally, with the tip pointing to the right. We can do this because we have rotated the current transformation by the angle of the line. For example, if the line is rotated 34.52 degrees, using *mdlCurrTrans_rotateByAngles* we will rotate the current transformation by -34.52, making everything "look" horizontal.

```
/* calculate angle of line */
zangle = atan2 ((tPts[0].y-tPts[1].y),(tPts[0].x-tPts[1].x));
mdlCurrTrans_rotateByAngles( 0.0, 0.0, zangle);
```

Working from the horizontal, it is very easy to calculate the points needed to create the arrowhead.

```
/* Create arrowhead */
tPts[1]    = tPts[0];
tPts[2].x = tPts[0].x - arrowsize;
tPts[2].y = tPts[0].y - (arrowsize/2);
tPts[0].x -= arrowsize;
tPts[0].y += arrowsize/2;
```

If we don't move the rotation origin to the tip of the arrowhead then the rotation will be around 0,0,0. Figure 6.6A shows the rotation without *mdlCurrTrans_translateOrigin* and Figure 6.6B is the correct method.

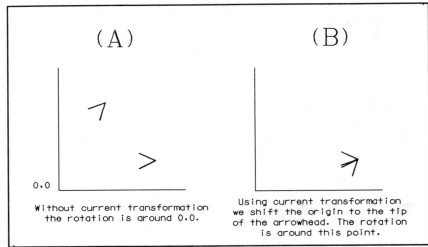

Figure 6.6 Rotation of the arrowhead

plcirc.mc

The *plcirc* application is similiar to *plbox*. We have introduced the function
`constIntersectionPoint` and added the current transformation into
`generateImage`. To load the application, enter *mdl l plcirc*. To execute the
application, enter PLACE TCIRC.

```
/*------------------------------------------------------------------+
| Copyright (C) 1991, Mach N. Dinh-Vu, All Rights Reserved          |
| Program    : plcirc.mc                                            |
| Revision   : 1.0.a                                                |
+------------------------------------------------------------------+
| Example MDL function to place a circle around                     |
| a text string with a leader line and an arrowhead.               |
+------------------------------------------------------------------*/
/*------------------------------------------------------------------+
|    Include Files                                                  |
+------------------------------------------------------------------*/
#include <mdl.h>       /* system include files */
#include <global.h>
#include <mselems.h>
#include <userfnc.h>
#include <rscdefs.h>
#include <tcb.h>
#include "plcirc.h"
/*------------------------------------------------------------------+
|    Private Global variables                                       |
+------------------------------------------------------------------*/
static char textin[128];
Dpoint3d    pntP[3];

/*------------------------------------------------------------------+
| name        main                                                 |
+------------------------------------------------------------------*/
main
(
)
  {
  RscFileHandle    rfHandle;

  /* load our command table */
  if (mdlParse_loadCommandTable (NULL) == NULL)
     mdlOutput_error ("Unable to load command table.");
  mdlResource_openFile (&rfHandle, NULL, FALSE);
  mdlOutput_error("Enter PLACE TCIRC to start");
  }

/*------------------------------------------------------------------+
| name        constIntersectionPoint                               |
+------------------------------------------------------------------*/
```

```
Private void constIntersectionPoint
(
Dpoint3d      *intersectionPt,        /* intersection point on circle */
double        *radius,                /* radius of circle */
Dpoint3d      *centerPt,              /* center of circle */
Dpoint3d      *directionPt            /* end point of arrowhead */
)
  {
  Dpoint3d      dirVector;

  mdlVec_subtractPoint (&dirVector, directionPt, centerPt);
  mdlVec_normalize (&dirVector);
  mdlVec_scale (&dirVector, &dirVector, *radius);
  mdlVec_addPoint (intersectionPt, centerPt, &dirVector);

}
/*_____+
| name    generateImage - dynamic function for complex case.          |
+_____*/
Private int generateImage
(
Dpoint3d      *pt,
int           view,
int           drawMode
)
{
  MSElementUnion    el;
  Dpoint3d          origin;
  Dpoint3d          tPts[3];
  double            zangle, radius;
  unsigned long     arrowsize;
  long              cellFilePos;

  arrowsize =  tcb->chheight / 2;
  radius = tcb->chheight * 2;
  pntP[1] = *pt;

  mdlCurrTrans_begin();
  mdlCurrTrans_identity();
  mdlCurrTrans_translateOrigin(&pntP[0]);
  mdlCurrTrans_invtransPointArray( tPts, pntP, 2 );
  origin = tPts[1];          /* origin of text */

  /* Create Text in dgnBuf for MicroStation Dynamics to display */
  mdlText_create (&el, NULL, textin, &tPts[1], NULL, NULL, NULL, NULL);
  mdlElement_display (&el, drawMode);
  if (drawMode == NORMALDRAW)
    {
    cellFilePos=mdlCell_begin("plcirc", NULL, NULL, 0);
    mdlElement_add(&el);
    }
```

```
   constIntersectionPoint(&tPts[1], &radius, &origin, &tPts[0]);

   mdlLine_create (&el, NULL, tPts);
   mdlElement_display (&el, drawMode);
   if (drawMode == NORMALDRAW) mdlElement_add(&el);

   /* Create arrowhead */
   mdlEllipse_create(&el, NULL, &origin, radius, radius, NULL, 0);
   mdlElement_display(&el, drawMode);
   if (drawMode == NORMALDRAW) mdlElement_add(&el);

   /* calculate angle of line */
   zangle = atan2 ((tPts[0].y-tPts[1].y),(tPts[0].x-tPts[1].x));
   mdlCurrTrans_rotateByAngles( 0.0, 0.0, zangle);

   /* Create arrowhead */
   tPts[1]   = tPts[0];
   tPts[2].x = tPts[0].x - arrowsize;
   tPts[2].y = tPts[0].y - (arrowsize/2);
   tPts[0].x -= arrowsize;
   tPts[0].y += arrowsize/2;

   mdlLineString_create (&el, NULL, tPts, 3);
   mdlElement_display (&el, drawMode);
   if (drawMode == NORMALDRAW)
   {
   mdlElement_add(&el);
   mdlCell_end(cellFilePos);
   }

   mdlCurrTrans_end();
   return  SUCCESS;
}
/*-------------------------------------------------------------------+
| name    keyinText                                                  |
+-------------------------------------------------------------------*/
Private void    keyinText
(
)
  {
  if (!*statedata.cmdstring)
     return;

  strncpy(textin, statedata.cmdstring, sizeof(textin));
  }

/*-------------------------------------------------------------------+
| name    placeCirc_secondPoint                                      |
+-------------------------------------------------------------------*/
Private void     placeCirc_secondPoint
```

```
(
Dpoint3d      *pt,
int           view
)
{
  generateImage(pt , view, NORMALDRAW);
}
/*—————————————————————————————————————————————+
| name        placeCirc_done                                 |
+———————————————————————————————————————————————*/
Private void    placeCirc_done
(
)
  {
  mdlState_restartCurrentCommand();
}
/*—————————————————————————————————————————————+
| name        placeCirc_firstPoint                           |
+———————————————————————————————————————————————*/
Private void    placeCirc_firstPoint
(
Dpoint3d      *pt,
int           view
)
  {
  pntP[0] = *pt;/* save first point */

  /* Set the datapoint state function for the second point. */
  mdlState_setFunction (STATE_KEYIN,      keyinText);
  mdlState_setFunction (STATE_DATAPOINT, placeCirc_secondPoint);
  mdlState_setFunction (STATE_RESET,      placeCirc_done);
  mdlOutput_rscPrintf (MSG_PROMPT, NULL, 0, 3);

  /* setup dynamics for the second point */
  mdlState_setFunction (STATE_COMPLEX_DYNAMICS, generateImage);
  }
/*—————————————————————————————————————————————+
| name        placeCirc_start                                |
+———————————————————————————————————————————————*/
cmdName      placeCirc_start
(
)
cmdNumber        CMD_PLACE_TCIRC
  {
  mdlState_startPrimitive (placeCirc_firstPoint, placeCirc_start, 1, 2);
  }
```

The file *plcirc.r* contains the command table and prompts.

plcirc.r

```
/*-----------------------------------------------------------------------+
| PLCIRC.R command table and messages for PLCIRC.MC                      |
+-----------------------------------------------------------------------*/
#include "rscdefs.h"
#include "cmdclass.h"

#define      CT_NONE           0
#define      CT_PLACE          2

Table   1 =
{
   { 1,  CT_PLACE,        PLACEMENT,        REQ,                         "PLACE" },
};

Table   CT_PLACE =
{
   { 1,  CT_NONE,         INHERIT,          NONE | CMDSTR (1),      "TCIRC" },
};


MessageList 0 =
{
   {
   { 0, "" },
   { 1, "MDL Place Text in Circle" },
   { 2, "Define Start point" },
   { 3, "Define Circle position" },
   }
```

plcirc.mke

The makefile uses the standard *seed.mke*, with all occurrences of seed substituted by plcirc.

```
#----------------------------------------------------------------
#          PLCIRC MDL Make File
#----------------------------------------------------------------
%include $(MS)/mdl/include/mdl.mki
#----------------------------------------------------------------
#          Define constants specific to this plcirc application
#----------------------------------------------------------------
progmdl          = d:/progmdl/disk/
baseDir          = $(progmdl)plcirc/
objectDir        = $(mdlexample)objects/
privateInc       = $(baseDir)

plcircObjs  =    $(objectDir)plcirc.mo
plcircRscs  =    $(objectDir)plcirc.rsc \
                 $(objectDir)plcirc.mp

$(privateInc)plcirc.h        : $(baseDir)plcirc.r

$(objectDir)plcirc.rsc       : $(baseDir)plcirc.r

$(objectDir)plcirc.mo        : $(baseDir)plcirc.mc

$(objectDir)plcirc.mp            : $(plcircObjs)
        $(msg)
        > $(objectDir)temp.cmd
        -a$@
        -s6000
        $(linkOpts)
        $(plcircObjs)
        <
        $(linkCmd) @$(objectDir)temp.cmd
        ~time

$(mdlapps)plcirc.ma              : $(plcircRscs)
        $(msg)
        > $(objectDir)temp.cmd
        -o$@
        $(plcircRscs)
        <
        $(rscLibCmd) @$(objectDir)temp.cmd
        ~time
```

Transformation Matrix Functions

MicroStation uses Geometric Transformation for translation, scaling and rotation. These three basic transformations can be combined and represented in a matrix. It is beyond the scope of this book to mathematically prove that one matrix can represent all three transformations. We will assume that this is so, and see how to do this with an MDL program.

Let's look at the available Transformation Matrix Functions.

mdlTMatrix_fromRMatrix	return the transformation matrix from a rotation matrix.
mdlTMatrix_getIdentity	set transformation matrix to the identity matrix.
mdlTMatrix_getTranslation	return the translation from a transformation matrix.
mdlTMatrix_masterToReference	returns the matrix that can transform elements from master file to reference file coordinate system.
mdlTMatrix_multiply	multiply two matrices together.
mdlTMatrix_referenceToMaster	returns the matrix that can transform elements from reference file to master file coordinate system.
mdlTMatrix_rotateByAngles	rotate the transformation matrix by angles in radians.
mdlTMatrix_rotateByRMatrix	rotate the transformation matrix by the rotation matrix.
mdlTMatrix_rotateScalePoint	rotate and scale the point by the transformation matrix.
mdlTMatrix_setOrigin	set the origin of the transformation matrix.
mdlTMatrix_scale	scale the transformation matrix by a factor.
mdlTMatrix_setTranslation	set the translation of the transformation matrix.

mdlTMatrix_transformPoint	transform a point by the transformation matrix.
mdlTMatrix_transformPointArray	transform an array of points by the transformation matrix.
mdlTMatrix_translate	shift origin of transformation matrix.
mdlTMatrix_transpose	swap rows and columns of transformation matrix.

Rotate, Scale and Translation

To prove that one matrix can represent rotation, scaling and translation we will write an MDL program to manipulate text, or a text node. The program *textrms.mc* will first prompt for the text or text node. It will then rotate it by the active angle, scale it by the active scale, and move it to a new position. In this program we will not provide selection set, or fence, manipulation. If you wish to expand *textrms.mc* to include these features, then refer to Chapter 4.

We will use *mdlState_startModifyCommand* as the state function to modify the element. The `transformElement` function defines the dynamics for our manipulation.

```
mdlLocate_noElemNoLocked();
mdlLocate_setElemSearchMask(sizeof(searchType)/sizeof(int), searchType);

mdlState_startModifyCommand(rotMove_start, rotMove_accept,
                    transformElement,NULL, NULL, 1, 0, TRUE, 0);
mdlLocate_init();
```

The `transformElement` function will rotate, scale and move the text. The order in which these are applied is very important, as the resultant transformation is dependant on the sequence. Figure 6.7 shows the correct sequence to transform a text string. The functions, *mdlTMatrix_rotateByAngles* and *mdlTMatrix_scale*, operate from the origin of the current transformation. Therefore, we need to establish a new transformation and make the point *pt* the origin of current transformation (see Figure 6.7b). This is done with the function *mdlCurrTrans_translateOrigin*.

Using *mdlTMatrix_getIdentity* is vital as it sets the transformation matrix to a known state. To scale the matrix we will use *mdlTMatrix_scale* and pass it the active scale. The *mdlTMatrix_rotateByAngles* rotates the matrix by the active angle. This function requires the angle to be in radians, therefore we need to convert the degree angle by multiplying it by *fc_piover180*.

```
mdlTMatrix_getIdentity(&tMatrix);
mdlTMatrix_scale(&tMatrix, &tMatrix, tcb->xactscle,
                            tcb->yactscle, tcb->zactscle);
mdlTMatrix_rotateByAngles(&tMatrix, &tMatrix, 0.0, 0.0
                            tcb->actangle*fc_piover180);
mdlTMatrix_translate(&tMatrix, &tMatrix, distance.x,
                            distance.y, distance.z);
```

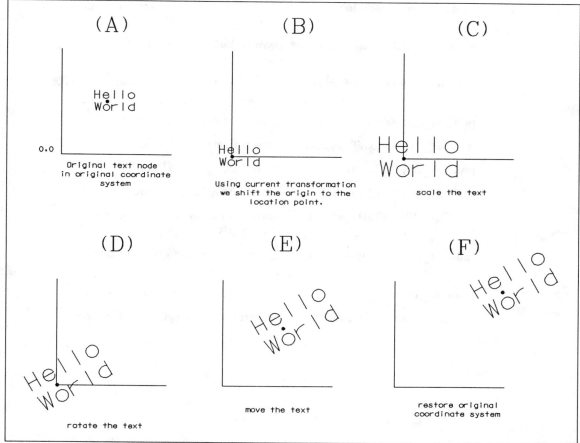

Figure 6.7 Transformation of Hello World

The move is performed by *mdlTMatrix_translate*. To apply the matrix to our text string we will use the function *mdlElement_transform*. The last step is to pop the current transformation matrix, which will put us back into the original coordinate system. Note: if AS = 1 and AA = 0 then this program will act the same as MOVE ELEMENT.

By using Transformation Matrices we have converted a very complicated mathematical problem into several lines of simple code.

Data Format

MicroStation and MDL supports several different types of data format. The data conversion functions to move between these formats are listed here.

mdlCnv_doubleFromFileFormat	convert floating point from file to internal format.
mdlCnv_doubleToFileFormat	convert floating point from internal to file format.
mdlCnv_doubleToNativeFloat	convert double to native float.
mdlCnv_nativeFloatToDouble	convert float to native double.
mdlCnv_DPointToIPoint	convert Dpoint3d to Point3d.
mdlCnv_IPointToDPoint	convert Point3d to Dpoint3d.
mdlCnv_DPointToIPointArray	convert an array of Dpoint3ds to an array of Point3ds.
mdlCnv_IPointToDPointArray	convert an array of Point3ds to an array of Dpoint3ds.
mdlCnv_fromAsciiToR50	convert ASCII string to RAD50 string.
mdlCnv_fromR50ToAscii	convert RAD50 string to ASCII string.

The function *mdlCnv_fromR50ToAscii* is of interest, as it allows the conversion between RAD50 and ASCII. The use of RAD50 dates back to the original Intergraph system on the DEC PDP11 series of mini computers. The advantage of RAD50 is that it stores 3 characters for every 16 bit word, whereas ASCII can only store 2 characters. The disadvantage of RAD50 is that it is restricted to a limited character set. Conversion to ASCII is required when we wish to extract the cell name, as shown here.

```
mdlCnv_fromR50ToAscii(6, &cellHeader->cell_lib_hdr.name, cellName);
mdlCnv_fromR50ToAscii(27, &cellHeader->cell_lib_hdr.descrip,
                      cellDescription);
```

mdlCnv_fromScanFormat	convert unsigned long in scan format to signed long number in internal format.
mdlCnv_roundDoubleToLong	convert a double to a long.
mdlCnv_roundDoubleToULong	convert a double to an unsigned long.
mdlCnv_swapWordArray	swap the words on an array of 4 byte integers.
mdlCnv_toScanFormat	convert signed long in internal format to unsigned long number in scan format.

Point Stack

Data points sent to MicroStation are placed on a point stack. The built-in variable *statedata.pointstack* holds this information. The element location logic stores the location point in integer world format, that is *Point3d*. Therefore, we need to convert the contents of *statedata.pointstack[0]* to *DPoint3d* with the function *mdlCnv_IPointToDPoint*. In the function `getMoveDistance` we will save the *anchor* point and calculate the *distance* to move using *mdlVec_subtractPoint*.

```
/* convert to DPoint */
mdlCnv_IPointToDPoint (&anchor, statedata.pointstack);

/* subtract anchor point from current point to get the distance */
mdlVec_subtractPoint (distance, pt, &anchor);
```

Here is the complete source for the TEXTRMS application. To load the application enter *mdl l textrms*. To execute the application enter TEXT RMS .

textrms.mc

```
/*----------------------------------------------------------------+
| Copyright (C) 1991, Mach N. Dinh-Vu, All Rights Reserved.       |
| Program    : textrms.mc                                         |
| Revision   : 1.0.a                                              |
+----------------------------------------------------------------+
|         This program will rotate, scale and move the identified |
|         text or text node by the active angle and active scale. |
+----------------------------------------------------------------*/
/*----------------------------------------------------------------+
|     Include Files                                               |
+----------------------------------------------------------------*/
#include <mdl.h>           /* system include files */
#include <global.h>
#include <mselems.h>
#include <userfnc.h>
#include <rscdefs.h>
#include <tcb.h>

#include "textrms.h"
/*----------------------------------------------------------------+
|     Private Global variables                                    |
+----------------------------------------------------------------*/
int           currFile;
ULong         filepos;
Transform     tMatrix;

void    rotMove_start ();
/*----------------------------------------------------------------+
| name      main                                                  |
+----------------------------------------------------------------*/
main()
{
 RscFileHandle    rfHandle;

 /* load our command table */
 if (mdlParse_loadCommandTable (NULL) == NULL)
        mdlOutput_error ("Unable to load command table.");
 mdlResource_openFile (&rfHandle, NULL, FALSE);
 mdlOutput_prompt("Key-in TEXT RMS to execute");
}
/*----------------------------------------------------------------+
| name      getMoveDistance                                       |
+----------------------------------------------------------------*/
```

```
Private void     getMoveDistance
(
Dpoint3d    *distance,            /* <= distance from anchor */
Dpoint3d    *pt                   /* => current point */
)
    {
    Dpoint3d    anchor;

    /* convert to DPoint */
    mdlCnv_IPointToDPoint (&anchor, statedata.pointstack);

    /* subtract anchor point from current point to get the distance */
    mdlVec_subtractPoint (distance, pt, &anchor);
    }
```

```
/*-----------------------------------------------------------------+
| name      transformElement                                       |
+------------------------------------------------------------------*/
Private void     transformElement
(
Dpoint3d    *pt          /* => current location of cursor */
)
    {
    Dpoint3d    distance, offset;

    getMoveDistance (&distance, pt);

    mdlCurrTrans_begin();
    mdlCurrTrans_identity();
    mdlCurrTrans_translateOrigin(pt);

    mdlTMatrix_getIdentity(&tMatrix);
    mdlTMatrix_scale(&tMatrix, &tMatrix, tcb->xactscle,
                        tcb->yactscle, tcb->zactscle);
    mdlTMatrix_rotateByAngles(&tMatrix, &tMatrix, 0.0, 0.0,
                        tcb->actangle*fc_piover180);
    mdlTMatrix_translate(&tMatrix, &tMatrix, distance.x,
                        distance.y, distance.z);

    mdlElement_transform (dgnBuf, dgnBuf, &tMatrix);
    mdlCurrTrans_end();
    }
```

```
/*-----------------------------------------------------------------+
| name   elementModify_move                                        |
+------------------------------------------------------------------*/
Private int      elementModify_move
(
MSElementUnion  *el,       /* <> element to be modified */
Dpoint3d        *pt        /* => from params in mdlModify_element... */
```

```
)
    {
    Dpoint3d      distance;

    getMoveDistance (&distance, pt);
    mdlCurrTrans_begin();
    mdlCurrTrans_identity();
    mdlCurrTrans_translateOrigin(pt);

    /* start from a known matrix */
    mdlTMatrix_getIdentity(&tMatrix);

    /* scale it by current active scale */
    mdlTMatrix_scale(&tMatrix, &tMatrix, tcb->xactscle,
                        tcb->yactscle, tcb->xactscle);

    /* rotate it by current active angle */
    mdlTMatrix_rotateByAngles(&tMatrix, &tMatrix, 0.0, 0.0,
                        tcb->actangle*fc_piover180);
    mdlTMatrix_translate(&tMatrix, &tMatrix, distance.x,
                        distance.y, distance.z);

    if (mdlElement_transform (el, el, &tMatrix))
        return  MODIFY_STATUS_ERROR;

    mdlCurrTrans_end();
    return  MODIFY_STATUS_REPLACE;
    }
```

```
/*----------------------------------------------------------------+
| name   rotMove_accept                                           |
+-----------------------------------------------------------------*/
Private void    rotMove_accept
(
Dpoint3d    *pt          /* => final point for move element */
)
    {
    Dpoint3d      distance;
    int           currFile;
    ULong         filePos;

    /* Get the file position and file number of the element to move. */
    filePos = mdlElement_getFilePos (FILEPOS_CURRENT, &currFile);

    /* Now move each element, no selection set */
    mdlModify_elementSingle (currFile, filePos, MODIFY_REQUEST_HEADERS,
                        MODIFY_ORIG, elementModify_move, pt, NULL);

    /* Save new anchor point (the current acceptance point) */
    mdlCnv_DPointToIPoint (statedata.pointstack, pt);
```

```
        /* Reload the dynamic buffer with the new element. */
        mdlDynamic_loadElement (NULL, currFile, filePos);

        /* a RESET will restart this command */
        mdlState_setFunction (STATE_RESET, rotMove_start);

        /* if in singleshot mode then restart default command */
        mdlState_checkSingleShot ();
        }
/*-------------------------------------------------------------------+
| name    rotMove_start                                              |
+-------------------------------------------------------------------*/
cmdName   void      rotMove_start ()
cmdNumber           CMD_TEXT_RMS
{
 static int searchType[] = {
                        TEXT_ELM,
                        TEXT_NODE_ELM
                        };

mdlLocate_noElemNoLocked();
mdlLocate_setElemSearchMask(sizeof(searchType)/sizeof(int), searchType);

mdlState_startModifyCommand(rotMove_start, rotMove_accept,
                        transformElement,NULL, NULL, 1, 0, TRUE, 0);
mdlLocate_init();
}
```

The makefile uses the standard *seed.mke*, with all occurrences of SEED substituted with TEXTRMS. To build the application enter *bmake -a textrms.*

textrms.mke

```
#--------------------------------------------------------------------
#         TEXTRMS MDL Make File
#--------------------------------------------------------------------
%include $(MS)/mdl/include/mdl.mki
#--------------------------------------------------------------------
#         Define constants specific to this textrms application
#--------------------------------------------------------------------
progmdl            = d:/progmdl/disk/
baseDir            = $(progmdl)textrms/
objectDir          = $(mdlexample)objects/
privateInc         = $(baseDir)

textrmsObjs = $(objectDir)textrms.mo
textrmsRscs         = $(objectDir)textrms.rsc \
                       $(objectDir)textrms.mp

$(privateInc)textrms.h        : $(baseDir)textrms.r

$(objectDir)textrms.rsc       : $(baseDir)textrms.r

$(objectDir)textrms.mo        : $(baseDir)textrms.mc

$(objectDir)textrms.mp           : $(textrmsObjs)
        $(msg)
        > $(objectDir)temp.cmd
        -a$@
        -s6000
        $(linkOpts)
        $(textrmsObjs)
        <
        $(linkCmd) @$(objectDir)temp.cmd
        ~time

$(mdlapps)textrms.ma             : $(textrmsRscs)
        $(msg)
        > $(objectDir)temp.cmd
        -o$@
        $(textrmsRscs)
        <
        $(rscLibCmd) @$(objectDir)temp.cmd
        ~time
```

The file *textrms.r* contains the command table and prompts.

textrms.r

```
/*----------------------------------------------------------------------+
| TEXTRMS.R command table and messages for TEXTRMS.MC                   |
+----------------------------------------------------------------------*/
#include "rscdefs.h"
#include "cmdclass.h"

#define    CT_NONE        0
#define    CT_TEXT        1
#define    CT_RMS         2

Table   CT_TEXT =
{
    { 1,  CT_RMS,      MANIPULATION,      REQ,         "TEXT" },
};

Table   CT_RMS =
{
    { 1,  CT_NONE,       INHERIT,        REQ,      "RMS" },
};


MessageList 0 =
{
    {
    { 0, "" },
    { 1, "Text Rotate Move Scale" },
    }
};
```

Rotation Matrix Functions

The rotation matrix is a subset of the transformation matrix. The process with which we rotate the element is the same. Consider the rotation of an element around P1 (see Figure 6.8). We would translate it to the origin, rotate it and move it back to the original P1. The translation is done with the *mdlCurrTrans_* functions and the rotation with the *mdlRMatrix_* functions.

A summary of the Rotation Matrix functions are listed here.

mdlRMatrix_from3Points   return a rotation matrix from 3 points on a plane.

mdlRMatrix_fromAngle   return a rotation matrix from the angle.

mdlRMatrix_fromColumnVector   return a rotation matrix based on vectors that define the column.

mdlRMatrix_fromNormalVector   return a rotation matrix from a direction vector.

mdlRMatrix_fromRowVector   return a rotation matrix based on vectors that define the row.

mdlRMatrix_fromQuat   extract rotation matrix from the quarternion.

mdlRMatrix_fromTMatrix   extract rotation and scaling from transformation matrix and place it in the rotation matrix.

mdlRMatrix_fromView   make a copy of the rotation matrix to another matrix.

mdlRMatrix_getColumnVector   extract a column from a rotation matrix into a vector.

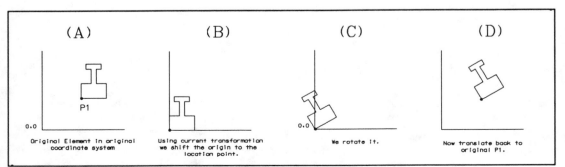

Figure 6.8 Rotation about point P1.

mdlRMatrix_getIdentity	set the rotation matrix to be the Identity Matrix.
mdlRMatrix_getInverse	return the inverse of the rotation matrix.
mdlRMatrix_getRowVector	extract a row from a rotation matrix into a vector.
mdlRMatrix_invert	return the transpose of the rotation matrix.
mdlRMatrix_multiply	multiply two matrices together.
mdlRMatrix_multiplyByTMatrix	multiply a transformation and a rotation matrix together.
mdlRMatrix_normalize	normalise the columns of the rotation matrix.
mdlRMatrix_rotate	rotate the rotation matrix by angle.
mdlRMatrix_rotatePointArray	rotate the rotation matrix by an array of points.
mdlRMatrix_rotateRange	scales and sets the range cube in the rotated coordinate system.
mdlRMatrix_toAngle	return the rotation angle for a 2D rotation matrix.
mdlRMatrix_toQuat	generates a quaternion from a 3D rotation matrix.
mdlRMatrix_unrotatePoint	rotate a point by the inverse of the rotation matrix.
mdlRMatrix_unrotatePointArray	rotate a series of points by the inverse of the rotation matrix.

To explain the rotation matrix we will look at the example *rotcell.mc*. In this application we rotate a cell so that it aligns with the active angle. For example, a cell was placed at an angle of 25°, and we then change the active angle to 45° and call *rotcell*. The cell will be modified to appear as if it was placed at 45°.

The bulk of the program is the same as *modsing*, found in Chapter 4. Using *mdlModify_elementMulti* we will call `rotcell` for the cell header and its component elements. Once we have the cell header, we will extract the rotation matrix and the rotation point with the function *mdlCell_extract*.

```
mdlCell_extract(&rotpoint, NULL, &rMatrix, NULL, NULL, el);
```

We need to build the transformation matrix that will allow us to align to a specific angle. The best method is to rotate the cell back to 0° and then rotate it by the active angle. The function *mdlRMatrix_invert* will swap the rows and columns of the rotation matrix (in effect, unrotate it). For example, if a cell was rotated by 45°, then calling *mdlRMatrix_invert* will unrotate the transformation matrix by 45° (i.e., rotate it by -45).

The following code sets the transformation matrix to a known state (the Identity Matrix). Then we calculate the amount to unrotate the cell. After calling *mdlTMatrix_rotateByRMatrix*, the transformation matrix will contain the rotation to set the cell at 0°.

```
mdlTMatrix_getIdentity(&tMatrix);
mdlRMatrix_invert(&rMatrix, &rMatrix);
mdlTMatrix_rotateByRMatrix(&tMatrix, &tMatrix, &rMatrix);
```

Our next step is to decide if we want the rotation in the local or the global coordinate system. If we are working in the local system, then we need to consider view rotation. The function *mdlRMatrix_fromView* extracts the rotation matrix in the view where we select the cell. Calling *mdlRMatrix_invert* unrotates the view and *mdlTMatrix_rotateByRMatrix* builds the view rotation into our transformation matrix.

```
mdlRMatrix_fromView(&rMatrix, rotview, FALSE);
mdlRMatrix_invert(&rMatrix, &rMatrix);
mdlTMatrix_rotateByRMatrix( &tMatrix, &tMatrix, &rMatrix);
```

Finally, we rotate the transformation matrix by the active angle.

```
mdlTMatrix_rotateByAngles( &tMatrix, &tMatrix, 0.0, 0.0,
                           tcb->actangle*fc_piover180);
```

Now that we have the transformation matrix, we can apply it to our element.
Using the current transformation sets the rotation origin to be at *rotpoint*.

```
mdlCurrTrans_begin();
mdlCurrTrans_identity();
mdlCurrTrans_translateOriginWorld(&rotpoint);

status = mdlElement_transform(el, el, &tMatrix);

mdlCurrTrans_end();
```

Putting all the code fragments together gives us our MDL application to rotate
the cell. The entire source code is given below. To load the application enter
mdl l rotcell. To execute the application enter ROTATE CELL.

rotcell.mc

```
/*----------------------------------------------------------------------+
|        Copyright (c) 1991 Mach Dinh-Vu, All Rights Reserved           |
|                                                                       |
|        rotcell.mc - rotate the cell so that it aligns with the        |
|        active angle                                                   |
|                         ROTATE CELL                                   |
+----------------------------------------------------------------------*/
#include        <mdl.h>
#include        <mselems.h>
#include        <rscdefs.h>
#include        <tcb.h>
#include        <global.h>
#include        <scanner.h>
#include        "rotcell.h"

Private int     rotview;
/*----------------------------------------------------------------------+
| name           main                                                   |
+----------------------------------------------------------------------*/
main ()
{
        RscFileHandle   rfHandle;

        /* --- load our command table --- */
        if (mdlParse_loadCommandTable (NULL) == NULL)
                mdlOutput_error ("Unable to load command table.");
        mdlOutput_prompt ("to execute, key-in ROTATE CELL");
        mdlResource_openFile (&rfHandle, NULL, FALSE);

}

/*----------------------------------------------------------------------+
| name           setSearchType                                          |
+----------------------------------------------------------------------*/
Private void setSearchType()
{
        static int searchType[]={CELL_HEADER_ELM, LINE_ELM,LINE_STRING_ELM,
                         SHAPE_ELM, TEXT_NODE_ELM, CURVE_ELM,CMPLX_STRING_ELM,
                         CONIC_ELM, CMPLX_SHAPE_ELM, ELLIPSE_ELM, ARC_ELM,
                         TEXT_ELM, SURFACE_ELM, SOLID_ELM};

        /* initialize search criteria to find nothing */
        mdlLocate_noElemNoLocked();
```

```
              /* add elements to search to list */
              mdlLocate_setElemSearchMask(sizeof(searchType)/sizeof(int),searchType);
}
/*-------------------------------------------------------------------------+
| name            rotCell                                                   |
+-------------------------------------------------------------------------*/
Private int rotCell
(
MSElementUnion *el
)
      {
      Dpoint3d    rotpoint;
      char        cellName[8];
      RotMatrix   rMatrix;
      Transform   tMatrix;
      int         status;

      /*   build transformation matrix from the cell header
           for each component element.                         */

      if (!el->hdr.ehdr.complex)
         {
         if (el->hdr.ehdr.type != CELL_HEADER_ELM)
         return (MODIFY_STATUS_NOCHANGE);

         /* get origin for the rotation point, and rotation matrix */
         mdlCell_extract(&rotpoint, NULL, &rMatrix, NULL, NULL, el);

         /* build transformation matrix with the rotation component
            of the cell.                                         */
         mdlTMatrix_getIdentity(&tMatrix);
         mdlRMatrix_invert(&rMatrix, &rMatrix);
         mdlTMatrix_rotateByRMatrix(&tMatrix, &tMatrix, &rMatrix);

         /* compensate for view rotation so the transformation is local*/
         mdlRMatrix_fromView(&rMatrix, rotview, FALSE);
         mdlRMatrix_invert(&rMatrix, &rMatrix);
         mdlTMatrix_rotateByRMatrix( &tMatrix, &tMatrix, &rMatrix);

         mdlTMatrix_rotateByAngles( &tMatrix, &tMatrix, 0.0, 0.0,
                                    tcb->actangle*fc_piover180);
         }

   mdlCurrTrans_begin();
   mdlCurrTrans_identity();
   mdlCurrTrans_translateOriginWorld(&rotpoint);

   status = mdlElement_transform(el, el, &tMatrix);
   mdlCurrTrans_end();
```

```
        return (status ? 0 : MODIFY_STATUS_REPLACE);
}
/*----------------------------------------------------------------------+
| name          mod_accept                                              |
+----------------------------------------------------------------------*/
Private void    mod_accept
(
Dpoint3d    *pt,
int         view
)
        {
        ULong   filePos, compOffset;
        int     currFile=0;

        rotview = view;
        filePos = mdlElement_getFilePos (FILEPOS_CURRENT, &currFile);
        if (mdlSelect_isActive())
            {
        mdlModify_elementMulti (currFile,    /* file to process */
                    filePos,      /* file position for element */
                    MODIFY_REQUEST_HEADERS, /* process complex headers */
                    MODIFY_ORIG, /* modify original element */
                    rotCell,     /* modify routine for each element */
                    NULL,        /* parameters for rotCell */
                    TRUE);       /* process graphic group */
            } else {
        mdlModify_elementSingle (currFile,
                    filePos,      /* file position for element */
                    MODIFY_REQUEST_HEADERS, /* process complex headers */
                    MODIFY_ORIG, /* modify original element */
                    rotCell,     /* modify routine for each element */
                    NULL,         /* parameters for rotCell */
                    FALSE); /* offset for component elements */
            }

        /* restart the element location process */
        mdlLocate_restart (FALSE);

}
/*----------------------------------------------------------------------+
| name          change_cell                                             |
+----------------------------------------------------------------------*/
Private void change_cell()
        {
        setSearchType();
        mdlState_startModifyCommand (
                    change_cell, /* function to call on RESET */
                    mod_accept,  /* function to call on DATA */
                    NULL,        /* function to call for DYNAMIC */
                    NULL,        /* function to call on SHOW */
                    NULL,        /* function to call on CLEAN */
```

```
                    1,                  /* index into MESSAGE LIST */
                    2,                  /* index into PROMPT LIST */
                    TRUE,               /* Modify SELECTION SET ? */
                    FALSE);             /* additional data points required */

        /* start element search from the beginning of file */
        mdlLocate_init ();
        }
/*----------------------------------------------------------------------------+
| name            rotcell                                                     |
+-----------------------------------------------------------------------------*/
cmdName        rotcell ()
cmdNumber      CMD_ROTATE_CELL
        {
        change_cell();
        }
```

rotcell.r contains the command table and messages for *rotcell.mc*.

rotcell.r

```
/*----------------------------------------------------------------------------+
| ROTCELL.R                                                                   |
+-----------------------------------------------------------------------------*/
#include "rscdefs.h"
#include "cmdclass.h"

#define    CT_NONE        0
#define    CT_ROTATE      1
#define    CT_CELL        2

Table   CT_ROTATE =
{
    { 1,  CT_CELL,       PLACEMENT,      REQ,            "ROTATE" },
};
Table   CT_CELL =
{
    { 1,  CT_NONE,       INHERIT,        DEF,            "CELL" },
};
MessageList 0 =
{
    {
    { 1, "Rotate Cell" },
    { 2, "Accept/Reject element" },
    }
};
```

To build the application, enter *bmake -a rotcell.*

rotcell.mke

```
#------------------------------------------------------------
#        ROTCELL MDL Make File
#------------------------------------------------------------
%include $(MS)/mdl/include/mdl.mki


#------------------------------------------------------------
#        Define constants specific to this ROTCELL application
#------------------------------------------------------------
progmdl           = d:/progmdl/disk/
baseDir           = $(progmdl)rotcell/
objectDir         = $(mdlexample)objects/
privateInc        = $(baseDir)

rotcellObjs = $(objectDir)rotcell.mo
rotcellRscs             = $(objectDir)rotcell.rsc \
                        $(objectDir)rotcell.mp


$(privateInc)rotcell.h      : $(baseDir)rotcell.r

$(objectDir)rotcell.rsc     : $(baseDir)rotcell.r

$(objectDir)rotcell.mo      : $(baseDir)rotcell.mc

$(objectDir)rotcell.mp          : $(rotcellObjs)
        $(msg)
        > $(objectDir)temp.cmd
        -a$@
        -s6000
        $(linkOpts)
        $(rotcellObjs)
        <
        $(linkCmd) @$(objectDir)temp.cmd
        ~time

$(mdlapps)rotcell.ma            : $(rotcellRscs)
        $(msg)
        > $(objectDir)temp.cmd
        -o$@
        $(rotcellRscs)
        <
        $(rscLibCmd) @$(objectDir)temp.cmd
        ~time
```

7 : Advanced Dialog Box

We have already seen that the dialog box is an extremely powerful user interface. In this chapter we will discuss some of the advanced features of the Dialog Box.

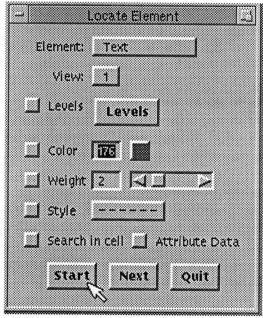

Figure 7.1 The LOCELE Dialog Box

We will write the LOCELE application which will explore the use of modal dialog box, synonym resources and dialog item communication.

The aim of the LOCELE application is to display a specified element using a search criteria. Each criteria has associated with it, a toggle button. If this button is on, then LOCELE locates elements that match the specified criteria. For example, if *Levels* is toggled 'on', then LOCELE will return only elements of the type specified, which are on the levels specified in the level mask.

Figure 7.1 shows the dialog box, associated with this application.

Files used in LOCELE are:

locele.mc	MDL source file.
loceldlg.r	Dialog Resource source file.
loceldlg.h	Include file containing dialog types.
locelmsg.r	Screen messages.
locelcmd.r	Command syntax.
loceltyp.mt	Data structure to publish.
locele.mke	Makefile for the application.

The first step in designing the LOCELE application, is to decide what criteria are required (and therefore, what goes onto the dialog box). We will use the structure *locElemInfoP*, shown here.

```
/*-----------------------------------------------------------------+
|    Local Structure Definitions                                   |
+-----------------------------------------------------------------*/
typedef struct loceleminfo
        {
        int     eleType;          /* element to search */
        int     View;             /* view to display element */
        int     colors;           /* boolean for toggle */
        int     weights;          /* boolean for toggle */
        int     styles;           /* boolean for toggle */
        int     levels;           /* boolean for toggle */
        int     cellElem;         /* boolean for toggle */
        int     attribData;       /* boolean for toggle */
        int     color;            /* search color */
        int     weight            /* search weight */
        int     style;            /* search style */
        short   level[4];         /* search levels */
        }
        LocElemInfoP;
```

Option Button Item

The Option Button dialog item is used in three areas - selecting the element to search, the view to display the element and the line style to search. Selecting the Element option will return the element type in *locElemInfoP->eleType* (See Figure 7.2). In our dialog resource file, *loceldlg.r* we will define the element search resource as:

```
DItem_OptionButtonRsc  OPTIONBUTTONID_EleType =
    {
    NOSYNONYM, NOHELP, MHELP, NOHOOK, NOARG,
    "Element:",
    "locElemInfoP->eleType",
    {
    {NOTYPE, NOICON, NOCMD, LCMD, 2, NOMASK, ON, "Cell"},
    {NOTYPE, NOICON, NOCMD, LCMD, 3, NOMASK, ON, "Line"},
    {NOTYPE, NOICON, NOCMD, LCMD, 4, NOMASK, ON, "Line String"},
    {NOTYPE, NOICON, NOCMD, LCMD, 6, NOMASK, ON, "Shape"},
    {NOTYPE, NOICON, NOCMD, LCMD, 7, NOMASK, ON, "Text Node"},
    {NOTYPE, NOICON, NOCMD, LCMD, 11, NOMASK, ON, "Curve"},
    {NOTYPE, NOICON, NOCMD, LCMD, 13, NOMASK, ON, "Conic"},
    {NOTYPE, NOICON, NOCMD, LCMD, 15, NOMASK, ON, "Ellipse"},
    {NOTYPE, NOICON, NOCMD, LCMD, 16, NOMASK, ON, "Arc"},
    {NOTYPE, NOICON, NOCMD, LCMD, 17, NOMASK, ON, "Text"},
    }
    };
```

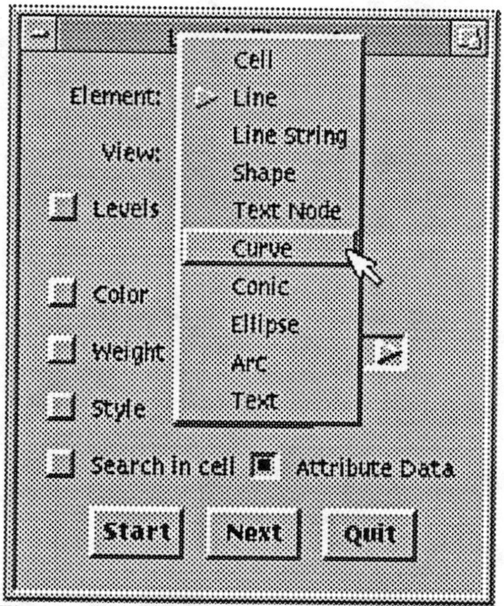

Figure 7.2 Selecting the element type

Also, we will use the Option Button to return the view in which we want to display the located element (see Figure 7.3). The resource is shown below.

```
DItem_OptionButtonRsc  OPTIONBUTTONID_View =
    {
    NOSYNONYM, NOHELP, MHELP, NOHOOK, NOARG,
    "View:",
    "locElemInfoP->View",
    {
        {NOTYPE, NOICON, NOCMD, LCMD, 1, NOMASK, ON, "1"},
        {NOTYPE, NOICON, NOCMD, LCMD, 2, NOMASK, ON, "2"},
        {NOTYPE, NOICON, NOCMD, LCMD, 3, NOMASK, ON, "3"},
        {NOTYPE, NOICON, NOCMD, LCMD, 4, NOMASK, ON, "4"},
        {NOTYPE, NOICON, NOCMD, LCMD, 5, NOMASK, ON, "5"},
        {NOTYPE, NOICON, NOCMD, LCMD, 6, NOMASK, ON, "6"},
        {NOTYPE, NOICON, NOCMD, LCMD, 7, NOMASK, ON, "7"},
        {NOTYPE, NOICON, NOCMD, LCMD, 8, NOMASK, ON, "8"},
    }
    };
```

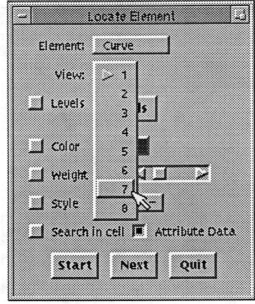

Figure 7.3 Selecting the View

To select the element style we will use icons to display the options (see Figure 7.4). These icons are defined in the include file < dlogids.h >.

```
DItem_OptionButtonRsc OPTIONBUTTONID_LoceleStyle =
    {
    NOSYNONYM, NOHELP, MHELP, NOHOOK, NOARG,
    "",
    "locElemInfoP->style",
    {
    {Icon, ICONID_LineStyle0, NOCMD, LCMD, 0, NOMASK, ON, ""},
    {Icon, ICONID_LineStyle1, NOCMD, LCMD, 1, NOMASK, ON, ""},
    {Icon, ICONID_LineStyle2, NOCMD, LCMD, 2, NOMASK, ON, ""},
    {Icon, ICONID_LineStyle3, NOCMD, LCMD, 3, NOMASK, ON, ""},
    {Icon, ICONID_LineStyle4, NOCMD, LCMD, 4, NOMASK, ON, ""},
    {Icon, ICONID_LineStyle5, NOCMD, LCMD, 5, NOMASK, ON, ""},
    {Icon, ICONID_LineStyle6, NOCMD, LCMD, 6, NOMASK, ON, ""},
    {Icon, ICONID_LineStyle7, NOCMD, LCMD, 7, NOMASK, ON, ""},
    }
    };
```

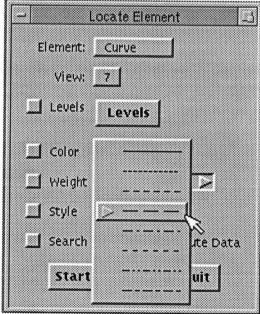

Figure 7.4 Selecting the Element Style

Level Map Item

The Level Map dialog item is used to display an eight by eight matrix of the display state of the design file levels. A black box around a level number indicates that the level is on. A black circle indicates the active level.

In our LOCELE application we use the level map to indicate which level to search. We do not use, or set the active level. Hence, the black circle is not shown. In Figure 7.5 we have specified to search levels 1,35,43,53,54 and 58.

Figure 7.5 The Level Map Dialog Item

The following line is the item list specification for our Level Map item.

```
{{X3, Y1, 0, 0}, LevelMap, LEVELMAPID_Levels,  ON, 0, "",""},
```

The structure of the Level Map resource dialog item is defined by the structure *ditem_levelmaprsc*.

```
typedef struct ditem_levelmaprsc
    {
    ULong   helpInfo;
    ULong   helpSource;
#if defined (resource)
    char    label[];
    char    accessStr[];
    char    activeLevelAccessStr[];
#else
    long    labelLength;
    char    label[1];
#endif
    } DItem_LevelMapRsc;
```

In our dialog resource file, *loceldlg.r* we define the Level Map resource as:

```
DItem_LevelMapRsc LEVELMAPID_Levels =
    {
    NOHELP, MHELP,
    "Levels",
    "locElemInfoP->level",
    ""
    };
```

Since we will not be setting the active level, we will not supply an
activeLevelAccessStr. The *accessStr* for the Level Map is
locElemInfoP->level. It is an array of four short integers, with each bit
designating a level. Figure 7.6 shows how the level mask works.

The variable *locElemInfoP->level* is defined as:

```
typedef struct loceleminfo
    {
    .
    .
    short   level[4];
    }
    LocElemInfo;
```

The other fields are discussed in Chapter 3, under the section Common Item
Resource Fields.

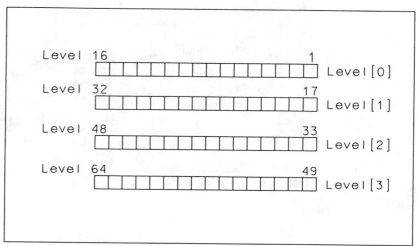

Figure 7.6 Using the level mask

Color Picker Item

The Color Picker dialog item displays the current color in a bevelled box from a palette of 255 colors. We use the Color Picker to select which color to search.

The following line is the item list specification for our Color Picker item.

```
{{X4, Y4, 0, 0}, ColorPicker, COLORPICKERID_Color, ON, 0, "", ""},
```

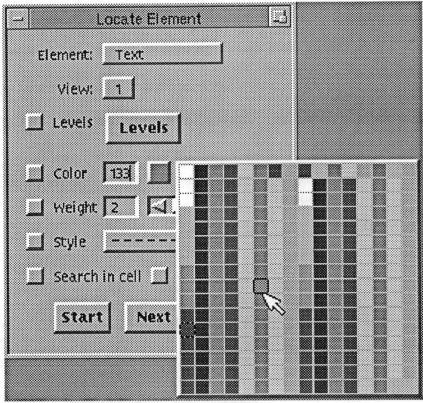

Figure 7.7 The Color Picker Dialog Item

The Color Picker resource dialog item is defined by the structure *ditem_colorpickerrsc*.

```
typedef struct ditem_colorpickerrsc
    {
    ULong   commandNumber;
    ULong   commandSource;
    long    synonymsId;
    ULong   helpInfo;
    ULong   helpSource;
    long    itemHookId;
    long    itemHookArg;
    long associatedTextId;
    ULong   mask;

#if defined (resource)
    char    label[];
    char    accessStr[];
#else
    long    labelLength;
    char    label[1];
#endif
    } DItem_ColorPickerRsc;
```

In our dialog resource file, *loceldlg.r* we define the Color Picker resource as:

```
DItem_ColorPickerRsc COLORPICKERID_Color =
    {
    NOCMD, MCMD, SYNONYMID_ColorLocele, NOHELP, MHELP, NOHOOK, NOARG,
    TEXTID_LoceleColor, NOMASK, "", "locElemInfoP->color"
    };
```

Synonym Resource Item

The *synonymsId*, SYNONYMID_ColorLocele, defines the corresponding dialog
item to change when this dialog item is modified. The definition is shown here:

```
DItem_SynonymsRsc SYNONYMID_ColorLocele =
    {
    {
    {Text,        TEXTID_LoceleColor},
    {ColorPicker, COLORPICKERID_Color},
    }
    };
```

In the Text Item we define its *synonymsId* to point to
SYNONYMID_ColorLocele. Whenever we change the text value, the
corresponding color will display in the bevelled box. Similarly, when we drag
the cursor across the color palette, the corresponding color number displays
in the text field.

```
DItem_TextRsc TEXTID_LoceleColor =
    {
    NOCMD, LCMD, SYNONYMID_ColorLocele, NOHELP, MHELP,
    NOHOOK, NOARG,
    3, "%-ld", "%ld", "0", "253", NOMASK, NOCONCAT,
    "",
    "locElemInfoP->color"
    };
```

Scroll Bar Item

The Scroll Bar displays a slider, which we can move between a range of values. We use the Scroll Bar to set the weight of the element to search. The orientation of the Scroll Bar is horizontal, if the *height* field is zero. If the *width* is zero, then a vertical bar is created. In our example we have set SBW to the *width* and zero to the *height*, thereby creating a horizontal bar.

Figure 7.8 The Scroll Bar and Text Item

The following line is the item list specification for our Scroll Bar item.

```
{{X4, Y5, SBW, 0}, ScrollBar, SCROLLBARID_Weight, ON, 0, "", ""},
```

The structure of the Scroll Bar resource dialog item is defined by the structure *ditem_scrollbarrsc*.

```
typedef struct ditem_scrollbarrsc
    {
    long    itemHookId;
    long    itemHookArg;
    int     minValue;
    int     maxValue;
    int     incAmount;
    int     pageIncAmount;
    double  sliderSize;
#if defined (resource)
    char    accessStr[];
#else
    long    accessStrLength;
    char    accessStr[1];
#endif
    } DItem_ScrollBarRsc;
```

We will design our Dialog Box so that when the slider moves it will display the corresponding weight value. Unfortunately, the structure *ditem_scrollbarrsc* does not provide a *synonymsId* field. Not to worry, we overcome this problem with a dialog item hook, HOOKITEMID_ScrollBar, which we will discuss in the next section.

minValue and *maxValue* set the range for the weight. These have been assigned 0 and 31 respectively, being the minimum and maximum weight an element can have.

incAmount is the amount to change the weight when we click on the arrows. We have set it to increase by 1 when we click the right arrow and decrease by 1 when we click the left arrow. The *pageIncAmount* is the amount to change the weight when we click the page area of the Scroll Bar.

sliderSize is the size of the slider, relative to the entire Scroll Bar. We will make our slider one tenth of the width of the Scroll Bar. The height of the slider will be the height of the Scroll Bar.

In our dialog resource file, *loceldlg.r* we define the Scroll Bar resource as:

```
DItem ScrollBarRsc SCROLLBARID_Weight =
    {
    HOOKITEMID ScrollBar, NOARG, 0, 31, 1, 5, 0.1,
    "locElemInfoP->weight"
    };
```

Advanced Dialog Hook

In Chapter 3 we saw the simple use of a dialog hook to launch a function. In this section we will trap and interpret the dialog item message, and manipulate the dialog item with calls to the *mdlDialog_item* functions.

As discussed earlier, the Scroll Bar does not have a *synonymsId* field and yet the Text Item does. This implies that we can define SYNONYMID_WeightLocele which will move the slider whenever the Text Item changes, but not vice versa.

```
DItem_TextRsc TEXTID_LoceleWeight =
    {
    NOCMD, LCMD, SYNONYMID_WeightLocele, NOHELP, MHELP,
    NOHOOK, NOARG,
    3, "%-ld", "%ld", "0", "31", NOMASK, NOCONCAT,
    "",
    "locElemInfoP->weight"
    };


DItem_SynonymsRsc SYNONYMID_WeightLocele =
    {
    {
    {Text,          TEXTID_LoceleWeight},
    {ScrollBar,     SCROLLBARID_Weight},
    }
    };
```

To overcome this problem we define a dialog item hook, HOOKITEMID_ScrollBar, which activates the function loceleScrollBarHook. In this function we simulate a synonym resource. When we move the slider, the corresponding weight value will be displayed in the Text item.

Dialog Item State

The Dialog Item has an internal value and an external state. The **internal value** is a simple C variable, which is referenced whenever the item is displayed. Therefore the internal value is what is shown on the screen.

The **external state** is the value of the data that we specified with *accessStr*. In our example, this is *locElemInfoP->weight*. When we manipulate the Scroll Bar dialog item, the internal value changes and the external state is updated accordingly.

Our problem is how to set the internal value of the Text Item used to display the weight. Using the debugger, we know that when we move the slider, the message sent is DITEM_MESSAGE_SETVALUE.

We will trap this message and do our own processing. First we need to set the external state of the Scroll Bar. Normally the dialog item handler would have taken care of this, but we have taken over the processing when we set *dmP->msgUnderstood = TRUE*.

There are a series of functions that we can use to manipulate dialog items. The three that we are interested in are:

mdlDialog_itemGetByTypeAndId return the pointer to the dialog item by specifying its resource type and ID.

mdlDialog_itemSetState   set the external state of an item.

mdlDialog_itemSetValue   set the internal value of an item.

We have to make sure that we are manipulating the correct dialog item. The function *mdlDialog_itemGetByTypeAndId* will return a pointer to the position of the Scroll Bar item. Using *mdlDialog_itemSetState* we will set the external state of the Scroll Bar.

We then call *mdlDialog_itemGetByTypeAndId* to return the pointer position of the Text item. Using *mdlDialog_itemSetValue* , we will set the internal value of the weight Text item. The dialog manager then updates the item's appearance on the screen.

The following code shows how we have taken over the processing and simulated a synonym resource.

```
switch (dimP->messageType)
    {
    case DITEM_MESSAGE_SETVALUE:
        {
        outFieldDiP = mdlDialog_itemGetByTypeAndId (dimP->db,
                          RTYPE_ScrollBar, SCROLLBARID_Weight, 0);
        mdlDialog_itemSetState (NULL, dimP->db,
                          outFieldDiP->itemIndex);
        outFieldDiP = mdlDialog_itemGetByTypeAndId (dimP->db,
                          RTYPE_Text, TEXTID_LoceleWeight, 0);
        sprintf(str,"%d\0",locElemInfoP->weight);
        mdlDialog_itemSetValue(NULL, 0, NULL, str,
                          dimP->db, outFieldDiP->itemIndex);
        break;
        }
```

Modal Dialog Box

So far we have used only modeless dialog boxes. These allow the user to interact with more than one dialog box at any given time. An example of this is the LOCELE application. Here, the user can locate an element, go off and do something else, then come back to the LOCELE dialog box to continue from where he left off.

A Modal Dialog Box requires all user interface to be focused on it. They are useful for situations when an application must have information before it can continue. The resource IDs PUSHBUTTONID_OK and PUSHBUTTONID_Cancel are provided to dismiss modal dialog boxes. We will use the modal dialog box to set the search levels.

The Push Button dialog item to launch the modal dialog box is shown below.

```
DItem_PushButtonRsc PUSHBUTTONID_OLevel =
    {
    NOT_DEFAULT_BUTTON, NOHELP, MHELP,
    HOOKITEMID_Dummy, 0, CMD_OPENMODAL, LCMD, "",
    "Levels"
    };
```

The following code segment in *locele.mc* supports the opening of the modal dialog box.

```
Public cmdName void level_openModal
(
char     *unparsedP  /* => unparsed part of command */
)
cmdNumber    CMD_OPENMODAL
    {
    int lastAction;

    /* open child modal dialog box */
    if (mdlDialog_openModal (&lastAction, NULL, DIALOGID_LevelModal))
        {
        mdlDialog_dmsgsPrint("Unable to open modal");
        return;
        }
    }
```

The definition for DIALOGID_LevelModal is shown below. Notice the use of DIALOGATTR_MODAL in the dialog attribute, to define that this is a modal dialog box. The use of the standard resource ID, PUSHBUTTONID_OK, automatically takes care of all the details needed to dismiss the modal dialog box.

```
/*----------------------------------------------------------------+
|    Level Modal Dialog, opened when PUSHBUTTONID_OLevel is activated    |
+----------------------------------------------------------------*/
DialogBoxRsc DIALOGID_LevelModal =
    {
    DIALOGATTR_DEFAULT | DIALOGATTR_MODAL,
    29*XC, 18*YC,
    NOHELP, MHELP, HOOKDIALOGID_Level, NOPARENTID,
    "Search",
{
    {{X3, Y1, 0, 0},    LevelMap, LEVELMAPID_Levels,    ON, 0, "",""},
    {{X8, Y7+YC, BW, 0},    PushButton, PUSHBUTTONID_OK,    ON, 0, "",""},
}
    };
```

Executing the Application

The Push Buttons "Start", "Next" and "Quit" all have dialog hooks that activate the LOCELE application. A "Start" sets the file search from the beginning of the design file. A "Next" continues the search from the last file position. A "Quit" makes a call to *mdlDialog_closeCommandQueue* to close the dialog box.

```
switch (dimP->dialogItemP->rawItemP->itemHookArg)
{
    case 1: /* start button */
            filePos = 0L;
            LocateElemString();
            break;
    case 2: /* next button */
            LocateElemString();
            break;
    case 3: /* quit button */
            mdlDialog_closeCommandQueue (dimP->db);
            break;
}
```

Unloading Dialog Boxes

In LOCELE we will use dialog hooks to trap the dialog message DIALOG_MESSAGE_DESTROY, and queue CMD_MDL_UNLOAD to call the unload function.

```
switch (dmP->messageType)
    {
    case DIALOG_MESSAGE_DESTROY:
        {
        /* unload this MDL task when the Locele Dialog is closed */
        mdlDialog_cmdNumberQueue (FALSE, CMD_MDL_UNLOAD,
                                mdlSystem_getCurrTaskID(), TRUE);
        break;
        };
    default:
        dmP->msgUnderstood = FALSE;
        break;
    }
```

Element Location

We will use the scanner to locate the desired element. Initially we set the *scanList.scantype* to locate all elements.

```
scanList.scantype    = ELEMTYPE | ELEMDATA | ONEELEM;
```

We have design the element type option button to return the actual element type number. Therefore, we need to set the correct bit in the element type search mask.

```
elemMask = 1 << (((locElemInfoP->eleType)-1) % 16);
if ((locElemInfoP->eleType) < 17)
    scanList.typmask[0]    = elemMask;
else
    scanList.typmask[1]    = elemMask;
```

If the Levels toggle button is 'on' then we will tell the scanner to return only those elements that match our level mask.

```
if (locElemInfoP->levels)
    {
    scanList.scantype  |= LEVELS;
    scanList.levmask[0] = locElemInfoP->level[0];
    scanList.levmask[1] = locElemInfoP->level[1];
    scanList.levmask[2] = locElemInfoP->level[2];
    scanList.levmask[3] = locElemInfoP->level[3];
    }
```

If "Search in cell" is toggled 'on' then we will include the cell header in the type mask.

```
if (locElemInfoP->cellElem)
    scanList.typmask[0]  |= CELL_HEADER_ELM;
```

If "Attribute Data" is toggled 'on' then we need the scanner to compare elements on properties and class. Attribute data is a property, therefore we will accept all classes by setting every bit in *scanList.clasmsk* (please refer to <scanner.h>). There are two variables that define the properties to search.

Every bit set in *scanList.pch.propmsk* must have the corresponding bit in *scanList.pcl.propval* set to 1 or 0, to show the desired search criteria. Bit 11 is the attribute data search bit. In the *propmsk* we tell the scanner to search for attribute data. In *propval* we want the scanner to return elements that have attribute data present.

```
if (locElemInfoP->attribData)
{
    scanList.scantype |= PROPCLAS;
    scanList.clasmsk = 0xFFFF;
    scanList.pcl.propval = 0x0800;
    scanList.pch.propmsk = 0x0800;
}
```

Element Symbology

As the scanner does not provide a search based on element symbology, we need to do the test ourselves. The function *mdlElement_getSymbology* returns the element's color, weight and style. Using simple 'if' statements we can eliminate those elements that do not match the search criteria.

```
mdlElement_getSymbology(&color, &weight, &style, &element);

if (locElemInfoP->colors)
    if (locElemInfoP->color != color) continue;

if (locElemInfoP->weights)
    if (locElemInfoP->weight != weight) continue;

if (locElemInfoP->styles)
    if (locElemInfoP->style != style) continue;
```

Once we have the desired element, we will window the element and display it in the specified view. We will use two windowing routines, one for text and one for the other elements. Before we can look at these routines, we must consider the view functions that are available.

```
switch (mdlElement_getType(&element))
    {
    case CELL_HEADER_ELM:
    case LINE_ELM:
    case LINE_STRING_ELM:
    case SHAPE_ELM:
    case CONIC_ELM:
    case CURVE_ELM:
    case ELLIPSE_ELM:
    case ARC_ELM:
        showElement (&element);
        return;
    case TEXT_ELM :
    case TEXT_NODE_ELM :
        showTextElement (&element);
        return;
    default :
        continue;
    }
```

View Functions

MDL provides several functions for manipulating and displaying design files in screen windows, called views. These functions are summarized here:

mdlView_attachNamed	attach and display a saved view.
mdlView_deleteNamed	delete a saved view from file.
mdlView_findNamed	search the file for a saved view.
mdlView_fit	fit master and/or reference files.
mdlView_getCamera	return the camera setting for the view.
mdlView_getDisplayControl	return view display information.
mdlView_getLevels	return the levels that are on for the view.
mdlView_getParameters	return view parameter information.
mdlView_getStandard	set rotation matrix with the standard view (e.g., ISO, TOP etc..)
mdlView_isActive	determine if the view is turned on.
mdlView_isStandard	determine whether a view is currently displaying a standard view.
mdlView_isVisible	determine if we can draw to the view.
mdlView_rotateToRMatrix	rotate the view to a rotation matrix.
mdlView_setArea	define the viewing area.
mdlView_saveNamed	save information about the view.
mdlView_setActiveDepth	set the active depth from the front clipping plane.
mdlView_setActiveDepthPoint	set active depth from a point.
mdlView_setDisplayControl	set view display information.
mdlView_setDisplayDepth	set the display depth from the front and back clipping plane.
mdlView_setDisplayDepthPoints	set display depth from an array of points.
mdlView_setFunction	define a view user function.

mdlView_setLevels	turn levels on/off for the view.
mdlView_turnOff	close a view.
mdlView_turnOn	open a view.
mdlView_updateMulti	update several views.
mdlView_updateSingle	update a single view.
mdlView_zoom	change the view extents.

Viewing Elements

In LOCELE, the function showElement will use the element's range for the
limits of the view window. This method will make the function generic as all
elements have a range.

The first step is to make sure that the user has specified a view that is active. A
simple test, using *mdlView_isVisible*, will confirm this.

```
if (!mdlView_isVisible(locElemInfoP->View-1))
{
    mdlDialog_openAlert ("View is inactive");
    return;
}
```

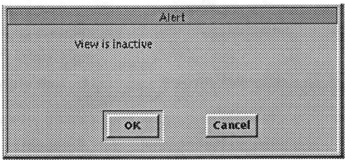

Figure 7.9 Using mdlDialog_openAlert

We will display the element in the ISO view, if we are in a 3D design file. *mdlView_getStandard* will extract the rotation matrix for the view.

```
if (tcb->ndices == 3)
    stdViewNum = STDVIEW_ISO;
else
    stdViewNum = STDVIEW_TOP;
mdlView_getStandard(&rMatrix, stdViewNum);
```

Due to historical reasons, the element range is stored in a different format from that used elsewhere in MicroStation. We will convert this format into *Dpoint3d* with the function *mdlCnv_fromScanFormat*.

```
memcpy(lRange, &element->ehdr.xlow, sizeof(lRange));
for (i=0; i<6; i++)
    lRange[i]=mdlCnv_fromScanFormat(lRange[i]);

viewRange[0].x = (double) (lRange[0]);
viewRange[0].y = (double) (lRange[1]);
viewRange[0].z = (double) (lRange[2]);
viewRange[1].x = (double) (lRange[3]);
viewRange[1].y = (double) (lRange[4]);
viewRange[1].z = (double) (lRange[5]);
```

Calls to *mdlRMatrix_rotateRange* and *mdlRMatrix_unrotatePointArray* will build a view range cube (for 3D file) or a view rectangle (for 2D file) for the element.

```
mdlRMatrix_rotateRange(&viewRange[0], &viewRange[1], &rMatrix);
mdlRMatrix_unrotatePointArray(viewRange, &rMatrix, 2);
```

Finally, we are ready to display the element. In a 3D file we need to supply *mdlView_setArea* with the display depth *range*. The call to *mdlView_updateSingle* will refresh the view that has our element. *mdlElement_display* will highlight the element in all views. Please note that *mdlElement_display* will only highlight simple elements. To highlight complex elements this program must be upgraded, using element descriptors.

```
range = fabs(viewRange[0].z - viewRange[1].z);

mdlView_setArea (locElemInfoP->View-1, viewRange, &viewRange[0],
                          range, range/2.0, &rMatrix);
mdlView_updateSingle (locElemInfoP->View-1);

mdlElement_display(element, HILITE);
```

This works for all elements. However, in the case of text and text nodes, it is better if we rotate the view so that the text always displays horizontally. The function showTextElement does this. The text's rotation matrix is extracted by using *mdlText_extract*. Using the matrix manipulation we discussed in Chapter 6, the text is unrotated (by *mdlRMatrix_invert*) to align with the view horizontal. The remaining windowing commands are the same as for showElement.

```
/* Find element's position and orientation */
mdlText_extract (&elemOrigin, NULL, NULL, NULL, NULL, &elemRMatrix,
        NULL, NULL, NULL, &elemSize, element);

/* Set up view to show elem element */
viewRange[0].x = viewRange[0].y = -2.0 * elemSize.height;
viewRange[1].x = elemSize.width + 2.0 * elemSize.height;
viewRange[1].y = elemSize.height * 3.0;
viewRange[0].z = viewRange[1].z = 0.0;
mdlRMatrix_rotatePointArray (viewRange, &elemRMatrix, 2);

mdlVec_addPointArray (viewRange, &elemOrigin, 2);

/* Display Text element */
mdlRMatrix_invert (&invElemMatrix, &elemRMatrix);

mdlView_setArea (locElemInfoP->View-1, viewRange, &viewRange[0],
        elemSize.width, elemSize.width/2.0, &invElemMatrix);
```

The complete source for our LOCELE application is given below. Don't forget that the optional companion disk will save you a lot of typing and reduce development time.

locele.mc

```
/*------------------------------------------------------------------+
|        Copyright (c) 1991 Mach Dinh-Vu, All Rights Reserved       |
|                                                                   |
|        locele.mc  - Display an element in a view, according to    |
|                     the search criteria.                          |
|                                                                   |
|                     LOCATE   ELEMENT                              |
+-------------------------------------------------------------------*/
#include     <mselems.h>
#include     <msdefs.h>
#include     <global.h>
#include     <scanner.h>
#include     <msinputq.h>
#include     <userfnc.h>
#include     <mdl.h>
#include     <cexpr.h>
#include     <rscdefs.h>
#include     <dlogitem.h>
#include     <cmdlist.h>
#include     <tcb.h>

#include     <dlogman.fdf>

#include     "locelcmd.h"  /* Generated by resource compiler (rcomp) */
#include     "loceldlg.h"  /* Need to know dialog id to open */

/*------------------------------------------------------------------+
|   Local function declarations                                     |
+-------------------------------------------------------------------*/
void    locele_dummyItemHook(), locele_dialogHook();

int     loceleButtonHook(), loceleScrollBarHook();

/*------------------------------------------------------------------+
|   Private Global variables                                        |
+-------------------------------------------------------------------*/
static LocElemInfo    *locElemInfoP;
static int            commandName;
static ULong          filePos;
static DialogMessage *dbP;
ExtScanlist           scanList;

static DialogHookInfo uHooks[] =
```

```
    {
    {HOOKITEMID_Button_Locele,   loceleButtonHook},
    {HOOKITEMID_ScrollBar,       loceleScrollBarHook},
    {HOOKITEMID_Dummy,           locele_dummyItemHook},
    {HOOKDIALOGID_Level,         locele_dialogHook},
    };
```

```
/*------------------------------------------------------------------------+
| name        unloadFunction                                              |
+------------------------------------------------------------------------*/
Private int unloadFunction ()
    {
    RscFileHandle    userPrefsH;
    LocElemInfo      *boxRscP;

    /* Open userpref.rsc to hold our small pref resource */
    mdlDialog_userPrefFileOpen (&userPrefsH);
    boxRscP = (LocElemInfo *)mdlResource_load (NULL, RTYPE_locElem,
                        RSCID_locElemPrefs);

    if (!boxRscP)
    {
        /* Our pref resource does not exist, so add it */
        mdlResource_add (userPrefsH, RTYPE_locElem, RSCID_locElemPrefs,
                locElemInfoP, sizeof(LocElemInfo), NULL);
    }
    else
    {
        *boxRscP = *locElemInfoP;

        /* Write out and free the updated resource */
        mdlResource_write (boxRscP);
        mdlResource_free (boxRscP);

    }
    /* Clean up */
    mdlResource_closeFile (userPrefsH);
    free(locElemInfoP);

    return (FALSE);
    }
/*------------------------------------------------------------------------+
|   name   main                                                           |
+------------------------------------------------------------------------*/
int      main
(
char          *pArgument
)
    {
    RscFileHandle   rfHandle, userPrefsH;
    LocElemInfo     *elemRscP;
```

```
    char            *setP;

    /* Open our file for access to command table and dialog */
    mdlResource_openFile (&rfHandle, NULL, FALSE);

    /* Load the command table */
    if (mdlParse_loadCommandTable (NULL) == NULL)
       mdlOutput_error ("Unable to load command table.");

    /* Publish the dialog item hooks */
    mdlDialog_hookPublish (sizeof(uHooks)/sizeof(DialogHookInfo), uHooks);

    /* Commands start in string list 0, prompts start in string 1 */
    mdlState_registerStringIds (0, 0);
    locElemInfoP = malloc(sizeof(LocElemInfo));

    /* Prepare to read resource */
    elemRscP = NULL;
    userPrefsH = NULL;
    mdlDialog_userPrefFileOpen(&userPrefsH);
    if (userPrefsH)
        elemRscP = (LocElemInfo *)mdlResource_load (NULL, RTYPE_locElem,
                                            RSCID_locElemPrefs);

    if (!elemRscP)
    {
    /* No resource was found */
        locElemInfoP->eleType = 3;
        locElemInfoP->color = 0;
        locElemInfoP->weight = 0;
        locElemInfoP->style = 0;
        locElemInfoP->level[0] = 0x0000;
        locElemInfoP->level[1] = 0x0000;
        locElemInfoP->level[2] = 0x0000;
        locElemInfoP->level[3] = 0x0000;
    }
    else
    {
    /* Copy resource into internal structure */
        *locElemInfoP = *elemRscP;

    /* This is unnecessary because the closeFile will free all resources,
     * but it is recommended practice */
    mdlResource_free (elemRscP);
    }

    if (userPrefsH)
       mdlResource_closeFile (userPrefsH);

    /* Set up and Publish locElemInfoP for access by the dialog manager */
```

```
    setP = mdlCExpression_initializeSet (VISIBILITY_DIALOG_BOX |
                    VISIBILITY_DEBUGGER, 0, FALSE);
    mdlDialog_publishComplexPtr (setP, "loceleminfo", "locElemInfoP",
                    &locElemInfoP);

    /* Make sure our function gets called at unload time */
    mdlSystem_setFunction (SYSTEM_UNLOAD_PROGRAM, unloadFunction);

    locateElem();
    return SUCCESS;
    }
/*------------------------------------------------------------------+
| name        showElement                                           |
+------------------------------------------------------------------*/
Private int showElement
(
MSElement *element
)
    {
    Dpoint3d    viewRange[2];
    RotMatrix   rMatrix;
    double      depth, range;
    long        lRange[6];
    int         stdViewNum, i;

    if (!mdlView_isVisible(locElemInfoP->View-1))
    {
        mdlDialog_openAlert ("View is inactive");
        return;
    }

    if (tcb->ndices == 3)
        stdViewNum = STDVIEW_ISO;
    else
        stdViewNum = STDVIEW_TOP;
    mdlView_getStandard(&rMatrix, stdViewNum);

    memcpy(lRange, &element->ehdr.xlow, sizeof(lRange));
    for (i=0; i<6; i++)
        lRange[i]=mdlCnv_fromScanFormat(lRange[i]);

    viewRange[0].x = (double) (lRange[0]);
    viewRange[0].y = (double) (lRange[1]);
    viewRange[0].z = (double) (lRange[2]);
    viewRange[1].x = (double) (lRange[3]);
    viewRange[1].y = (double) (lRange[4]);
    viewRange[1].z = (double) (lRange[5]);
    mdlRMatrix_rotateRange(&viewRange[0], &viewRange[1], &rMatrix);
    mdlRMatrix_unrotatePointArray(viewRange, &rMatrix, 2);
```

```
        range = fabs(viewRange[0].z - viewRange[1].z);

        mdlView_setArea (locElemInfoP->View-1, viewRange, &viewRange[0],
                              range, range/2.0, &rMatrix);
        mdlView_updateSingle (locElemInfoP->View-1);

        mdlElement_display(element, HILITE);
        return SUCCESS;
        }
/*--------------------------------------------------------------------+
| name          showTextElement                                       |
+---------------------------------------------------------------------*/
Private int showTextElement
(
MSElement *element
)
    {
    Dpoint3d    elemOrigin, viewRange[2];
    TextSize    elemSize;
    RotMatrix   elemRMatrix, invElemMatrix;

    /* Find elem element's position and orientation */
    mdlText_extract (&elemOrigin, NULL, NULL, NULL, NULL, &elemRMatrix,
            NULL, NULL, NULL, &elemSize, element);

    /* Set up view to show elem element */
    viewRange[0].x = viewRange[0].y = -2.0 * elemSize.height;
    viewRange[1].x = elemSize.width + 2.0 * elemSize.height;
    viewRange[1].y = elemSize.height * 3.0;
    viewRange[0].z = viewRange[1].z = 0.0;
    mdlRMatrix_rotatePointArray (viewRange, &elemRMatrix, 2);

    mdlVec_addPointArray (viewRange, &elemOrigin, 2);

    /* Display Text element */
    mdlRMatrix_invert (&invElemMatrix, &elemRMatrix);

    mdlView_setArea (locElemInfoP->View-1, viewRange, &viewRange[0],
        elemSize.width, elemSize.width/2.0, &invElemMatrix);

    mdlView_updateSingle (locElemInfoP->View-1);

    mdlElement_display(element, HILITE);
    return SUCCESS;
    }
/*--------------------------------------------------------------------+
| name          LocateElemString                                      |
+---------------------------------------------------------------------*/
Private void    LocateElemString ()
    {
```

```
int             scanWords, status;
int             elemMask, color, weight, style;
MSElement       element;

mdlScan_initScanlist (&scanList);
mdlScan_noRangeCheck (&scanList);

scanList.scantype   = ELEMTYPE | ELEMDATA | ONEELEM;

/* if user wants to restrict search to levels then set the scanner */
if (locElemInfoP->levels)
   {
   scanList.scantype  |= LEVELS;
   scanList.levmask[0] = locElemInfoP->level[0];
   scanList.levmask[1] = locElemInfoP->level[1];
   scanList.levmask[2] = locElemInfoP->level[2];
   scanList.levmask[3] = locElemInfoP->level[3];
   }

elemMask = 1 << (((locElemInfoP->eleType)-1) % 16);
if ((locElemInfoP->eleType) < 17)
   scanList.typmask[0]    = elemMask;
else
   scanList.typmask[1]    = elemMask;

if (locElemInfoP->cellElem)
   scanList.typmask[0] |= CELL_HEADER_ELM;

if (locElemInfoP->attribData)
{
   scanList.scantype  |= PROPCLAS;
   scanList.clasmsk = 0xFFFF;
   scanList.pcl.propval = 0x0800;
   scanList.pch.propmsk = 0x0800;
}

scanList.extendedType  = FILEPOS;
scanList.sector        = DGN_BLOCK(filePos);
scanList.offset        = DGN_OFFSET(filePos);

mdlScan_initialize (0, &scanList);

/* loop through the file until one matching the criteria is found */
while ((status = mdlScan_file (&element, &scanWords, sizeof(element),
        &filePos)), (scanWords != 0))
   {
   mdlElement_getSymbology(&color, &weight, &style, &element);

   if (locElemInfoP->colors)
      if (locElemInfoP->color != color) continue;
```

```
            if (locElemInfoP->weights)
                if (locElemInfoP->weight != weight) continue;

            if (locElemInfoP->styles)
                if (locElemInfoP->style != style) continue;

            switch (mdlElement_getType(&element))
                {
                case CELL_HEADER_ELM:
                case LINE_ELM:
                case LINE_STRING_ELM:
                case SHAPE_ELM:
                case CONIC_ELM:
                case CURVE_ELM:
                case ELLIPSE_ELM:
                case ARC_ELM:
                    showElement (&element);
                    return;
                case TEXT_ELM :
                case TEXT_NODE_ELM :
                    showTextElement (&element);
                    return;
                default :
                    continue;
                }
            }

    /* Display an alert and return result to caller */
    mdlDialog_openAlert ("End of File!");
    return;
    }
/*-----------------------------------------------------------------+
| name            locele_dialogHook                                |
+-----------------------------------------------------------------*/
Private void     locele_dialogHook
(
DialogMessage    *dmP            /* => a ptr to a dialog message */
)
    {
    /* ignore any messages being sent to modal dialog hook */
    if (dmP->dialogId != DIALOGID_LocateElem)
        return;

    dmP->msgUnderstood = TRUE;
    switch (dmP->messageType)
        {
        case DIALOG_MESSAGE_DESTROY:
            {
            /* unload this MDL task when the Locele Dialog is closed */
```

```
            mdlDialog_cmdNumberQueue (FALSE, CMD_MDL_UNLOAD,
                                       mdlSystem_getCurrTaskID(), TRUE);
            break;
            };

        default:
            dimP->msgUnderstood = FALSE;
            break;
        }
    }
/*-------------------------------------------------------------------+
| name             loceleButtonHook                                  |
+-------------------------------------------------------------------*/
Private int       loceleButtonHook (dimP)
DialogItemMessage    *dimP;
    {
    char *pResult;
    if ((dimP->messageType != DITEM_MESSAGE_BUTTON) ||
    (dimP->u.button.buttonTrans != BUTTONTRANS_UP))
        {
        /* Tell the dialog manager that we didn't handle this message */
        dimP->msgUnderstood = FALSE;
        return;
        }

    /* Tell the dialog manager that we are handling this message */
    dimP->msgUnderstood = TRUE;

    /*-----------------------------------------------------------+
    Call mdlState_startPrimitive to terminate current command and
    identify the current command.
    +-----------------------------------------------------------*/
    mdlState_startPrimitive (NULL, NULL, 1, 0);

    switch (dimP->dialogItemP->rawItemP->itemHookArg)
        {
        case 1: /* start button */
                filePos = 0L;
                LocateElemString();
                break;
        case 2: /* next button */
                LocateElemString();
                break;
        case 3: /* quit button */
                mdlDialog_closeCommandQueue(dimP->db);
                break;

        }
    }
/*-------------------------------------------------------------------+
| name             loceleScrollBarHook                               |
```

```
+--------------------------------------------------------------------*/
Private int        loceleScrollBarHook (dimP)
DialogItemMessage    *dimP;
    {
    DialogItem  *outFieldDiP;
    char        str[3];

    /* Tell the dialog manager that we are handling this message */
    dimP->msgUnderstood = TRUE;
    switch (dimP->messageType)
        {
        case DITEM_MESSAGE_SETVALUE:
            {
            outFieldDiP = mdlDialog_itemGetByTypeAndId (dimP->db,
                            RTYPE_ScrollBar,
                            SCROLLBARID_Weight, 0);
            mdlDialog_itemSetState (NULL, dimP->db,
                            outFieldDiP->itemIndex);

            outFieldDiP = mdlDialog_itemGetByTypeAndId (dimP->db,
                            RTYPE_Text,
                            TEXTID_LoceleWeight, 0);
            sprintf(str,"%d\0",locElemInfoP->weight);
            mdlDialog_itemSetValue(NULL, 0, NULL, str,
                            dimP->db, outFieldDiP->itemIndex);
            break;
            }

        default:
            {
            /* Tell the dialog manager to handle this message */
            dimP->msgUnderstood = FALSE;
            break;
            }
        }
    }
/*--------------------------------------------------------------------+
| name        locele_dummyItemHook                                    |
+--------------------------------------------------------------------*/
Private void locele_dummyItemHook
(
DialogItemMessage    *dimP    /* => a ptr to a dialog item message */
)
    {
    dimP->msgUnderstood = TRUE;

    switch (dimP->messageType)
        {
        default:
            dimP->msgUnderstood = FALSE;
```

```
                  break;
              }
      }
}
/*---------------------------------------------------------------+
| name              level_openModal                              |
+---------------------------------------------------------------*/
Public cmdName void level_openModal
(
char    *unparsedP  /* => unparsed part of command */
)
cmdNumber   CMD_OPENMODAL
    {
    int lastAction;

    /* open child modal dialog box */
    if (mdlDialog_openModal (&lastAction, NULL, DIALOGID_LevelModal))
        {
        mdlDialog_dmsgsPrint("Unable to open modal");
        return;
        }
    }
/*---------------------------------------------------------------+
| name              locateElem                                   |
+---------------------------------------------------------------*/
cmdName        locateElem()
cmdNumber      CMD_LOCATE_ELEMENT
    {
    /* Initialize view */
    locElemInfoP->View = (tcb->lstvw)+1;
    filePos = 0L;    /* start search from begining of file */

    dbP = (DialogBox *) mdlDialog_open (NULL, DIALOGID_LocateElem);
    }
```

localdlg.h is the application header file, defining constants and data structures used by the application LOCELE.

localdlg.h

```
/*----------------------------------------------------------------+
|    Dialog Box IDs                                               |
+----------------------------------------------------------------*/
#define DIALOGID_LocateElem         1
#define DIALOGID_LevelModal         2
/*----------------------------------------------------------------+
|    Option Button Item IDs                                       |
+----------------------------------------------------------------*/
#define OPTIONBUTTONID_EleType               1
#define OPTIONBUTTONID_View                  2
#define OPTIONBUTTONID_LoceleStyle           3
/*----------------------------------------------------------------+
|    Resource Type and ID for Prefs                               |
+----------------------------------------------------------------*/
#define RTYPE_locElem               'loEt'
#define RSCID_locElemPrefs          1
/*----------------------------------------------------------------+
|    Elem Item IDs                                                |
+----------------------------------------------------------------*/
#define TEXTID_LoceleColor          1
#define TEXTID_LoceleWeight         2
/*----------------------------------------------------------------+
|    Color Picker  IDs                                            |
+----------------------------------------------------------------*/
#define COLORPICKERID_Color         1
/*----------------------------------------------------------------+
|    Scroll Bar IDs                                               |
+----------------------------------------------------------------*/
#define SCROLLBARID_Weight          1
/*----------------------------------------------------------------+
|    LevelMap      IDs                                            |
+----------------------------------------------------------------*/
#define LEVELMAPID_Levels           1
/*----------------------------------------------------------------+
|    Toggle Button IDs                                            |
+----------------------------------------------------------------*/
#define TOGGLEID_Colors             1
#define TOGGLEID_Weights            2
#define TOGGLEID_Styles             3
#define TOGGLEID_Levels             4
#define TOGGLEID_CellElem           5
#define TOGGLEID_AttribData         6
```

```
/*-------------------------------------------------------------------+
|    PushButton Item IDs                                             |
+-------------------------------------------------------------------*/
#define PUSHBUTTONID_OLevel          1
#define PUSHBUTTONID_Start           2
#define PUSHBUTTONID_Next            3
#define PUSHBUTTONID_Quit            4
/*-------------------------------------------------------------------+
|    Synonym Id's                                                    |
+-------------------------------------------------------------------*/
#define SYNONYMID_WeightLocele               1
#define SYNONYMID_ColorLocele                2
/*-------------------------------------------------------------------+
|    Message Id's                                                    |
+-------------------------------------------------------------------*/
#define STRINGID_Messages            1
#define STRINGID_Errors              2
/*-------------------------------------------------------------------+
|    Hook Id's                                                       |
+-------------------------------------------------------------------*/
#define HOOKITEMID_Button_Locele             1
#define HOOKITEMID_Dummy                     2
#define HOOKITEMID_ScrollBar                 3
#define HOOKDIALOGID_Level                   4
/*-------------------------------------------------------------------+
|    Local Structure Definitions                                    |
+-------------------------------------------------------------------*/
typedef struct loceleminfo
    {
    int     eleType;                /* element to search */
    int     View;                   /* view to display element */
    int     colors;                 /* boolean for toggle */
    int     weights;                /* boolean for toggle */
    int     styles;                 /* boolean for toggle */
    int     levels;                 /* boolean for toggle */
    int     cellElem;               /* boolean for toggle */
    int     attribData;             /* boolean for toggle */
    int     color;                  /* search color */
    int     weight;                 /* search weight */
    int     style;                  /* search style */
    short   level[4];               /* search levels */
    }
    LocElemInfo;
```

loceldlg.r

The file *loceldlg.r* contains the definition of the LOCELE application's resources.

```
/*-----------------------------------------------------------------+
|    loceldlg.r  - Dialog Resources for MDL program  locele.mc     |
+-----------------------------------------------------------------*/
#include <rscdefs.h>
#include <dlogbox.h>
#include <dlogids.h>
#include "loceldlg.h"
#include "locelcmd.h"


/*-----------------------------------------------------------------+
|    Locate Elem Dialog Box                                        |
+-----------------------------------------------------------------*/
#define   OVERALLWIDTH     32 * XC
#define   OVERALLHEIGHT    19 * YC
#define   NEWLINE           2 * YC
#define   BW       6.5 * XC          /* button width - 6 chars    */
#define   SBW       11 * XC          /* scroll bar width */

#define   X1       11 * XC          /* String elem */
#define   X2       13 * XC          /* Option menus */
#define   X3        2 * XC          /* View */
#define   X4       16 * XC          /* Cell Elem */
#define   X5        5 * XC          /* left button */
#define   X6       21 * XC          /* right button */
#define   X7       28 * XC          /* modal width */
#define   X8      X7/2-(3*XC)       /* position of OK button */

#define   Y1       YC                        /* String elem item */
#define   Y2       Y1 + NEWLINE               /* EleType Option menu */
#define   Y3       Y2 + NEWLINE               /* Interactive toggle */
#define   Y4       Y3 + 3 * YC             /* Execute Buttons */
#define   Y5       Y4 + NEWLINE            /* Execute Buttons */
#define   Y6       Y5 + NEWLINE            /* Execute Buttons */
#define   Y7       Y6 + NEWLINE            /* Execute Buttons */
#define   Y8       Y7 + NEWLINE            /* Execute Buttons */


/*-----------------------------------------------------------------+
|    Main Dialog                                                   |
+-----------------------------------------------------------------*/
DialogBoxRsc DIALOGID_LocateElem =
    {
    DIALOGATTR_DEFAULT | DIALOGATTR_SINKABLE,
    OVERALLWIDTH, OVERALLHEIGHT,
```

```
        NOHELP, MHELP, HOOKDIALOGID_Level, NOPARENTID,
        "Locate Element",
{
        {{X1, Y1, 0, 0},    OptionButton, OPTIONBUTTONID_EleType,   ON, 0, "",""},
        {{X1, Y2, 0, 0},    OptionButton, OPTIONBUTTONID_View,      ON, 0, "",""},
        {{X1, Y3, 0, 0},      PushButton, PUSHBUTTONID_OLevel,      ON, 0, "",""},
        {{X3, Y3, 0, 0},    ToggleButton, TOGGLEID_Levels,          ON, 0, "",""},

        {{X3, Y4, 0, 0},    ToggleButton, TOGGLEID_Colors,          ON, 0, "",""},
        {{X1, Y4, 4*XC, 0},         Text, TEXTID_LoceleColor,       ON, 0, "", ""},
        {{X4, Y4, 0, 0},     ColorPicker, COLORPICKERID_Color,      ON, 0, "", ""},

        {{X3, Y5, 0, 0},    ToggleButton, TOGGLEID_Weights,         ON, 0, "",""},
        {{X1, Y5, 4*XC, 0},         Text, TEXTID_LoceleWeight,      ON, 0, "", ""},
        {{X4, Y5, SBW, 0},     ScrollBar, SCROLLBARID_Weight,       ON, 0, "", ""},

        {{X3, Y6, 0, 0},    ToggleButton, TOGGLEID_Styles,          ON, 0, "",""},
        {{X1, Y6, 0, 0},    OptionButton, OPTIONBUTTONID_LoceleStyle,
                                                                    ON, 0, "",""},
        {{X3, Y7, 0, 0},    ToggleButton, TOGGLEID_CellElem,        ON, 0, "",""},
        {{X4, Y7, 0, 0},    ToggleButton, TOGGLEID_AttribData,      ON, 0, "",""},
        {{X5, Y8, BW, 0},     PushButton, PUSHBUTTONID_Start,       ON, 0, "",""},
        {{X2, Y8, BW, 0},     PushButton, PUSHBUTTONID_Next,        ON, 0, "",""},
        {{X6, Y8, BW, 0},     PushButton, PUSHBUTTONID_Quit,        ON, 0, "",""},
}
    };
/*-------------------------------------------------------------------------------+
|    Level Modal Dialog, opened when PUSHBUTTONID_OLevel is activated            |
+-------------------------------------------------------------------------------*/
DialogBoxRsc DIALOGID_LevelModal =
    {
    DIALOGATTR_DEFAULT | DIALOGATTR_MODAL,
    29*XC, 18*YC,
    NOHELP, MHELP, HOOKDIALOGID_Level, NOPARENTID,
    "Search",
{
        {{X3, Y1, 0, 0},        LevelMap, LEVELMAPID_Levels,      ON, 0, "",""},
        {{X8, Y7+YC, BW, 0},   PushButton, PUSHBUTTONID_OK,       ON, 0, "",""},
}
    };
/*-------------------------------------------------------------------------------+
|      Dialog items                                                              |
+-------------------------------------------------------------------------------*/
/*-------------------------------------------------------------------------------+
|      Option Items                                                              |
+-------------------------------------------------------------------------------*/
DItem_OptionButtonRsc  OPTIONBUTTONID_EleType =
    {
    NOSYNONYM, NOHELP, MHELP, NOHOOK, NOARG,
    "Element:",
```

```
            "locElemInfoP->eleType",
            {
            {NOTYPE, NOICON, NOCMD, LCMD, 2, NOMASK, ON, "Cell"},
            {NOTYPE, NOICON, NOCMD, LCMD, 3, NOMASK, ON, "Line"},
            {NOTYPE, NOICON, NOCMD, LCMD, 4, NOMASK, ON, "Line String"},
            {NOTYPE, NOICON, NOCMD, LCMD, 6, NOMASK, ON, "Shape"},
            {NOTYPE, NOICON, NOCMD, LCMD, 7, NOMASK, ON, "Text Node"},
            {NOTYPE, NOICON, NOCMD, LCMD, 11, NOMASK, ON, "Curve"},
            {NOTYPE, NOICON, NOCMD, LCMD, 13, NOMASK, ON, "Conic"},
            {NOTYPE, NOICON, NOCMD, LCMD, 15, NOMASK, ON, "Ellipse"},
            {NOTYPE, NOICON, NOCMD, LCMD, 16, NOMASK, ON, "Arc"},
            {NOTYPE, NOICON, NOCMD, LCMD, 17, NOMASK, ON, "Text"},
            }
            };
  DItem_OptionButtonRsc  OPTIONBUTTONID_View =
            {
            NOSYNONYM, NOHELP, MHELP, NOHOOK, NOARG,
            "View:",
            "locElemInfoP->View",
            {
                {NOTYPE, NOICON, NOCMD, LCMD, 1, NOMASK, ON, "1"},
                {NOTYPE, NOICON, NOCMD, LCMD, 2, NOMASK, ON, "2"},
                {NOTYPE, NOICON, NOCMD, LCMD, 3, NOMASK, ON, "3"},
                {NOTYPE, NOICON, NOCMD, LCMD, 4, NOMASK, ON, "4"},
                {NOTYPE, NOICON, NOCMD, LCMD, 5, NOMASK, ON, "5"},
                {NOTYPE, NOICON, NOCMD, LCMD, 6, NOMASK, ON, "6"},
                {NOTYPE, NOICON, NOCMD, LCMD, 7, NOMASK, ON, "7"},
                {NOTYPE, NOICON, NOCMD, LCMD, 8, NOMASK, ON, "8"},
            }
            };
  DItem_OptionButtonRsc OPTIONBUTTONID_LoceleStyle =
            {
            NOSYNONYM, NOHELP, MHELP, NOHOOK, NOARG,
            "",
            "locElemInfoP->style",
            {
            {Icon, ICONID_LineStyle0, NOCMD, LCMD, 0, NOMASK, ON, ""},
            {Icon, ICONID_LineStyle1, NOCMD, LCMD, 1, NOMASK, ON, ""},
            {Icon, ICONID_LineStyle2, NOCMD, LCMD, 2, NOMASK, ON, ""},
            {Icon, ICONID_LineStyle3, NOCMD, LCMD, 3, NOMASK, ON, ""},
            {Icon, ICONID_LineStyle4, NOCMD, LCMD, 4, NOMASK, ON, ""},
            {Icon, ICONID_LineStyle5, NOCMD, LCMD, 5, NOMASK, ON, ""},
            {Icon, ICONID_LineStyle6, NOCMD, LCMD, 6, NOMASK, ON, ""},
            {Icon, ICONID_LineStyle7, NOCMD, LCMD, 7, NOMASK, ON, ""},
            }
            };
/*-------------------------------------------------------------------+
|    Toggle Buttons                                                  |
+-------------------------------------------------------------------*/
DItem_ToggleButtonRsc TOGGLEID_Colors =
```

```
    {
    NOCMD, MCMD, NOSYNONYM, NOHELP, MCMD, NOHOOK, NOARG,
    NOMASK, NOINVERT,
    "Color",
    "locElemInfoP->colors"
    };
DItem_ToggleButtonRsc TOGGLEID_Weights =
    {
    NOCMD, MCMD, NOSYNONYM, NOHELP, MCMD, NOHOOK, NOARG,
    NOMASK, NOINVERT,
    "Weight",
    "locElemInfoP->weights"
    };
DItem_ToggleButtonRsc TOGGLEID_Styles =
    {
    NOCMD, MCMD, NOSYNONYM, NOHELP, MCMD, NOHOOK, NOARG,
    NOMASK, NOINVERT,
    "Style",
    "locElemInfoP->styles"
    };
DItem_ToggleButtonRsc TOGGLEID_Levels =
    {
    NOCMD, MCMD, NOSYNONYM, NOHELP, MCMD, NOHOOK, NOARG,
    NOMASK, NOINVERT,
    "Levels",
    "locElemInfoP->levels"
    };
DItem_ToggleButtonRsc TOGGLEID_CellElem =
    {
    NOCMD, MCMD, NOSYNONYM, NOHELP, MCMD, NOHOOK, NOARG,
    NOMASK, NOINVERT,
    "Search in cell",
    "locElemInfoP->cellElem"
    };
DItem_ToggleButtonRsc TOGGLEID_AttribData =
    {
    NOCMD, MCMD, NOSYNONYM, NOHELP, MCMD, NOHOOK, NOARG,
    NOMASK, NOINVERT,
    "Attribute Data",
    "locElemInfoP->attribData"
    };
/*-------------------------------------------------------------+
|       Push Button Items                                      |
+-------------------------------------------------------------*/
DItem_PushButtonRsc PUSHBUTTONID_Start =
    {
    NOT_DEFAULT_BUTTON, NOHELP, MHELP,
    HOOKITEMID_Button_Locele, 1, NOCMD, MCMD, "",
    "Start"
    };
```

```
DItem_PushButtonRsc PUSHBUTTONID_Next =
    {
    NOT_DEFAULT_BUTTON, NOHELP, MHELP,
    HOOKITEMID_Button_Locele, 2, NOCMD, MCMD, "",
    "Next"
    };
DItem_PushButtonRsc PUSHBUTTONID_Quit =
    {
    NOT_DEFAULT_BUTTON, NOHELP, MHELP,
    HOOKITEMID_Button_Locele, 3, NOCMD, MCMD, "",
    "Quit"
    };
DItem_PushButtonRsc PUSHBUTTONID_OLevel =
    {
    NOT_DEFAULT_BUTTON, NOHELP, MHELP,
    HOOKITEMID_Dummy, 0, CMD_OPENMODAL, LCMD, "",
    "Levels"
    };
/*-------------------------------------------------------------------+
|    Level Resources                                                 |
+-------------------------------------------------------------------*/
DItem_LevelMapRsc LEVELMAPID_Levels =
    {
    NOHELP, MHELP,
    "Levels",
    "locElemInfoP->level",
    ""
    };
/*-------------------------------------------------------------------+
|    Color Picker Item Resources                                     |
+-------------------------------------------------------------------*/
DItem_ColorPickerRsc COLORPICKERID_Color =
    {
    NOCMD, MCMD, SYNONYMID_ColorLocele, NOHELP, MHELP, NOHOOK, NOARG,
    TEXTID_LoceleColor, NOMASK, "", "locElemInfoP->color"
    };
/*-------------------------------------------------------------------+
|    Scroll Bar Resources                                            |
+-------------------------------------------------------------------*/
DItem_ScrollBarRsc SCROLLBARID_Weight =
    {
    HOOKITEMID_ScrollBar, NOARG, 0, 31, 1, 5, 0.1,
    "locElemInfoP->weight"
    };
/*-------------------------------------------------------------------+
|    Text Item Resources                                             |
+-------------------------------------------------------------------*/
DItem_TextRsc TEXTID_LoceleColor =
    {
    NOCMD, LCMD, SYNONYMID_ColorLocele, NOHELP, MHELP,
```

```
    NOHOOK, NOARG,
    3, "%-ld", "%ld", "0", "253", NOMASK, NOCONCAT,
    "",
    "locElemInfoP->color"
    };
DItem_TextRsc TEXTID_LoceleWeight =
    {
    NOCMD, LCMD, SYNONYMID_WeightLocele, NOHELP, MHELP,
    NOHOOK, NOARG,
    3, "%-ld", "%ld", "0", "31", NOMASK, NOCONCAT,
    "",
    "locElemInfoP->weight"
    };
/*--------------------------------------------------------------------+
|    Item Synonyms                                                    |
+--------------------------------------------------------------------*/
DItem_SynonymsRsc SYNONYMID_ColorLocele =
    {
    {
    {Text,        TEXTID_LoceleColor},
    {ColorPicker, COLORPICKERID_Color},
    }
    };
DItem_SynonymsRsc SYNONYMID_WeightLocele =
    {
    {
    {Text,        TEXTID_LoceleWeight},
    {ScrollBar,   SCROLLBARID_Weight},
    }
    };
```

localmsg.r contains the messages for the LOCELE application.

localmsg.r

```
/*------------------------------------------------------------------+
|   locelmsg.r                                                      |
+------------------------------------------------------------------*/
#include <rscdefs.h>
#include <cmdclass.h>

MessageList 0 =
{
  {
    { 0, "Locate Element" },
  }
};
```

locelcmd.r contains the command table for the LOCELE application.

locelcmd.r

```
/*------------------------------------------------------------------+
|   locelcmd.r   - command table for locele application            |
+------------------------------------------------------------------*/
#include <rscdefs.h>
#include <cmdclass.h>

#define    CT_NONE                    0
#define    CT_LOCATE                  1
#define    CT_ELEMENT                 2

Table   CT_LOCATE =
    {
        { 1, CT_ELEMENT, SHOW,      REQ,        "LOCATE" },
        { 2, CT_NONE,    INPUT,     NONE,    "OPENMODAL" }
    };

Table   CT_ELEMENT =
    {
        { 1, CT_NONE,    INHERIT,   NONE,       "ELEMENT" }
    };
```

Publish structure for Dialog Manager.

loceltyp.mt

```
/*————————————————————————————————————————————————————————+
|    loceltyp.mt — Locate Element Dialog Types             |
+—————————————————————————————————————————————————————————*/
#include     "loceldlg.h"

publishStructures (loceleminfo);
```

To build the LOCELE application, enter *bmake -a locele*.

locele.mke

```
#————————————————————————————————————————————————————————————
#       LOCELE MDL Makefile
#————————————————————————————————————————————————————————————
%include $(MS)/mdl/include/mdl.mki

#————————————————————————————————————————————————————————————
#       Define constants specific to this example
#————————————————————————————————————————————————————————————
progmdl      = d:/progmdl/disk/
baseDir      = $(progmdl)locele/
objectDir    = $(mdlexample)objects/
privateInc   = $(baseDir)

loceleObjs   = $(objectDir)locele.mo \
               $(mdlLibs)ditemlib.ml

loceleRscs   = $(objectDir)locelcmd.rsc \
               $(objectDir)loceldlg.rsc \
               $(objectDir)loceltyp.rsc \
               $(objectDir)locelmsg.rsc \
               $(objectDir)locele.mp

#————————————————————————————————————————————————————————————
#       Generate Command Tables
#————————————————————————————————————————————————————————————
$(PrivateInc)locelcmd.h          : $(baseDir)locelcmd.r

$(objectDir)locelcmd.rsc         : $(baseDir)locelcmd.r

#————————————————————————————————————————————————————————————
```

```
#       Compile Dialog Resources
#----------------------------------------------------------------
$(objectDir)loceldlg.rsc : $(baseDir)loceldlg.r $(PrivateInc)locelcmd.h

#----------------------------------------------------------------
#       Prompts and command numbers
#----------------------------------------------------------------
#   Don't generate an include file for the prompts and command numbers
$(objectDir)locelmsg.rsc : $(baseDir)locelmsg.r

#----------------------------------------------------------------
#       Make resource to publish structure(s)
#----------------------------------------------------------------
$(objectDir)loceltyp.r : $(baseDir)loceltyp.mt $(privateInc)loceldlg.h

$(objectDir)loceltyp.rsc : $(objectDir)loceltyp.r

#----------------------------------------------------------------
#       Compile and link MDL Application
#----------------------------------------------------------------
$(objectDir)locele.mo : $(baseDir)locele.mc $(PrivateInc)locelcmd.h

$(objectDir)locele.mp          : $(objectDir)locele.mo
        $(msg)
        >$(objectDir)temp.cmd
        -a$@
        -s6000
        -g
        $(loceleObjs)
        $(mdlLibs)ditemlib.ml
        <
        $(linkCmd) @$(objectDir)temp.cmd
        ~time

#----------------------------------------------------------------
#       Merge Objects into one file
#----------------------------------------------------------------
$(mdlapps)locele.ma            : $(loceleRscs)
        $(msg)
        >$(objectDir)temp.cmd
        -o$@
        $(loceleRscs)
        <
        $(rscLibCmd) @$(objectDir)temp.cmd
        ~time
```

View Hooks

MDL allows us to define a function that will execute when the view updates, or when the cursor moves in a view. This powerful feature opens up many possibilities.

View User Function

MDL provides the facility to call User functions when certain view events occur. Please note that the function name in italics is not the actual name of the function. Replace it with the function name that you use in your program.

userView_update	function to call when views are updated.
userView_motion	function to call when the cursor moves in a view.
userView_noMotion	function to call when the cursor stops moving in a view.

We will write a simple application to highlight all active points in the design file. This program will execute after the view updates and it will draw a circle to the screen using *mdlElement_display*.

The HIGHAP application will call *mdlView_setFunction* to define the function to call, when the view updates. We can have our function called before the screen updates, with UPDATE_PRE, or after the screen updates, with UPDATE_POST. The available options are:

UPDATE_PRE	call user function before screen updates.
UPDATE_POST	call user function after screen updates.
VIEW_NOMOTION	call user function when cursor moves.
VIEW_MOTION	call user function when cursor stops moving.
UPDATE_EACH_ELEMENT	calls user function as each element is updated. This could be useful for hiding elements or changing their symbology.
PLOTUPDATE_PRE	call before each plotting update (i.e., before generating a plotfile).
PLOTUPDATE_POST	call after each plotting update (i.e., after generating a plotfile).

Since we will draw a circle onto the screen after it updates, we will use UPDATE_POST. If we are going to use UPDATE_PRE, then we must return a zero value from our function, to tell MicroStation to continue updating. Otherwise, it will stop.

The main function calls *mdlView_setFunction* to establish a user function `handleUpdate`.

```
main ()
    {
    mdlView_setFunction (UPDATE_POST, handleUpdate);
    }
```

When we update the screen with any of the view commands, like ZOOM, WINDOW, UPDATE or FIT, the function `handleUpdate` is activated. It scans for active points that are in view 1 and places a highlighted circle around each.

To restrict the search area, we pass to the scanner, the scan range. In this example it is the extents of view 1. Using *mdlView_getParameters* we can retrieve the origin and the size of the view.

```
mdlView_getParameters(&origin, NULL, &delta, NULL, NULL, SCANVIEW);
```

For to historical reasons, the MicroStation scanner uses a coordinate format that differs from all other formats used within MicroStation. We need to convert the *origin* and *delta*, which is *Dpoint3d* to a *Point3d*.

```
mdlCnv_DPointToIPoint(&lorigin, &origin);
mdlCnv_DPointToIPoint(&ldelta, &delta);
```

We then convert the *long*, from *Point3d* to an unsigned long, using *mdlCnv_toScanFormat*.

```
scanList.xlowlim = mdlCnv_toScanFormat(lorigin.x);
scanList.ylowlim = mdlCnv_toScanFormat(lorigin.y);
scanList.zlowlim = mdlCnv_toScanFormat(lorigin.z);
scanList.xhighlim = mdlCnv_toScanFormat(lorigin.x) +
                         mdlCnv_toScanFormat(ldelta.x);
scanList.yhighlim = mdlCnv_toScanFormat(lorigin.y) +
```

```
                              mdlCnv_toScanFormat(ldelta.y);
        scanList.zhighlim = mdlCnv_toScanFormat(lorigin.z) +
                              mdlCnv_toScanFormat(ldelta.z);
```

Finally, we call *mdlScan_viewRange*. This sets the range members of the *scanList* to find only elements in the SCANVIEW, and from the MASTERFILE.

```
mdlScan_viewRange(&scanList, SCANVIEW, MASTERFILE);
```

When handleUpdate finds a line that matches the search criteria, it calls the function highlight.

The first thing we do, inside highlight, is to check if we have a line element.

```
if (el->ehdr.type != LINE_ELM)
    return (MODIFY_STATUS_NOCHANGE);
```

We then extract the points and test if they are the same, with *mdlVec_pointEqual*. The definition of an active point is a zero length line, with identical begin and end points.

```
mdlLinear_extract(pnts, &numVerts, el, MASTERFILE);
if (!mdlVec_pointEqual(&pnts[0], &pnts[1]))
    return (MODIFY_STATUS_NOCHANGE);
```

In the last step, we create a circle with *mdlEllipse_create* and write it to the screen. We use the current text height as the radius of the circle.

```
mdlEllipse_create(&circle, NULL, &pnts[0], RADIUS, RADIUS,
                  NULL, NULL);
mdlElement_display(&circle, HILITE);
return (MODIFY_STATUS_NOCHANGE);
```

Notice that we always exit with MODIFY_STATUS_NOCHANGE. In this way we do not alter the element, even though we used *mdlModify_elementSingle* to manipulate the element.

highap.mc

The complete listing for the program HIGHAP is shown below. When you load the application, the program immediately establishes the view state function. Therefore, we do not be use a command table or resource file. To load the application, enter *mdl l highap*.

```
/*-------------------------------------------------------------------+
|        Copyright (c) 1991 Mach Dinh-Vu, All Rights Reserved        |
|                                                                    |
|        highap.mc -       Highlight the active points in the file.  |
|                                                                    |
+-------------------------------------------------------------------*/
#include        <mdl.h>
#include        <mselems.h>
#include        <tcb.h>
#include        <global.h>
#include        <scanner.h>
#include        <userfnc.h>
#include        <mstypes.h>

#define     RADIUS          tcb->chheight
#define     SCANVIEW        0       /* view 1 */
/*-------------------------------------------------------------------+
| name            highlight                                          |
+-------------------------------------------------------------------*/
Private int highlight
(
MSElementUnion  *el
)
        {
        Dpoint3d            pnts[2];
        int                 numVerts, viewMask;
        MSElementUnion      circle;

        if (el->ehdr.type != LINE_ELM)
           return (MODIFY_STATUS_NOCHANGE);

        mdlLinear_extract(pnts, &numVerts, el, MASTERFILE);

        if (!mdlVec_pointEqual(&pnts[0], &pnts[1]))
           return (MODIFY_STATUS_NOCHANGE);

        mdlEllipse_create(&circle, NULL, &pnts[0], RADIUS, RADIUS,
                          NULL, NULL);

        mdlElement_display(&circle, HILITE);
        return (MODIFY_STATUS_NOCHANGE);
        }
```

```
/*─────────────────────────────────────────────────────────────────+
| name          handleUpdate                                        |
+──────────────────────────────────────────────────────────────────*/
Private int handleUpdate
(
int                 preUpdate,
int                 eraseMode,
long                *fileMask,
int                 numberRegions,
Asynch_update_view  regions[],
Rectangle           *coverLists [],
int                 numCovers[],
MSDisplayDescr      *displayDescr []
)
{
        ULong           elemAddr[50], eofPos, filePos;
        int             scanWords, status, i, numAddr;
        ExtScanlist     scanList;
        char            buffer[50];
        Dpoint3d        origin, delta;
        Point3d         lorigin, ldelta;

        mdlScan_initScanlist (&scanList);
        mdlOutput_message("Scanning file ....");

        scanList.scantype       = ELEMTYPE | ONEELEM;
        scanList.extendedType   = FILEPOS;
        scanList.typmask[0]     = TMSK0_LINE;

        mdlView_getParameters(&origin, NULL, &delta, NULL, NULL, SCANVIEW);

        mdlCnv_DPointToIPoint(&lorigin, &origin);
        mdlCnv_DPointToIPoint(&ldelta, &delta);

        scanList.xlowlim = mdlCnv_toScanFormat(lorigin.x);
        scanList.ylowlim = mdlCnv_toScanFormat(lorigin.y);
        scanList.zlowlim = mdlCnv_toScanFormat(lorigin.z);
        scanList.xhighlim = mdlCnv_toScanFormat(lorigin.x) +
                        mdlCnv_toScanFormat(ldelta.x);
        scanList.yhighlim = mdlCnv_toScanFormat(lorigin.y) +
                        mdlCnv_toScanFormat(ldelta.y);
        scanList.zhighlim = mdlCnv_toScanFormat(lorigin.z) +
                        mdlCnv_toScanFormat(ldelta.z);

        mdlScan_viewRange(&scanList, SCANVIEW, MASTERFILE);
        eofPos  = mdlElement_getFilePos (FILEPOS_EOF, NULL);
        filePos = 0L;            /* start seacrh from top of file */

        mdlScan_initialize (MASTERFILE, &scanList);
        /* loop through all line elements in file */
```

```
      do {
         scanWords = sizeof(elemAddr)/sizeof(short);
         status    = mdlScan_file (elemAddr, &scanWords,
                          sizeof(elemAddr),&filePos);
         numAddr   = scanWords / sizeof(short);

         for (i=0; i < numAddr; i++)
         {
             if (elemAddr[i] >= eofPos)  break;
             mdlModify_elementSingle (0, elemAddr[i],
                         MODIFY_REQUEST_NOHEADERS, MODIFY_ORIG,
                         highlight, NULL, 0L);
         }
      } while (status == BUFF_FULL);
      mdlOutput_message(" ");
}

/*----------------------------------------------------------------------------+
| name          main                                                          |
+----------------------------------------------------------------------------*/
main ()
   {
   mdlView_setFunction (UPDATE_POST, handleUpdate);
   }
```

To build the HIGHAP application, enter *bmake -a highap*.

highap.mke

```
#------------------------------------------------------------
#        highap MDL Make File
#------------------------------------------------------------
%include $(MS)/mdl/include/mdl.mki


#------------------------------------------------------------
#        Define constants specific to this highap application
#------------------------------------------------------------
progmdl      = d:/progmdl/disk/
baseDir      = $(progmdl)highap/
objectDir    = $(mdlexample)objects/
privateInc   = $(baseDir)

highapObjs   = $(objectDir)highap.mo

highapRscs   = $(objectDir)highap.mp

$(objectDir)highap.mo            : $(baseDir)highap.mc

$(objectDir)highap.mp            : $(highapObjs)
        $(msg)
        > $(objectDir)temp.cmd
        -a$@
        -s6000
        $(linkOpts)
        $(highapObjs)
        <
        $(linkCmd) @$(objectDir)temp.cmd
        ~time

$(mdlapps)highap.ma              : $(highapRscs)
        $(msg)
        > $(objectDir)temp.cmd
        -o$@
        $(highapRscs)
        <
        $(rscLibCmd) @$(objectDir)temp.cmd
        ~time
```

Chapter 7 - Summary

The Dialog Box is a very powerful user interface which needs to be exploited. In chapter 3 and in this chapter we looked at the many different approaches to using the dialog box. There are features which we did not cover, which you may wish to follow up. These are:

- Building Menu Bars.
- Icon Palettes.
- creating icons using *rasticon.ma*.

The DLOGDEMO program (supplied as a MicroStation MDL demo) is an excellent example of Dialog Box usage. This program is a good source where dialog item definitions can be "cut" from to be "pasted" into other applications. Also, the DLOGDEMO application shows the use of DMSG, which we discussed in chapter 3.

8 : Input Queue

All input to MicroStation must first go through the **input queue**. This allows us to pre-process the input, before it gets to the state dispatcher. One of the most common requests from the MicroStation User group is a 'view only' copy of MicroStation. The intention here is to restrict the operator to view commands like WINDOW AREA or ZOOM. As a drawing reaches a stable state, it is advantageous to have the drawing available for review and plotting, thereby stopping any further changes.

How it works

Figure 8.1 shows the general operation of the dispatching loop that controls the input queue. We can see from the diagram that user supplied functions will be called when certain events occur in MicroStation. We will supply our own user function for *userInput_commandFilter*.

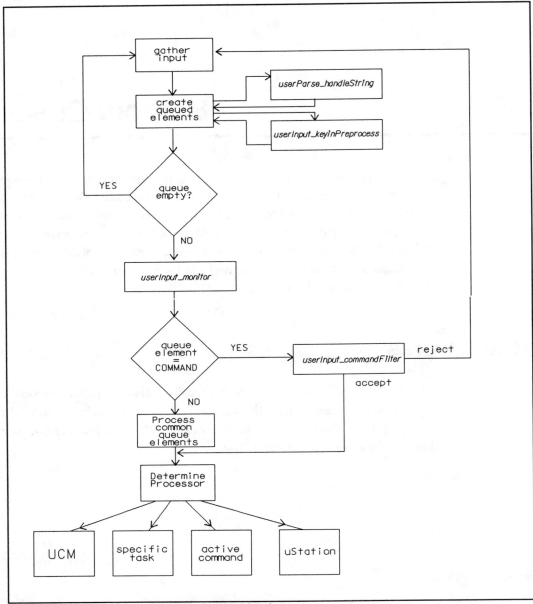

Figure 8.1 MicroStation's main dispatching loop

Input Queue Functions

MDL provides several functions that allow the trapping and manipulation of queued elements. These functions are summarized here:

mdlInput_commandState   return whether the command is a view or primitive command.

mdlInput_disableCommandClass disable command classes.

mdlInput_enableCommandClass enable command classes.

mdlInput_endCommand   stop the "active command" status.

mdlInput_getMessage   copy most recent queued element into a specified area.

mdlInput_getTabletType   determine if we are using a tablet or mouse.

mdlInput_pause   stop MicroStation, and wait for a keystroke.

mdlInput_requeueLastInput   requeue last queued element for MicroStation to process.

mdlInput_sendCommand   create and queue a CMDNUM queue element.

mdlInput_sendKeyin   create and queue a KEYIN queue element.

mdlInput_sendMessage   create and queue a queue element.

mdlInput_sendReset   create and queue a RESET queue element.

mdlInput_sendResume   place a resume message at the start of the queue.

mdlInput_sendUORPoint   create and queue a data point element.

mdlInput_sendCommand   create and queue a CMDNUM element.

mdlInput_setMonitorFunction specify a user function to process queue elements before they enter the queue.

mdlInput_startCommand   request active command status for
                                   current task.

mdlInput_waitForMessage   suspends the MDL task, until it receives
                                   another message.

User Functions

We can specify functions that are called when certain events occur in the
MicroStation queue processing. Function names, shown here in italics, are not
the actual names of the functions. Replace them with the function names you
use in your program.

userInput_commandFilter function to call when INPUT_COMMAND_FILTER
                                   is specified as a parameter in mdlInput_setFunction.

userInput_monitor   function to call when the user function name is
                                   specified in a call to mdlInput_setMonitorFunction.

userInput_preprocessKeyin function to call when INPUT_KEYIN_PREPROCESS
                                   is specified as a parameter in mdlInput_setFunction.

userInput_receive   function to call when INPUT_MESSAGE_RECEIVED is
                                   specified as a parameter in mdlInput_setFunction.

Queued Elements

The structure of the queued element *Inputq_element* is defined in
< msinputq.h >. Each queued element has a header *Inputq_header* followed
by a union of input queue types.

```
typedef struct inputq_element
    {
    Inputq_header hdr;
    union
    {
    Inputq_keyin        keyin;      /* keyed in (not command) */
    Inputq_datapnt      data;       /* data point */
    Inputq_command      cmd;        /* parsed command */
    Inputq_tentpnt      tent;       /* tentative point */
```

```
    Inputq_reset        reset;           /* reset */
    Inputq_partial      partial;         /* incomplete keyin */
    Inputq_unassignedcb cursbutn;        /* unassigned cursor button */
    Inputq_menumsg      menumsg;         /* menu message to be posted */
    Inputq_submenu      submenu;         /* submenu to be displayed */
    Inputq_menuwait     menuwait;        /* go back, get another input */
    Inputq_contents     contents;        /* menu entry contents */
    Inputq_null         nullqelem;       /* NULL event */
    Inputq_tutkeyin     tutkeyin;        /* Tutorial keyin */
    Inputq_nullcmd      nullcmd;         /* NULL command elem */
    Inputq_rawButton    rawButton;       /* raw button information */
    Inputq_rawKeyStroke rawKeyStroke;    /* raw keystroke information */
    Inputq_rawIconEvent rawIconEvent;    /* raw Icon event information */
    Inputq_timerEvent   timerEvent;      /* timer event information */
    char fill[480];                      /* make sure it's big enough */
    } u;
      } Inputq_element;

typedef struct inputq_header
    {
    short   cmdtype;                     /* type of input following */
    short   bytes;                       /* bytes in queue element */
    short   source;                      /* source of input (user, app, etc) */
    short   uc_fno_value;                /* value to put in tcb-uc fno */
    int     sourcepid;                   /* source pid for queue element */
    char    taskId[16];                  /* destination child task */
    } Inputq_header;
```

In our application, we are interested only in the command class and, therefore, the structure *Inputq_command*.

```
typedef struct inputq_command
    {
    int     class;                       /* command class */
    int     immediate;                   /* has immediate mode */
    long command;                        /* unique command id */
    char taskId[16];                     /* destination child task */
    char unparsed[1];                    /* Unparsed portion (if any) */
    } Inputq_command;
```

Command Filter

To make the design file 'view only' we will filter the commands before they get into the input queue. We will pass INPUT_COMMAND_FILTER to the function *mdlInput_setFuntion*. This will establish our user function `commandFilter`.

```
mdlInput_setFunction (INPUT_COMMAND_FILTER, commandFilter);
```

In the user function `commandFilter` we will test the class of the queue elements. If it belongs to any of the following classes then it is passed onto MicroStation. Otherwise it is rejected, and a warning message is displayed. The viewing classes are VIEWING, VIEWPARAM and VIEWIMMED. We will allow the user to make measurements with MEASURE. The dialog manager classes, WINDOWMAN and DIALOGMAN are important, as they support the PLOT dialog box. The last requirement is the ability to exit the design file with EXIT (INPUT class).

The break-down of which command belongs to which class is found in the include file < cmdclass.h >.

```
switch (queueElementP->u.cmd.class)
    {
    case VIEWING:
    case MEASURE:
    case VIEWPARAM:
    case VIEWIMMED:
    case WINDOWMAN:
    case DIALOGMAN:
    case INPUT:
    case PLOT:
        return INPUT_COMMAND_ACCEPT;
        break;
    default:
        mdlUtil_beep(1);
        mdlOutput_error ("WARNING: This is a VIEW only file.");
        return INPUT_COMMAND_REJECT;
```

Autoexecution of MDL applications

MicroStation provides two environment variables, MS_DGNAPPS and MS_INITAPPS, which specify programs to load when MicroStation starts up. MS_INITAPPS defines the MDL application to execute before MicroStation enters graphics. The MicroStation Manager (mm.ma) is a good example of this front-end facility.

MS_DGNAPPS specifies the MDL application to load when a design file is opened. We will assign our *viewonly* application to this environment variable.

To make the assignment, we place the following line in our *uconfig.dat* file:

```
MS_DGNAPPS=viewonly
```

Note that we can have multiple startup applications. They must be delimeted by a semi-colon in the MS_DGNAPPS assignment. If no directory is supplied then the startup application will be searched in the directory defined by MS_MDL.

viewonly.mc

This program is different to the others we have seen. There is no command table and hence no command resource file. When the application is loaded, it starts executing from **main** and then it terminates. To load the program, enter *mdl l viewonly* or use the startup environment variable discussed on the previous page.

```
/*------------------------------------------------------------------+
| Copyright (C) 1991, Mach N. Dinh-Vu, All Rights Reserved          |
| Program   : viewonly.mc                                           |
| Revision  : 1.0.a                                                 |
+-------------------------------------------------------------------+
|           Set the file into VIEW ONLY mode                        |
+-----------------------------------------------------------------*/
/*------------------------------------------------------------------+
|   Include Files                                                   |
+-----------------------------------------------------------------*/
#include     <mdl.h>          /* system include files */
#include     <global.h>
#include     <userfnc.h>
#include     <msinputq.h>
#include     <cmdlist.h>
#include     <cmdclass.h>

/*------------------------------------------------------------------+
| name       commandFilter                                          |
+-----------------------------------------------------------------*/
Private int commandFilter
(
Inputq_element   *queueElementP
)
    {
    /* If this is not a MicroStation command, just return. */
    if ((queueElementP->u.cmd.taskId != '\0') &&
        (strcmp (queueElementP->u.cmd.taskId, ustnTaskId) != 0))
        return INPUT_COMMAND_ACCEPT;

    switch (queueElementP->u.cmd.class)
        {
        case VIEWING:
        case MEASURE:
        case VIEWPARAM:
        case VIEWIMMED:
        case WINDOWMAN:
        case DIALOGMAN:
        case INPUT:
        case PLOT:
            return INPUT_COMMAND_ACCEPT;
            break;
```

```
        default:
            mdlUtil_beep(1);
            mdlOutput_error ("WARNING: This is a VIEW only file.");
            return INPUT_COMMAND_REJECT;
        }
    }
/*———————————————————————————————————————————————————————————+
| name          main                                         |
+———————————————————————————————————————————————————————————*/
main()
{
 mdlInput_setFunction (INPUT_COMMAND_FILTER, commandFilter);
 mdlOutput_prompt("file set to VIEW ONLY");
}
```

The VIEWONLY makefile is a scaled down version as there is no command resource table to compile.

viewonly.mke

```
#——————————————————————————————————————————————————————————————
#     Makefile for VIEWONLY
#——————————————————————————————————————————————————————————————

%include $(MS)/mdl/include/mdl.mki

#——————————————————————————————————————————————————————————————
#       Define constants specific to this example
#——————————————————————————————————————————————————————————————
baseDir     = $(mdlexample)viewonly/
objectDir   = $(mdlexample)objects/
privateInc  = $(baseDir)

viewonlyObjs  = $(objectDir)viewonly.mo

viewonlyRscs  = $(objectDir)viewonly.mp

$(objectDir)viewonly.mo        : $(baseDir)viewonly.mc

$(objectDir)viewonly.mp        : $(viewonlyObjs)
        $(msg)
        > $(objectDir)temp.cmd
        -a$@
        -s6000
        $(linkOpts)
        $(viewonlyObjs)
        <
        $(linkCmd) @$(objectDir)temp.cmd
```

```
        ~time

$(mdlapps)viewonly.ma            : $(viewonlyRscs)
        $(msg)
        > $(objectDir)temp.cmd
        -o$@
        $(viewonlyRscs)
        <
        $(rscLibCmd) @$(objectDir)temp.cmd
        ~time
```

Disabling the Command Class

In the VIEWONLY example we are checking every command on the input
queue. MDL provides an alternative method to do this with two functions -
mdlInput_disableCommandClass and *mdlInput_enableCommandClass*. In
the next example, VWCLASS we will use these two functions. First, we will
disable all command classes and then re-enable the ones that we need to use.
This method is not as elegant as VIEWONLY as it is not dynamic. It allows the
user to select a command, only to find that it will not do anything. VWCLASS
is shown here as an example of the functions *mdlInput_disableCommandClass*
and *mdlInput_enableCommandClass*.

Input to *mdlInput_disableCommandClass* is two 32 bit masks. The first mask is
from class 1 to class 32 and the second mask from class 33 to class 64. Since
there are only 29 classes, we need to concern ourselves only with the first
mask.

First, we disable all classes. We do this by setting every bit in the variable *mask*, assigning it the Hex value 0xffffffff. Then we enable the specific class, as in the example VIEWONLY, by clearing those bits corresponding to the allowed command classes.

```
/* disable all class */
mask = 0xffffffff;
mdlInput_disableCommandClass( mask, 0L);

/* enable specific classes */
mask = 1 < (VIEWING - 1);
mask |= 1 < (PLOT - 1);
mask |= 1 < (MEASURE - 1);
mask |= 1 < (INPUT - 1);
mask |= 1 < (VIEWPARAM - 1);
mask |= 1 < (VIEWIMMED - 1);
mask |= 1 < (WINDOWMAN - 1);
mask |= 1 < (DIALOGMAN - 1);
mdlInput_enableCommandClass( mask, 0L );
```

 To load the application enter *mdl l vwclass*. It will start executing from `main` and then terminate.

vwclass.mc

```
/*-----------------------------------------------------------------------------+
|  Copyright (C) 1991, Mach N. Dinh-Vu, All Rights Reserved                     |
|  Program   : vwclass.mc                                                       |
|  Revision  : 1.0.a                                                            |
+-------------------------------------------------------------------------------+
|     Set the file into VIEW ONLY mode by disabling command class               |
+-----------------------------------------------------------------------------*/
/*-----------------------------------------------------------------------------+
|    Include Files                                                              |
+-----------------------------------------------------------------------------*/
#include     <mdl.h>          /* system include files */
#include     <global.h>
#include     <userfnc.h>
#include     <msinputq.h>
#include     <cmdlist.h>
#include     <cmdclass.h>

/*-----------------------------------------------------------------------------+
|  name         main                                                            |
+-----------------------------------------------------------------------------*/
main()
```

```
{
 long mask;

 /* disable all class */
 mask = 0xffffffff;
 mdlInput_disableCommandClass( mask, 0L);

 /* enable specific classes */
 mask = 1 < (VIEWING - 1);
 mask |= 1 < (PLOT - 1);
 mask |= 1 < (MEASURE - 1);
 mask |= 1 < (INPUT - 1);
 mask |= 1 < (VIEWPARAM - 1);
 mask |= 1 < (VIEWIMMED - 1);
 mask |= 1 < (WINDOWMAN - 1);
 mask |= 1 < (DIALOGMAN - 1);
 mdlInput_enableCommandClass( mask, 0L );
 mdlOutput_prompt("file set to VIEW ONLY");
}
```

 The makefile for VWCLASS is similiar to VIEWONLY. There is no
resource file to compile.

vwclass.mke

```
#------------------------------------------------------------------------
#      Makefile for VWCLASS
#------------------------------------------------------------------------

%include $(MS)/mdl/include/mdl.mki

#------------------------------------------------------------------------
#          Define constants specific to this example
#------------------------------------------------------------------------
baseDir     = $(mdlexample)viewonly/
objectDir   = $(mdlexample)objects/
privateInc  = $(baseDir)

vwclassObjs = $(objectDir)vwclass.mo

vwclassRscs = $(objectDir)vwclass.mp

$(objectDir)vwclass.mo          : $(baseDir)vwclass.mc

$(objectDir)vwclass.mp          : $(vwclassObjs)
        $(msg)
        > $(objectDir)temp.cmd
        -a$@
        -s6000
```

```
        $(linkOpts)
        $(vwclassObjs)
        <
        $(linkCmd) @$(objectDir)temp.cmd
        ~time

$(mdlapps)vwclass.ma                : $(vwclassRscs)
        $(msg)
     > $(objectDir)temp.cmd
       -o$@
        $(vwclassRscs)
        <
        $(rscLibCmd) @$(objectDir)temp.cmd
        ~time
```

System Functions

MDL provides several System Functions that we can use with the VIEWONLY application. The function of interest is *mdlSystem_createStartupElement*, which installs a startup element into the design file. When MicroStation enters a design file, it will scan for a type 66, level 10, startup element. If it finds the startup element, it will queue the command to start the MDL program. When MicroStation finishes loading the design file, it begins processing all queued commands, including those from the startup elements.

mdlSystem_abortRequested	determine if user tries to abort an MDL task.
mdlSystem_cancelTimer	cancel the timer request.
mdlSystem_closeDesignFile	if MS_INITAPPS is defined then execute it, otherwise terminate MicroStation and close the design file.
mdlSystem_createStartupElement	create a startup element, which can start an MDL application.
mdlSystem_deleteStartupElement	delete the startup element.
mdlSystem_enterGraphics	startup MicroStation graphic.
mdlSystem_exit	abort and exit MDL task.
mdlSystem_fileDesign	save current settings.
mdlSystem_getChar	get a character from the keyboard.
mdlSystem_getenv	return the value of the environment variable.
mdlSystem_getMdlTaskList	return the names of installed Tasks.
mdlSystem_getTaskStatistics	return the statistics of the specified task.
mdlSystem_getTicks	return the elapsed time.
mdlSystem_loadMdlProgram	load a specified MDL program.

mdlSystem_newDesignFile   close the current file and open a new one.

mdlSystem_pauseTicks   pause MicroStation for a period of time.

mdlSystem_putenv   set the value of an environment variable.

mdlSystem_setFunction   designate a *userSystem* user function
                                    (see below).

mdlSystem_setTimerFunction   set user function to call when timer expires.

mdlSystem_unloadMdlProgram   unload specified MDL program.

mdlSystem_userAbortEnable   control whether a user can abort the
                                    MDL task.

User Functions

We can specify functions to call when certain system events occur. The function names, shown here in italics, are not the actual names of the functions. Replace them with the function names you use in your program.

userSystem_mdlChildTerminated   function to call when a child task termi-
                                   nates.

userSystem_newDesignFile   function to call when MicroStation loads
                                   a new design file.

userSystem_reloadProgram   function to call when a load request is from
                                   a program that is already loaded.

userSystem_timerExpired   function to call when a timer expires.

userSystem_unloadProgram   function to call when a program unloads.

userSystem_writeToFile   function to call whenever MicroStation
                                   writes to the design file.

Automatic Startup

The *instvo.mc* program will create a startup element in the current file. The program is straightforward. It first calls *mdlSystem_createStartupElement* with the application name. We then add the startup element with *mdlElement_add*.

instvo.mc

```
/*------------------------------------------------------------------+
| Copyright (C) 1991, Mach N. Dinh-Vu, All Rights Reserved          |
| Program   : instvo.mc                                             |
| Revision  : 1.0.a                                                 |
+-------------------------------------------------------------------+
|    install VIEWONLY startup command line                          |
|                                                                 --*/
/*------------------------------------------------------------------+
|    Include Files                                                  |
|                                                                 --*/
#include     <mdl.h>          /* system include files */
#include     <global.h>
#include     <mselems.h>

/*------------------------------------------------------------------+
| name            main                                              |
+----------------------------------------------------------------- --*/
main()
{
 MSElementUnion  startel;

 if (!mdlSystem_createStartupElement(&startel, "VIEWONLY"))
 {
    mdlElement_add(&startel);
    mdlOutput_prompt("file set to VIEW ONLY");
  } else {
    mdlOutput_prompt("unable to install start up element");
  }
}
```

The INSTVO application does not require a command table resource as it
executes direct from `main` when it is loaded. To compile the application, enter
bmake -a instvo.

instvo.mke

```
#-------------------------------------------------------------------
#          INSTVO MDL Make File
#-------------------------------------------------------------------
%include $(MS)/mdl/include/mdl.mki


#-------------------------------------------------------------------
#          Define constants specific to this INSTVO application
#-------------------------------------------------------------------
progmdl     = d:/progmdl/disk/
baseDir     = $(progmdl)viewonly/
objectDir   = $(mdlexample)objects/
privateInc  = $(baseDir)

instvoObjs  = $(objectDir)instvo.mo

instvoRscs  = $(objectDir)instvo.mp

$(objectDir)instvo.mo            : $(baseDir)instvo.mc

$(objectDir)instvo.mp            : $(instvoObjs)
        $(msg)
        >$(objectDir)temp.cmd
        -a$@
        -s6000
        $(linkOpts)
        $(instvoObjs)
        <
        $(linkCmd) @$(objectDir)temp.cmd
        ~time

$(mdlapps)instvo.ma              : $(instvoRscs)
        $(msg)
        >$(objectDir)temp.cmd
        -o$@
        $(instvoRscs)
        <
        $(rscLibCmd) @$(objectDir)temp.cmd
        ~time
```

Demo Program

The System Functions provide the ability to write a demo program. Such a program would provide the full capabilities of the application but only for a restricted period. This is the same as running MicroStation without a hardware lock. It will exit when the 10 minutes demo period expires.

Our application DEMOMODE will run VIEWONLY for 5 minutes and then exit MicroStation. The system function *mdlSystem_setTimerFunction* will call our function demoExpired when the DEMOPERIOD expires. The time is based on a tick, which is approximately one-sixtieth of a second. The user function pauses for 5 seconds, to display the message "Demo period expired", and then calls *mdlSystem_closeDesignFile* to exit MicroStation.

demomode.mc

The source for *demomode.mc* is shown below. There is no command table associated with this application, as the load command will execute the main function. Enter *mdl l demomode* to load the application.

```
/*-----------------------------------------------------------------+
| Copyright (C) 1991, Mach N. Dinh-Vu, All Rights Reserved         |
| Program    : demomode.mc                                         |
| Revision   : 1.0.a                                               |
+-----------------------------------------------------------------+
|        Set the file into DEMO mode using the VIEWONLY facilities |
+-----------------------------------------------------------------*/
/*-----------------------------------------------------------------+
|    Include Files                                                 |
+-----------------------------------------------------------------*/
#include     <mdl.h>          /* system include files */
#include     <global.h>
#include     <userfnc.h>
#include     <msinputq.h>
#include     <cmdlist.h>
#include     <cmdclass.h>

#define      TICK        (1/60)
#define      ASECOND     (60*TICK)
#define      AMINUTE     (60*ASECOND)
#define      DEMOPERIOD  (5*AMINUTE)

Private  int   timerHandle;
```

```
/*-----------------------------------------------------------------+
| name            commandFilter                                    |
+-----------------------------------------------------------------*/
Private int commandFilter
(
Inputq_element   *queueElementP
)
    {
    /* If this is not a MicroStation command, just return. */
    if ((queueElementP->u.cmd.taskId != '\0') &&
        (strcmp (queueElementP->u.cmd.taskId, ustnTaskId) != 0))
        return INPUT_COMMAND_ACCEPT;

    switch (queueElementP->u.cmd.class)
        {
        case VIEWING:
        case MEASURE:
        case VIEWPARAM:
        case VIEWIMMED:
        case WINDOWMAN:
        case DIALOGMAN:
        case INPUT:
        case PLOT:
            return INPUT_COMMAND_ACCEPT;
            break;
        default:
            mdlUtil_beep(1);
            mdlOutput_error ("WARNING: This is a VIEW only file.");
            return INPUT_COMMAND_REJECT;
        }
    }
/*-----------------------------------------------------------------+
| name            demoExpired                                      |
+-----------------------------------------------------------------*/
demoExpired()
{
 mdlOutput_message("Demo period expired");
 mdlSystem_pauseTicks(5*ASECOND);
 mdlSystem_closeDesignFile();
}
/*-----------------------------------------------------------------+
| name            main                                             |
+-----------------------------------------------------------------*/
main()
{
 mdlSystem_setTimerFunction(&timerHandle, DEMOPERIOD,demoExpired, 0, TRUE);
 mdlInput_setFunction (INPUT_COMMAND_FILTER, commandFilter);
 mdlOutput_prompt("DEMO MODE : File set to VIEW ONLY");
}
```

To build the DEMOMODE application enter *bmake -a demomode.*

demomode.mke

```
#----------------------------------------------------------------------
#          DEMOMODE MDL Make File
#----------------------------------------------------------------------
%include $(MS)/mdl/include/mdl.mki


#----------------------------------------------------------------------
#          Define constants specific to this DEMOMODE application
#----------------------------------------------------------------------
progmdl      = d:/progmdl/disk/
baseDir      = $(progmdl)viewonly/
objectDir    = $(mdlexample)objects/
privateInc   = $(baseDir)

demomodeObjs  = $(objectDir)demomode.mo

demomodeRscs  = $(objectDir)demomode.mp


#----------------------------------------------------------------------
#          Compile Resources
#----------------------------------------------------------------------
$(objectDir)demomode.mo            : $(baseDir)demomode.mc

$(objectDir)demomode.mp            : $(demomodeObjs)
        $(msg)
        >$(objectDir)temp.cmd
        -a$@
        -s6000
        $(linkOpts)
        $(demomodeObjs)
        <
        $(linkCmd) @$(objectDir)temp.cmd
        ~time

$(mdlapps)demomode.ma              : $(demomodeRscs)
        $(msg)
        >$(objectDir)temp.cmd
        -o$@
        $(demomodeRscs)
        <
        $(rscLibCmd) @$(objectDir)temp.cmd
        ~time
```

Compiling UCMs

To compile a User Command we must be inside a design file and enter "ucc = " followed by the filename. If we have a list of UCMs to compile then we can enter the names of our UCMs into a list file and use the @ symbol to prefix the list filename. If our list file is *ucms.lst* then to compile it we would enter *ucc = @ucms.lst*.

We can simplify all this by using the input queue and file manipulation functions.

File Functions

Since MicroStation can exist on multiple platforms, it is difficult to cater for the differences in the operating systems. The file functions allow portability of the MDL program between these platforms.

mdlFile_buildName	build complete filename from device name, directory specification, root filename or extension.
mdlFile_copy	copy a file.
mdlFile_create	create a file based on the root filename, environment variable or file extension.
mdlFile_find	find a file based on the root filename, environment variable or file extension.
mdlFile_findFiles	find a series of files based on a search criteria.
mdlFile_getcwd	return the current working directory.
mdlFile_getDiskFree	return the number of bytes available on the file system.
mdlFile_getDrive	return the current drive number (PC only).
mdlFile_getFileAttributes	return the attributes of a given file.

mdlFile_parseName   parse the specified file and return the device name,
                           directory specification, root filename and extension.

mdlFile_setDefaultShare establish the sharing mode used by fopen
                        (PC only).

mdlFile_setDrive   set the current drive number (PC only).

We will write a program using file functions to compile all files with the
extension ".ucm". The bulk of the work is done in the function
compucm_start. The MDL function *mdlFile_findFiles* will locate all files in
the current directory with the extension ".ucm". The next step is to loop
through all the names of the files, prefix them with "ucc=", and put them onto
the input queue with the function *mdlInput_sendKeyin*. The compilation does
not start until the function compucm_start returns to MicroStation.

```
cmdName             compucm_start()
cmdNumber           CMD_COMPUCM
{
    FindFileInfo    *finfoP;
    char            fspec[40];
    char            keyin[80];
    int             fcount, i;

    finfoP=malloc(sizeof(FindFileInfo));
    strcpy(fspec,"*.UCM");
    mdlFile_findFiles(&finfoP, &fcount, fspec, FF_NORMAL);
    for (i=0; i < fcount; i++)
    {
        strcpy(keyin,"UCC=");
        strcat(keyin,finfoP[i].name);
        mdlInput_sendKeyin(keyin, 0, i, NULL);
    }

    free(finfoP);
}
```

To load the application enter *mdl l compucm*. To execute the application enter COMPUCM.

compucm.mc

```
/*------------------------------------------------------------------+
|  Copyright (C) 1991, Mach N. Dinh-Vu, All Rights Reserved         |
|  Program    : compucm.mc                                          |
|  Revision   : 1.0.a                                               |
+------------------------------------------------------------------+
|         compile all UCMs in the current directory                 |
+------------------------------------------------------------------*/
/*------------------------------------------------------------------+
|    Include Files                                                  |
+------------------------------------------------------------------*/
#include     <mdl.h>              /* system include files */
#include     <global.h>
#include     <mselems.h>
#include     <userfnc.h>
#include     <system.h>
#include     <msinputq.h>
#include     <rscdefs.h>
#include     <tcb.h>

#include     "compucm.h"
/*------------------------------------------------------------------+
|  name           main                                              |
+------------------------------------------------------------------*/
main
(
)
    {
    RscFileHandle    rfHandle;

    /* load our command table */
    if (mdlParse_loadCommandTable (NULL) == NULL)
        mdlOutput_error ("Unable to load command table.");
    else
        mdlOutput_error ("To execute enter COMPUCM");
    mdlResource_openFile (&rfHandle, NULL, FALSE);
    }

/*------------------------------------------------------------------+
|  name           compucm_start                                     |
+------------------------------------------------------------------*/
cmdName          compucm_start()
cmdNumber        CMD_COMPUCM
```

```
{
    FindFileInfo      *finfoP;
    char              fspec[40];
    char              keyin[80];
    int               fcount, i;

    finfoP=malloc(sizeof(FindFileInfo));
    strcpy(fspec,"*.UCM");
    mdlFile_findFiles(&finfoP, &fcount, fspec, FF_NORMAL);
    for (i=0; i < fcount; i++)
    {
        strcpy(keyin,"UCC=");
        strcat(keyin,finfoP[i].name);
        mdlInput_sendKeyin(keyin, 0, i, NULL);
    }

    free(finfoP);
}
```

     The makefile for COMPUCM.

compucm.mke

```
#-------------------------------------------------------------
#     Makefile for COMPUCM
#-------------------------------------------------------------
%include $(MS)/mdl/include/mdl.mki
#-------------------------------------------------------------
#        Define constants specific to this example
#-------------------------------------------------------------
baseDir      = $(mdlexample)compucm/
objectDir    = $(mdlexample)objects/
privateInc   = $(baseDir)

compucmObjs  = $(objectDir)compucm.mo

compucmRscs  = $(objectDir)compucm.rsc \
               $(objectDir)compucm.mp


#-------------------------------------------------------------
#        Compile Resources
#-------------------------------------------------------------
$(privateInc)compucm.h          : $(baseDir)compucm.r

$(objectDir)compucm.rsc         : $(baseDir)compucm.r

$(objectDir)compucm.mo          : $(baseDir)compucm.mc
```

```
$(objectDir)compucm.mp            : $(compucmObjs)
        $(msg)
        > $(objectDir)temp.cmd
        -a$@
        -s6000
        $(linkOpts)
        $(compucmObjs)
        <
        $(linkCmd) @$(objectDir)temp.cmd
        ~time

$(mdlapps)compucm.ma              : $(compucmRscs)
        $(msg)
        > $(objectDir)temp.cmd
        -o$@
        $(compucmRscs)
        <
        $(rscLibCmd) @$(objectDir)temp.cmd
        ~time
```

Where to from here?

While we have tried to expose you to the many aspects of MDL, we did not
cover databases and external programs. Both of these topics requires the
purchase of extra software. The former being Oracle, and the latter being
MetaWare High C. If you feel confident with MDL, you may want to
investigate these areas further.

The MDL examples, supplied with MicroStation, is worth careful look.
Compile and execute each application and see how they work. Other examples
are found on the MicroStation Information Center (the bulletin board). One
example of interest is DRAWCOMP.

There are many third-party books and tools to support MDL. The notable
book is *101 MDL Commands* by Bill Steinbock. If you believe in learning by
example, then this book is a must.

Now that you have made it this far, you must be as excited about MDL as we
are. MDL opens a new world to the application developers. Programs are
now limited only by the imagination, not the tool. Good Luck and Good
Programming.

Appendix A : Include Files

Appendix A, lists the most used files in the *\ustation\mdl\include* directory. These are:

File	Page	Description
basetype.h	A-2	Basic Type definitions for MicroStation/MDL
global.h	A-7	Structure definitions for global data areas in MicroStation.
mdl.h	A-10	Main include file for MDL applications.
mdl.mki	A-16	Make include file.
msdefs.h	A-19	Defines for MicroStation data structures.
mselems.h	A-22	Structures that define MicroStation elements.
scanner.h	A-39	Typedefs and Defines for using the scanner.
tcb.h	A-41	Typedefs and Defines for Terminal Control Block. Contains all current information about the design file being edited.

```
/*-----------------------------------------------------------------+
|  basetype.h -- Basic Type definitions for MicroStation/MDL       |
+------------------------------------------------------------------*/
typedef unsigned long        ULong;
typedef unsigned short       UShort;
typedef unsigned int         UInt;
typedef unsigned char        UChar;
typedef int                  ErrorCode;  /* 0 means no error, see also mdlerrs.h */

typedef struct versionnumber
    {
    UShort     release:8;
    UShort     major:8;
    UShort     minor:8;
    UShort     subMinor:8;
    } VersionNumber;

typedef struct point2d
    {
    long     x;
    long     y;
    } Point2d;

typedef struct point3d
    {
    long     x;
    long     y;
    long     z;
    } Point3d;

typedef struct dpoint2d
    {
    double   x;
    double   y;
    } Dpoint2d, DPoint2d;

typedef struct dpoint3d
    {
    double   x;
    double   y;
    double   z;
    } Dpoint3d, DPoint3d;

typedef struct spoint2d
    {
    short    x;
    short    y;
    } Spoint2d, SPoint2d;

typedef struct uspoint2d
```

```
    {
    unsigned short   x;
    unsigned short   y;
    } Uspoint2d;

typedef struct spoint3d
    {
    short     x;
    short     y;
    short     z;
    } Spoint3d, SPoint3d;

typedef struct uspoint3d
    {
    unsigned short   x;
    unsigned short   y;
    unsigned short   z;
    } Uspoint3d;

typedef struct upoint2d
    {
    unsigned long    x;
    unsigned long    y;
    } Upoint2d;

typedef struct upoint3d
    {
    unsigned long    x;
    unsigned long    y;
    unsigned long    z;
    } Upoint3d;

typedef struct vector2d
    {
    Point2d  org;
    Point2d  end;
    } Vector2d;

typedef struct vector3d
    {
    Point3d  org;
    Point3d  end;
    } Vector3d;

typedef struct svector2d
    {
    SPoint2d org;
    SPoint2d end;
    } Svector2d, SVector2d;
```

```
typedef struct svector3d
    {
    SPoint3d org;
    SPoint3d end;
    } Svector3d, SVector3d;

typedef struct dvector2d
    {
    DPoint2d org;
    DPoint2d end;
    } Dvector2d, DVector2d;

typedef struct dvector3d
    {
    DPoint3d org;
    DPoint3d end;
    } Dvector3d, DVector3d;

typedef struct extent
    {
    SPoint2d origin;                    /* upper left */
    short    width;
    short    height;
    } Sextent;

typedef struct rectangle
    {
    Point2d origin;
    Point2d corner;
    } Rectangle;

typedef struct srectangle
    {
    SPoint2d origin;
    SPoint2d corner;
    } Srectangle;

typedef struct drectangle
    {
    DPoint2d origin;
    DPoint2d corner;
    } Drectangle;

typedef struct urectangle
    {
    Uspoint2d        origin;
    Uspoint2d        corner;
    } Urectangle;

typedef struct transform3d
```

```
    {
    double    element[3][3];
    } Transform3d;

typedef struct transform2d
    {
    double    element[2][2];
    } Transform2d;

typedef struct assocpoint
    {
    ULong     tagValue;
    long      assoc[2];
    } AssocPoint;

typedef union rotMatrix
    {
    double    form2d[2][2];
    double    form3d[3][3];
    } RotMatrix;

typedef union transform
    {
    double    form2d[2][3];
    double    form3d[3][4];
    } Transform;

typedef struct ritransform
    {
    Transform         trans;
    union
      {
      long    matrix2d[2][2];
      long    matrix3d[3][3];
      } rot;
    union
      {
      Point2d org2d;
      Point3d org3d;
      } view;
    union
      {
      Point2d org2d;
      Point3d org3d;
      } screen;
    } RITransform;

typedef union types_u
    {
    char          c;
```

```
    unsigned char   uc;
    short           s;
    unsigned short  us;
    long            l;
    unsigned long   ul;
    int             i;
    float           f;
    double          d;
    char            *pc;
    }
Types_u;

/*------------------------------------------------------------------+
|    Color Structures                                               |
+------------------------------------------------------------------*/
typedef struct rgbColorDef
    {
    unsigned char   red;
    unsigned char   green;
    unsigned char   blue;
    } RGBColorDef;

typedef struct hsvcolor
    {
    int       hue;        /* red=0, yellow, green, cyan, blue, magenta */
                          /* 0 - 360 */
    int       saturation;/* 0=white, 100=no white, tints */
    int       value;     /* 0=black, 100=no black, shades */
    } HSVColor;

typedef struct RGBFACTOR
    {
    double red;          /* 0.0  intensity  1.0 */
    double green;        /* 0.0  intensity  1.0 */
    double blue;         /* 0.0  intensity  1.0 */
    } RGBFactor;
```

```
/*--------------------------------------------------------------------+
|      global.h - structure definitions for global data areas in      |
|              MicroStation.                                          |
+--------------------------------------------------------------------*/
/*--------------------------------------------------------------------+
|     MGDS modes structure                                            |
+--------------------------------------------------------------------*/
typedef struct mgds_modes
    {
    byte        three_d;                /* drawing is 3-d */
    byte        loc_ele_hilited;        /* is an element currently hilited */
    byte        rangedisplay;           /* show ranges (for debugging) */
    byte        libindexed;             /* cell library is indexed */
    short       tmp_element;            /* temporary element is on the screen */
    byte        noDgnFile;              /* There is no design file */
    byte        workFileWritten;        /* the work file has been written */
    byte        dgn_read_only;          /* design file is read only */
    byte        cell_read_only;         /* cell file is read only */
    byte        fb_only;                /* file builder only */
    byte        always_read_only;       /* MicroStation started read_only */
#if defined (ip32)
    byte        use_blitsymbols;        /* use blit symbols */
    byte        noMenubar;              /* no menu bar */
#endif
    byte        dontCheckLock;          /* don't check file locking */
    byte        enableFork;             /* enable forking to operating system */
    byte        filemode;               /* direct or workfile mode */
    byte        panZoomActive;          /* in a pan/zoom */
    byte        noIntTransform;         /* don't use integer scale algorithm */
    byte        recording;              /* we are currently recording */
    byte        playback;               /* we are currently playing back */
    byte        noReferenceFiles;       /* dont bring up reference files */
    } Mgds_modes;


/*--------------------------------------------------------------------+
|      Graphics Configuration                                         |
+--------------------------------------------------------------------*/
typedef struct msGraphConfig
    {
    short           numScreens;     /* number of physical screens */
    short           currentScreen;  /* displayed screen w 2 virt scrns */
    short           windowBorderStyle;  /* 0 normal, 1-9 = wide, 128 = none */
    struct msDisplayDescr *displayDescrP[MAX_PHYSSCREEN];
    short           swapPossible;   /* TRUE if screen can swap */
    short           needUpdateOnSwap;/* TRUE if we need update on a swap */
    Rectangle       swapUpdateRect; /* Rectangle we need update for */
    void            *updateHereBack; /* frontmost wind that needs update */
    } MSGraphConfig;
```

```
/*------------------------------------------------------------------+
|       MicroStation State data                                     |
+------------------------------------------------------------------*/
typedef struct
    {
    Point3d   rawUors;          /* database coordinates */
    Point3d   uors;             /* database coords (adjusted for locks) */
    Uspoint3d input;            /* input device coordinates */
    Spoint2d  screen;           /* screen coordinate system */
    GuiWindow *gwP;             /* M/S window we are in */
    short     region;           /* region on input device */
    short     screenNumber;     /* screen cursor is in */
    short     view;             /* view cursor is in */
    short     buttonTrans;      /* button transition type */
    short     qualifierMask;    /* keyboard qualifiers */
    } CursorInfo;

typedef struct    msStateData
    {
    CursorInfo    current;      /* current cursor information */
    CursorInfo    old;          /* last time through cursor information */
    CursorInfo    inPoint;      /* datapoint entered by user */
    CursorInfo    tentative;    /* tentative point information */
    short    viewflags[MAX_VIEWS];/ views command will operate on */
    short    precision;         /* indicates precision input */
    Point3d  *pointstack;       /* database point stack */
    Dpoint3d *dPointStack;      /* double precision version */
    short    pointpntr;         /* point stack pointer */
    Point3d  viewpntstack[5];   /* point stack for view commands */
    short    vwpntpntr;         /* view point stack pointer */
    short    tntPointActive;    /* data point should go to tentative pt */
    short    snappedElement;    /* tent point identified an element */
    char     cmdstring[128];    /* commandstring */
    short    datapnt3d_active;  /* first part of 3D data entered */
    Point3d  datapnt3d;         /* first part 3D data point */
    short    datapnt3d_view;    /* view for first part of 3D data pnt */
    short    tentpnt3d_active;  /* first part of 3D tent pt entered */
    Point3d  tentpnt3d;         /* first part of 3D tent point */
    short    tentpnt3d_view;    /* view for first part of 3D tent pnt */
    byte     pointFlags[16];    /* flag array to parallel point stack   */
    struct
      {
      unsigned short      dragging:1;
      unsigned short      mouseup:1;
      unsigned short      closeCmd:1;
      unsigned short      unused:13;
      } flags;
    } MSStateData;

typedef struct msDisplayDescr
```

```
{
short      id;           /* card identity */
short      colors;       /* number of colors supported */
short      xResolution;  /* x resolution (pixels) */
short      yResolution;  /* y resolution (pixels) */
short      screenWidth;  /* physical size of screen used, x */
short      screenHeight; /* physical size of screen used, y */
double     aspect;       /* aspect ratio of screen */
short      charHeight;   /* character height (pixels) */
short      charWidth;    /* width of characters (pixels) */
short      cursorWidth;  /* 1/2 of graphics cursor width */
short      cursorHeight; /* 1/2 of graphics cursor height */
short      xorColor;     /* exclusive or color */
short      hiliteColor;  /* color used for hilight */
byte       *colormap;    /* mapping from dgn to display color */
short      nPlanes;      /* number of planes on screen */
byte       ditherShades[256];  /* 8 bit intensity to avail resolutn. */
byte       rgb9BitToCtbl[512]; /* 9 bit rgb to colortbl-index map. */
byte       menuColors[NUM_MENU_COLORS+1];   /* number of menu colors */
} MSDisplayDescr;
```

```
/*------------------------------------------------------------------------+
|    mdl.h -- Main include file for MDL applications.  Defines|
|          structures and constants used by MDL library functions.        |
+-----------------------------------------------------------------------*/
/*------------------------------------------------------------------------+
|       Constants for standard views                                      |
+-----------------------------------------------------------------------*/
#define          STDVIEW_TOP        1
#define          STDVIEW_BOTTOM     2
#define          STDVIEW_LEFT       3
#define          STDVIEW_RIGHT      4
#define          STDVIEW_FRONT      5
#define          STDVIEW_BACK       6
#define          STDVIEW_ISO        7


/*------------------------------------------------------------------------+
|       Text creation routine parameters                                  |
+-----------------------------------------------------------------------*/
#define          TXT_NO_TRANSFORM   0x8000
#define          TXT_BY_TILE_SIZE   1
#define          TXT_BY_MULT        2
#define          TXT_BY_TEXT_SIZE   3
#define          TXT_BY_WIDTH_ASPECT 4

/*    Text Justifications    */
#define          TXTJUST_LT          0         /* Left Top */
#define          TXTJUST_LC          1         /* Left Center */
#define          TXTJUST_LB          2         /* Left Bottom */
#define          TXTJUST_LMT         3         /* Left Margin Top */
#define          TXTJUST_LMC         4         /* Left Margin Center */
#define          TXTJUST_LMB         5         /* Left Margin Bottom */
#define          TXTJUST_CT          6         /* Center Top */
#define          TXTJUST_CC          7         /* Center Center */
#define          TXTJUST_CB          8         /* Center Bottom */
#define          TXTJUST_RMT         9         /* Right Margin Top */
#define          TXTJUST_RMC         10        /* Right Margin Center */
#define          TXTJUST_RMB         11        /* Right Margin Bottom */
#define          TXTJUST_RT          12        /* Right Top */
#define          TXTJUST_RC          13        /* Right Center */
#define          TXTJUST_RB          14        /* Right Bottom */

/* Text Symbol Type */
#define          TXTFONT_NORMAL   0      /* Normal font */
#define          TXTFONT_SYMBOL   1      /* Symbol font */
/* Text Vector Size */
#define          TXTFONT_BYTEVEC  1      /*  8-bits used for vector */
#define          TXTFONT_WORDVEC  2      /* 16-bits used for vector */
/* Text Representation Size */
#define          TXTFONT_BYTEREP  0      /*  8-bits represents font */
#define          TXTFONT_WORDREP  1      /* 16-bits represents font */
```

```
/* Text Type */
#define          TXTFONT_VECTOR   0        /* Vector font */
#define          TXTFONT_RASTER   1        /* Raster font */

typedef struct textSize
    {
    double    width;
    double    height;
    } TextSize;

typedef struct textSizeParam
    {
    int            mode;
    TextSize size;
    double    aspectRatio;
    } TextSizeParam;

typedef struct textParam
    {
    int            font;
    int            just;
    int            style;
    int            viewIndependent;
    } TextParam;

typedef struct textEDField
    {
    byte      start;
    byte      len;
    byte      just;
    } TextEDField;

typedef struct textEDParam
    {
    int              numEDFields;
    TextEDField      *edField;
    } TextEDParam;

typedef struct textScale
    {
    double      x; /* magnification of vectors within tile */
    double      y; /* magnification of vectors within tile */
    } TextScale;

typedef struct textFlags
    {
    UShort        upper:1;        /* upper case */
    UShort        lower:1;        /* lower case */
    UShort        fract:1;        /* fractions */
```

```
    UShort          intl:1;         /* international */
    UShort          fast:1;         /* fast */
    UShort          reserved:4;            /* reserved */
    } TextFlags;

typedef struct textStyleInfo
    {
    int             font;
    short   style;
    } TextStyleInfo;

typedef struct textFontInfo
    {
    TextFlags       lettersType;    /* upper, lower, fractions, intl */
    byte            charType;       /* symbol or normal */
    byte            vectorSize;     /* byte or word */
    byte            graphicType;    /* rastor or vector */
    byte            charSize;       /* 8 or 16 bit representation of font */
    short           tileSize;       /* size of "tile" making up characters */
    long            dataSize;       /* size of file including header */
    Point2d         origin;         /* origin of char in the "tile" */
    TextScale       scale;          /* scale factor of font */
    } TextFontInfo;
```

```
/*-------------------------------------------------------------------+
|    Defines for mdlElement_getFilePos & mdlElement_setFilePos routines. |
+-------------------------------------------------------------------*/
#define FILEPOS_EOF                     0
#define FILEPOS_CURRENT                 1
#define FILEPOS_FIRST_ELE               2
#define FILEPOS_NEXT_ELE                3
#define FILEPOS_WORKING_SET             4
#define FILEPOS_WORKING_WINDOW          5
#define FILEPOS_COMPONENT               6
/*-------------------------------------------------------------------+
|    Defines for mdlElmdscr_ routines                                |
+-------------------------------------------------------------------*/
#define     ELMD_ELEMENT            (1<<0)
#define     ELMD_PRE_HDR            (1<<1)
#define     ELMD_POST_HDR           (1<<2)
#define     ELMD_PRE_NESTEDHDR      (1<<3)
#define     ELMD_POST_NESTEDHDR     (1<<4)
#define     ELMD_ALL_ONCE           (ELMD_ELEMENT | ELMD_PRE_HDR |
                                     ELMD_PRE_NESTEDHDR)
#define ELMD_HDRS_ONCE              (ELMD_PRE_HDR | ELMD_PRE_NESTEDHDR)
/*-------------------------------------------------------------------+
|    Parameters for mdlModify_ routines          |
+-------------------------------------------------------------------*/
typedef struct
    {
```

```
      int       reserved1;
      int       reserved2;
      void      *reserved3;
      } MdlCopyParams;

#define MODIFY_ORIG                 (1<<1)
#define MODIFY_COPY                 0
#define MODIFY_DRAWINHILITE         (1<<3)
#define MODIFY_DONTDRAWNEW          (1<<4)
#define MODIFY_DONTERASEORIG        (1<<5)

#define MODIFY_REQUEST_NOHEADERS 0
#define MODIFY_REQUEST_HEADERS      (1<<0)
#define MODIFY_REQUEST_ONLYONE      (1<<1)

#define MODIFY_STATUS_NOCHANGE      0
#define MODIFY_STATUS_REPLACE       (1<<0)
#define MODIFY_STATUS_DELETE        (1<<1)
#define MODIFY_STATUS_ABORT         (1<<2)
#define MODIFY_STATUS_FAIL          (1<<3)
#define MODIFY_STATUS_REPLACEDSCR(1<<4)
#define MODIFY_STATUS_MODIFIED      (1<<5)
#define MODIFY_STATUS_ERROR         (MODIFY_STATUS_FAIL | MODIFY_STATUS_ABORT)

/*--------------------------------------------------------------------+
    |   Defines for mdlView_getDisplayControls() &                    |
    |             mdlView_setDisplayControls()                        |
    +--------------------------------------------------------------------*/
#define VIEWCONTROL_FAST_CURVE            0
#define VIEWCONTROL_FAST_TEXT             1
#define VIEWCONTROL_FAST_FONT             2
#define VIEWCONTROL_LINE_WEIGHTS          3
#define VIEWCONTROL_PATTERNS              4
#define VIEWCONTROL_TEXT_NODES            5
#define VIEWCONTROL_ED_FIELDS             6
#define VIEWCONTROL_GRID                  9
#define VIEWCONTROL_LEV_SYMB              10
#define VIEWCONTROL_POINTS                11
#define VIEWCONTROL_CONSTRUCTION          12
#define VIEWCONTROL_DIMENSIONS            13
#define VIEWCONTROL_AREA_FILL             16
#define VIEWCONTROL_RASTER_TEXT           17
#define VIEWCONTROL_AUX_DISPLAY           18
#define VIEWCONTROL_CAMERA                22
#define VIEWCONTROL_RENDERMODE            23
#define VIEWCONTROL_BACKGROUND            26
#define VIEWCONTROL_REF_BOUND             27
#define VIEWCONTROL_FAST_BOUND_CLIP       28
#define VIEWCONTROL_DEPTH_CUE             29
#define VIEWCONTROL_NO_DYNAMICS           30
```

```
#define VIEWMODE_WIREFRAME         0
#define VIEWMODE_CROSSSECTION      1
#define VIEWMODE_WIREMESH          2
#define VIEWMODE_HIDDENLINE        3
#define VIEWMODE_FILLEDHLINE       4
#define VIEWMODE_CONTANTSHADE      5
#define VIEWMODE_SMOOTHSHADE       6
#define VIEWMODE_PHONGSHADE        7


/*-------------------------------------------------------------------+
|    Defines for mdlParams_getActive() & mdlParams_setActive()       |
+-------------------------------------------------------------------*/
#define        ACTIVEPARAM_COLOR              1
#define        ACTIVEPARAM_COLOR_BY_NAME      2
#define        ACTIVEPARAM_LINESTYLE          3
#define        ACTIVEPARAM_LINEWEIGHT         4
#define        ACTIVEPARAM_LEVEL              5
#define        ACTIVEPARAM_ANGLE              6
#define        ACTIVEPARAM_FONT               7
#define        ACTIVEPARAM_GRIDUNITS          8
#define        ACTIVEPARAM_GRIDREF            9
#define        ACTIVEPARAM_TEXTHEIGHT        10
#define        ACTIVEPARAM_TEXTWIDTH         11
#define        ACTIVEPARAM_UNITROUNDOFF      12
#define        ACTIVEPARAM_TEXTJUST          13
#define        ACTIVEPARAM_NODEJUST          14
#define        ACTIVEPARAM_CELLNAME          15
#define        ACTIVEPARAM_LINELENGTH        16
#define        ACTIVEPARAM_LINESPACING       17
#define        ACTIVEPARAM_TERMINATOR        18
#define        ACTIVEPARAM_TAGINCREMENT      19
#define        ACTIVEPARAM_TAB               20
#define        ACTIVEPARAM_STREAMDELTA       21
#define        ACTIVEPARAM_STREAMTOLERANCE   22
#define        ACTIVEPARAM_STREAMANGLE       23
#define        ACTIVEPARAM_STREAMAREA        24
#define        ACTIVEPARAM_POINT             25
#define        ACTIVEPARAM_KEYPOINT          26
#define        ACTIVEPARAM_PATTERNDELTA      27
#define        ACTIVEPARAM_PATTERNANGLE      28
#define        ACTIVEPARAM_PATTERNSCALE      29
#define        ACTIVEPARAM_PATTERNCELL       30
#define        ACTIVEPARAM_AREAMODE          31
#define        ACTIVEPARAM_AXISANGLE         32
#define        ACTIVEPARAM_CLASS             33
#define        ACTIVEPARAM_CAPMODE           34
#define        ACTIVEPARAM_GRIDMODE          35
#define        ACTIVEPARAM_GRIDRATIO         36
#define        ACTIVEPARAM_FILLMODE          37
```

```
#define ACTIVEPARAM_SCALE              38
#define ACTIVEPARAM_TERMINATORSCALE    39
#define ACTIVEPARAM_DIMCOMPAT          40
#define ACTIVEPARAM_MLINECOMPAT        41
#define ACTIVEPARAM_AXISORIGIN         42
#define ACTIVELOCK_ASSOCIATION         500
/*-------------------------------------------------------------------+
|    Defines for mdlOutput_printf.                                    |
+-------------------------------------------------------------------*/
#define MSG_MESSAGE        0
#define MSG_ERROR          1
#define MSG_PROMPT         2
#define MSG_STATUS         3
#define MSG_COMMAND        4
#define MSG_KEYIN          5
/*-------------------------------------------------------------------+
|    Constants for dimension and multiline points                     |
+-------------------------------------------------------------------* /
#define POINT_CHECK              0
#define POINT_ASSOC              1
#define POINT_STD                2
/* Arc association options */
#define ASSOC_ARC_ANGLE          0
#define ASSOC_ARC_CENTER         1
#define ASSOC_ARC_START          2
#define ASSOC_ARC_END            3
/*-------------------------------------------------------------------+
|    Constants for mdlMline functions             |                   |
+-------------------------------------------------------------------*/
#define MLBREAK_FROM_JOINT 0x8000
#define MLBREAK_TO_JOINT   0x4000
#define MLBREAK_STD        0
#define MLCAP_NONE         0x0
#define MLCAP_LINE         0x1
#define MLCAP_OUTER_ARCS   0x2
#define MLCAP_INNER_ARCS   0x4
#define MLCAP_CLOSE        0x8
#define SHIFT_BREAKS       0x2
/*-------------------------------------------------------------------+
|    Constants for mdlLevel functions             |                   |
+-------------------------------------------------------------------*/
#define DUPLICATE_GROUP          2227
#define DUPLICATE_LEVEL          2228
/*-------------------------------------------------------------------+
|    Constants for mdlText functions              |                   |
+-------------------------------------------------------------------*/
#define     FRACTIONS            (1<<1)
#define     INTERNATIONAL        (1<<2)
#define     CONTROL              (1<<3)
```

```
#------------------------------------------------------------------------
#     Make Include File For Example Mdl Applications
#
#     Note: define environment variable MS pointing to your MicroStation
#           root directory.
#------------------------------------------------------------------------
msg     =        |[== Building $@, ($=) ==]
#------------------------------------------------------------------------
#     Define paths and other things that might need to be overridden
#     for BSI internal use.
#------------------------------------------------------------------------
toolsPath    = $(MS)/mdl/bin/
publishInc   = $(MS)/mdl/include/
stdlibInc    = $(MS)/mdl/include/stdlib
rscDir       = $(MS)/resource/
o            = $(MS)/mdl/objects/
src          = $(MS)/mdl/examples/
#------------------------------------------------------------------------
#     Machine independent
#------------------------------------------------------------------------
mdlapps      = $(MS)/mdlapps/
mdlexample   = $(MS)/mdl/examples/
mdlLibs      = $(MS)/mdl/library/

%ifdef unix
#------------------------------------------------------------------------
#     Unix Macros
#------------------------------------------------------------------------
compCmd      = $(toolsPath)mcomp
linkCmd      = $(toolsPath)mlink
libCmd       = $(toolsPath)mlib
rscCompCmd   = $(toolsPath)rcomp
rscTypeName  = $(toolsPath)rsctype
rscLibCmd    = $(toolsPath)rlib
deleteCmd    = rm
CCompCmd     = cc -Xa -c
oext         = .o

%elif msdos
#------------------------------------------------------------------------
#     MSDos Macros
#------------------------------------------------------------------------
compCmd      = $(msdosRunCmd) $(toolsPath)mcomp
linkCmd      = $(msdosRunCmd) $(toolsPath)mlink
libCmd       = $(msdosRunCmd) $(toolsPath)mlib
rscCompCmd   = $(msdosRunCmd) $(toolsPath)rcomp
rscTypeName  = $(msdosRunCmd) $(toolsPath)rsctype
rscLibCmd    = $(msdosRunCmd) $(toolsPath)rlib
deleteCmd    = del
CCompCmd     = hc386p
```

```
oext          = .obj
%endif

%ifdef debug
compOpts = -g          # add debugging info
linkOpts = -g          # retain debugging info
%elif  production
compOpts =             # don't need anything
linkOpts = -go         # strip out debugging info
%endif
#-------------------------------------------------------------
#      Inference Rules
#-------------------------------------------------------------
.mc.mo:
     $(msg)
     > $(objectDir)temp.cmd
     -c
     -o$@
     -i$(publishInc)
     -i$(stdlibInc)
%ifdef privateInc
     -i$(privateInc)
%endif
     $(compOpts)
     $%$*.mc
     <
     $(compCmd) @$(objectDir)temp.cmd
     ~time

%ifdef unix
.c.o:
     $(msg)
     $(CCompCmd) -I$(publishInc) $%$*.c
     @mv $*.o $@
     ~time
%endif
%ifdef msdos
.c.obj:
     $(msg)
     $(CCompCmd) $%$*.c -ob $@
     ~time
%endif

.mo.ma:
     $(msg)
     > $(objectDir)temp.cmd
     -a$@
     $(linkOpts) $%$*.mo
     <
     $(linkCmd) @$(objectDir)temp.cmd
```

```
        ~time

.mt.r:
        $(msg)
        > $(objectDir)temp.cmd
        -o$@
%ifdef privateInc
        -i$(privateInc)
%endif
        -i$(publishInc)
        $%$*.mt
        <
        $(rscTypeName)          @$(objectDir)temp.cmd
        ~time

.r.rsc:
        $(msg)
        > $(objectDir)temp.cmd
        -w
        -o$@
%ifdef privateInc
        -i$(privateInc)
%endif
        -i$(publishInc)
        $%$*.r
        <
        $(rscCompCmd) @$(objectDir)temp.cmd
        ~time

.r.h:
        $(msg)
        > $(objectDir)temp.cmd
        -ho$@
        -o$(objectDir)$*.rsc
%ifdef privateInc
        -i$(privateInc)
%endif
        -i$(publishInc)
        $%$*.r
        <
        $(rscCompCmd) @$(objectDir)temp.cmd
        ~time
```

```
/*-----------------------------------------------------------------------+
|    msdefs.h -- Defines for MicroStation data structures         |
+-----------------------------------------------------------------------*/
#define        MAX_REFS              255
#define        MAX_REFCLIPPNTS       100    /* maximum reference clip points
#define        MAX_REFBOUNDS         50     /* maximum bounds + voids */
#define        MAX_FILEMASK          8      /* enough for 255 refs and main */
#define        MAX_VIEWS             8
#define        MAX_VERTICES          101
#define        MAX_EDFIELDS          20     /* max enter data fields / line */
#define        MAX_ATTRIBSIZE        650    /* largest attributes (words) */
#define        MAX_PHYSSCREEN        2      /* max number of graphic screens
#define        MAX_ELEMENT_SIZE      (768*2)
#define        MAX_FONTS             128
#define        MAXFILELENGTH         128
#define        MAXDEVICELENGTH       32
#define        MAXDIRLENGTH          128
#define        MAXNAMELENGTH         64
#define        MAXEXTENSIONLENGTH    32
#define        MAXVERSIONLENGTH      16
#define        MAXKEYINPROMPT        40
#define        MAX_CMAPENTRIES       256

#define        CELL_LIB              256
#define        MASTERFILE            0

#define        TASK_ID_SIZE          16
/*-----------------------------------------------------------------------+
|        File Filter Masks - Used for specifying file filter attributes   |
|                       for mdlFile_findFirst                             |
+-----------------------------------------------------------------------*/
#define        FFILTER_READONLY      0x0001
#define        FFILTER_SUBDIR        0x0002
/*-----------------------------------------------------------------------+
|    DISCONNECT is a coordinate value that signifies a disconnected       |
|        vertex in a string of points.  These vertices can occur in       |
|        linestrings or reference file clip boundaries.                   |
+-----------------------------------------------------------------------*/
#define DISCONNECT  (-2147483647L  - 1L)
/*-----------------------------------------------------------------------+
|    Dialog Box Color Constants                                           |
+-----------------------------------------------------------------------*/
#if !defined (NUM_MENU_COLORS)
#define        NUM_MENU_COLORS       12          /* number of menu colors */
#endif

/*  Basic Color Indexes */
#define BLACK_INDEX 0
#define BLUE_INDEX  1
#define GREEN_INDEX 2
```

```
#define CYAN_INDEX              3
#define RED_INDEX               4
#define MAGENTA_INDEX           5
#define YELLOW_INDEX            6
#define WHITE_INDEX             7
#define LGREY_INDEX             8
#define DGREY_INDEX             9
#define MGREY_INDEX             10
#define PSEUDOWHITE_INDEX 11                      /* actually BLACK on mono screens */

/* icon style constants */
#define ICON_STYLE_NORMAL       0
#define ICON_STYLE_LGREY        1
#define ICON_STYLE_DGREY        2
#define ICON_STYLE_DISABLED 3
/*----------------------------------------------------------------------+
|     MicroStation Raster Font constants                                |
+----------------------------------------------------------------------*/
#define FONT_INDEX_NUMBER 6

#define FONT_INDEX_SYSTEM 0        /* cmd window, screen menus */
#define FONT_INDEX_BORDER 1        /* window borders */
#define FONT_INDEX_DIALOG 2        /* most dialog boxes */
#define FONT_INDEX_BOLD   3        /* bold text in dialog boxes */
#define FONT_INDEX_FIXED  4        /* fixed width font */
#define FONT_INDEX_FIXEDBOLD    5      /* bold fixed width font */
/*----------------------------------------------------------------------+
|    These are drawing modes for mdlElement_display.                    |
+----------------------------------------------------------------------*/
#define         NORMALDRAW          0        /* drawing mode = set */
#define         ERASE               1        /* erase from screen */
#define         HILITE              2        /* highlight */
#define         TEMPDRAW            3        /* draw temporarily */
#define         TEMPERASE           4        /* erase temporarily drawn */
#define         TEMPROTATE          5        /* exclusive-or and halftone */
#define         XORDRAW             6        /* use exclusive or */
#define         SET_ALLOWBGCOLOR    7

#define         RMINI4              (-2147483648.)
#define         LMAXI4              2147483647L
#define         LMINI4              (-2147483647L)
#define         RMAXI4              2147483647.
#define         RMAXUI4             4294967295.
/*----------------------------------------------------------------------+
|    These are the Viewing Modes for 3D files                           |
+----------------------------------------------------------------------*/
#define WIREFRAME           0
#define CROSSSECTION        1
#define WIREMESH            2
#define HIDDENLINE          3
```

```
#define SOLIDFILL        4
#define CONSTANTSHADE    5
#define SMOOTHSHADE      6
#define PHONG            7
/*-----------------------------------------------------------------------+
|    Many MicroStation internal data structures that hold the address of  |
|    elements in a design file are defined in terms of "Block and         |
|    Byte" for compatibility with VAX based IGDS.  All MDL functions       |
|    accept arguments in the more logical concept of "File Position".      |
|    The following macros are provide for conversion between              |
|    block/byte and file position.                                         |
+-----------------------------------------------------------------------*/
#define          DGN_FILEPOS(x,y) (((x)<<9) + (y))
#define          DGN_BLOCK(x)     ((x)>>9)
#define          DGN_OFFSET(x)    ((x)&511)
/*-----------------------------------------------------------------------+
|    Types of Button Transitions                                          |
+-----------------------------------------------------------------------*/
#define BUTTONTRANS_UP            0x0001
#define BUTTONTRANS_DOWN          0x0002
#define BUTTONTRANS_TIMEOUT       0x0004
#define BUTTONTRANS_MOTION        0x0008
#define BUTTONTRANS_CLICK         0x0010
#define BUTTONTRANS_STARTDRAG     0x0020
/*-----------------------------------------------------------------------+
|    These are the window corner designations for resizing windows        |
+-----------------------------------------------------------------------*/
#define CORNER_UPPERLEFT  0
#define CORNER_LOWERLEFT  1
#define CORNER_LOWERRIGHT 2
#define CORNER_UPPERRIGHT 3
#define CORNER_ALL        4
/*-----------------------------------------------------------------------+
|    Auxilliary Coordinate System (ACS) types                             |
+-----------------------------------------------------------------------*/
#define ACS_RECTANGULAR      1
#define ACS_CYLINDRICAL      2
#define ACS_SPHERICAL        3
```

```
/*-----------------------------------------------------------------------+
|     mselems.h -- This file contains the structures that define         |
|               MicroStation elements.                                   |
+----------------------------------------------------------------------*/
#define        FIXEDDEPTH          0        /* Fixed Z depth */
#define        ELEMHIGH            1        /* High range value of Z range */
#define        ELEMLOW             2        /* Low range value of Z range */

#define        CELL_LIB_ELM              1
#define        CELL_HEADER_ELM           2
#define        LINE_ELM                  3
#define        LINE_STRING_ELM           4
#define        GROUP_DATA_ELM            5
#define        SHAPE_ELM                 6
#define        TEXT_NODE_ELM             7
#define        DIG_SETDATA_ELM           8
#define        DGNFIL_HEADER_ELM         9
#define        LEV_SYM_ELM              10
#define        CURVE_ELM                11
#define        CMPLX_STRING_ELM         12
#define        CONIC_ELM                13
#define        CMPLX_SHAPE_ELM          14
#define        ELLIPSE_ELM              15
#define        ARC_ELM                  16
#define        TEXT_ELM                 17
#define        SURFACE_ELM              18
#define        SOLID_ELM                19
#define        BSPLINE_POLE_ELM         21
#define        POINT_STRING_ELM         22
#define        CONE_ELM                 23
#define        BSPLINE_SURFACE_ELM      24
#define        BSURF_BOUNDARY_ELM       25
#define        BSPLINE_KNOT_ELM         26
#define        BSPLINE_CURVE_ELM        27
#define        BSPLINE_WEIGHT_ELM       28
#define        DIMENSION_ELM            33
#define        SHAREDCELL_DEF_ELM       34
#define        SHARED_CELL_ELM          35
#define        MULTILINE_ELM            36
#define        TEXT_ARRAY_ELM           58
#define        TEXT_STACK_ELM           59
#define        MICROSTATION_ELM         66
#define        RASTER_HDR               87
#define        RASTER_COMP              88

/*-----------------------------------------------------------------------+
|   Element Type Masks - Can be used to set up type masks for scanner    |
|      or element modification commands                                  |
+----------------------------------------------------------------------*/
/* The following masks must be 'OR'ed with typemask[0] */
```

```
#define ELMBITMSK(elmNum)          (1<<((elmNum-1)%16))
#define TMSK0_CELL_LIB             ELMBITMSK (CELL_LIB_ELM)
#define TMSK0_CELL_HEADER          ELMBITMSK (CELL_HEADER_ELM)
#define TMSK0_LINE                 ELMBITMSK (LINE_ELM)
#define TMSK0_LINE_STRING          ELMBITMSK (LINE_STRING_ELM)
#define TMSK0_GROUP_DATA           ELMBITMSK (GROUP_DATA_ELM)
#define TMSK0_SHAPE                ELMBITMSK (SHAPE_ELM)
#define TMSK0_TEXT_NODE            ELMBITMSK (TEXT_NODE_ELM)
#define TMSK0_DIG_SETDATA          ELMBITMSK (DIG_SETDATA_ELM)
#define TMSK0_DGNFIL_HEADER        ELMBITMSK (DGNFIL_HEADER_ELM)
#define TMSK0_LEV_SYM              ELMBITMSK (LEV_SYM_ELM)
#define TMSK0_CURVE                ELMBITMSK (CURVE_ELM)
#define TMSK0_CMPLX_STRING         ELMBITMSK (CMPLX_STRING_ELM)
#define TMSK0_CONIC                ELMBITMSK (CONIC_ELM)
#define TMSK0_CMPLX_SHAPE          ELMBITMSK (CMPLX_SHAPE_ELM)
#define TMSK0_ELLIPSE              ELMBITMSK (ELLIPSE_ELM)
#define TMSK0_ARC                  ELMBITMSK (ARC_ELM)

/* These following masks must be 'OR'ed with typemask[1] */
#define TMSK1_TEXT                 ELMBITMSK (TEXT_ELM)
#define TMSK1_SURFACE              ELMBITMSK (SURFACE_ELM)
#define TMSK1_SOLID                ELMBITMSK (SOLID_ELM)
#define TMSK1_BSPLINE_POLE         ELMBITMSK (BSPLINE_POLE_ELM)
#define TMSK1_POINT_STRING         ELMBITMSK (POINT_STRING_ELM)
#define TMSK1_CONE                 ELMBITMSK (CONE_ELM)
#define TMSK1_BSPLINE_SURFACE      ELMBITMSK (BSPLINE_SURFACE_ELM)
#define TMSK1_BSURF_BOUNDARY       ELMBITMSK (BSURF_BOUNDARY_ELM)
#define TMSK1_BSPLINE_KNOT         ELMBITMSK (BSPLINE_KNOT_ELM)
#define TMSK1_BSPLINE_CURVE        ELMBITMSK (BSPLINE_CURVE_ELM)
#define TMSK1_BSPLINE_WEIGHT       ELMBITMSK (BSPLINE_WEIGHT_ELM)
/* These following masks must be 'OR'ed with typemask[2] */
#define TMSK2_DIMENSION            ELMBITMSK (DIMENSION_ELM)
#define TMSK2_SHAREDCELL_DEF       ELMBITMSK (SHAREDCELL_DEF_ELM)
#define TMSK2_SHARED_CELL          ELMBITMSK (SHARED_CELL_ELM)
#define TMSK2_MULTILINE            ELMBITMSK (MULTILINE_ELM)
/* These following masks must be 'OR'ed with typemask[3] */
#define TMSK3_TEXT_ARRAY           ELMBITMSK (TEXT_ARRAY_ELM)
#define TMSK3_TEXT_STACK           ELMBITMSK (TEXT_STACK_ELM)
/* These following masks must be 'OR'ed with typemask[5] */
#define     TMSK5_RASTER_HDR       ELMBITMSK (RASTER_HDR)
#define     TMSK5_RASTER_COMP      ELMBITMSK (RASTER_COMP)

/*-------------------------------------------------------------------------------------+
|      Level definitions                                              |
+-------------------------------------------------------------------------------------*/
#define         MSDIM_LEVEL             1
#define         MSREF_LEVEL             5
#define         MSLEVELNAME_LEVEL       6
#define         MSDIG_LEVEL             8
#define         MSTCB_LEVEL             9
```

```
#define          MSVIEW_LEVEL        7
#define          MSSTARTAPP_LEVEL   10

/* NOTE: database control elements have levels 11-19 reserved */
#define          MSDB_LEVEL          10       /* dBASE         */
#define          MSIX_LEVEL          11       /* Informix      */
#define          MSRIS_LEVEL         12       /* RIS           */
#define          MSORACLE_LEVEL      13       /* Oracle        */
#define          MSAPPINFO_LEVEL     20
#define          MSSTARTMDL_LEVEL    21
#define          MSMLINE_LEVEL       22
/*-----------------------------------------------------------------------+
|      Class definitions                                  |
+-----------------------------------------------------------------------*/
#define          PRIMARY_CLASS                0
#define          PATTERN_COMPONENT_CLASS      1
#define          CONSTRUCTION_CLASS           2
#define          DIMENSION_CLASS              3
#define          PRIMARY_RULE_CLASS           4
#define          LINEAR_PATTERNED_CLASS       5
#define          CONSTRUCTION_RULE_CLASS      6
/*-----------------------------------------------------------------------+
|      Element transformation structures                                 |
+-----------------------------------------------------------------------*/
typedef struct lTrans2d
    {
    long    t11;
    long    t12;
    long    t21;
    long    t22;
    } LTrans2d;

typedef struct lTrans3d
    {
    long    t11;
    long    t12;
    long    t13;
    long    t21;
    long    t22;
    long    t23;
    long    t31;
    long    t32;
    long    t33;
    } LTrans3d;


/*-----------------------------------------------------------------------+
|    Element Header structure - common to all MicroStation elements      |
+-----------------------------------------------------------------------*/
typedef struct elm_hdr
    {
```

```
#if !defined (mc68000)
    unsigned        level:6;     /* level element is on */
    unsigned        igresvd:1;   /* reserved by Intergraph */
    unsigned        complex:1;   /* part of complex element (cell) if set */
    unsigned        type:7;      /* type of element */
    unsigned        deleted:1;   /* set if element is deleted */
#else                            /* bit fields in reverse order for 680x0 */
    unsigned        deleted:1;   /* set if element is deleted */
    unsigned        type:7;      /* type of element */
    unsigned        complex:1;   /* part of complex element (cell) if set */
    unsigned        igresvd:1;   /* reserved by Intergraph */
    unsigned        level:6;     /* level element is on */
#endif
    unsigned short  words;   /* number of words to follow in element */
    unsigned long   xlow;    /* range of element - low (reversed longs) */
    unsigned long   ylow;
    unsigned long   zlow;
    unsigned long   xhigh;   /* range of element - high (reversed longs) */
    unsigned long   yhigh;
    unsigned long   zhigh;
    } Elm_hdr;
```

```
/*----------------------------------------------------------------------+
|   Extended Level Element Header Structure - used for 127 level cases   |
+----------------------------------------------------------------------*/
typedef struct extlev_hdr
    {
#if !defined (mc68000)
    unsigned        level:7;   /* level element is on */
    unsigned        complex:1; /* part of complex element (cell) if set */
    unsigned        type:7;    /* type of element */
    unsigned        deleted:1; /* set if element is deleted */
#else                          /* bit fields in reverse order for 680x0 */
    unsigned        deleted:1; /* set if element is deleted */
    unsigned        type:7;    /* type of element */
    unsigned        complex:1; /* part of complex element (cell) if set */
    unsigned        level:7;   /* level element is on */
#endif
    unsigned short  words;   /* number of words to follow in element */
    unsigned long   xlow;    /* range of element - low (reversed longs) */
    unsigned long   ylow;
    unsigned long   zlow;
    unsigned long   xhigh;   /* range of element - high (reversed longs) */
    unsigned long   yhigh;
    unsigned long   zhigh;
    } Extlev_hdr;
```

```
/*----------------------------------------------------------------------+
|   Display header - common to all displayed MicroStation elements       |
+----------------------------------------------------------------------*/
```

```
typedef struct disp_hdr
    {
    unsigned short  grphgrp;        /* graphics group number */
    short           attindx; /* words between this and attribute linkage */

    union
      {
      short      s;
      struct
        {
#if !defined (mc68000)
        unsigned class:4;     /* element class */
        unsigned :4;          /* reserved by Intergraph */
        unsigned l:1;         /* locked */
        unsigned n:1;         /* new */
        unsigned m:1;         /* modified */
        unsigned a:1;         /* attributes present */
        unsigned r:1;         /* relative to: 0=database 1=screen */
        unsigned p:1;         /* planar */
        unsigned s:1;         /* 0=snappable, 1=nonsnappable */
        unsigned h:1;         /* hole or solid (usually) */
#else
        unsigned h:1;         /* hole or solid (usually) */
        unsigned s:1;         /* 0=snappable, 1=nonsnappable */
        unsigned p:1;         /* planar */
        unsigned r:1;         /* relative to: 0=database 1=screen */
        unsigned a:1;         /* attributes present */
        unsigned m:1;         /* modified */
        unsigned n:1;         /* new */
        unsigned l:1;         /* locked */
        unsigned :4;          /* reserved by Intergraph */
        unsigned class:4;      /* element class */
#endif
        } b;
      } props;

    union
      {
      short      s;
      Symbology  b;
      } symb;

    } Disp_hdr;

typedef struct header
    {
    Elm_hdr    ehdr;
    Disp_hdr   dhdr;
    } Header;
/*-------------------------------------------------------------------+
```

```
|    Cell Library Header Element (type 1, only in cell libraries)            |
+---------------------------------------------------------------------------*/
typedef struct cell_lib_hdr
    {
    Elm_hdr        ehdr;          /* element header */
    short          celltype;      /* cell type */
    short          attindx;       /* attribute linkage */
    long           name;          /* radix-50 cell name */
    unsigned short numwords;      /* number of words in descriptions */
    short          properties;    /* properties */
    short          dispsymb;      /* display symbology */
    short          class;         /* cell class (always 0) */
    short          levels[4];     /* levels used in cell */
    short          descrip[9];    /* cell description */
    } Cell_Lib_Hdr;
/*-------------------------------------------------------------------------+
|    2-D Cell Element (complex element, type 2)                            |
+---------------------------------------------------------------------------*/
typedef struct cell_2d
    {
    Elm_hdr        ehdr;          /* element header */
    Disp_hdr       dhdr;          /* display header */
    unsigned short totlength;           /* total length of cell */
    long           name;          /* radix 50 name */
    short          class;         /* class bit map */
    short          levels[4];     /* levels used in cell */
    Point2d        rnglow;        /* range block lo */
    Point2d        rnghigh;       /* range block hi */
    LTrans2d       trans;         /* transformation matrix */
    Point2d        origin;        /* cell origin */
    } Cell_2d;
/*-------------------------------------------------------------------------+
|    3-D Cell Element (complex element, type 3)                            |
+---------------------------------------------------------------------------*/
typedef struct cell_3d
    {
    Elm_hdr        ehdr;          /* element header */
    Disp_hdr       dhdr;          /* display header */
    unsigned short totlength;           /* total length of cell */
    long           name;          /* radix 50 name */
    short          class;         /* class bit map */
    short          levels[4];     /* levels used in cell */
    Point3d        rnglow;        /* range block lo */
    Point3d        rnghigh;       /* range block hi */
    LTrans3d       trans;         /* transformation matrix */
    Point3d        origin;        /* cell origin */
    } Cell_3d;
/*-------------------------------------------------------------------------+
|    2-D Line Element (type 3)                                             |
+---------------------------------------------------------------------------*/
```

```
typedef struct line_2d
    {
    Elm_hdr  ehdr;        /* element header */
    Disp_hdr dhdr;        /* display header */
    Point2d  start;       /* starting point */
    Point2d  end;         /* ending point */
    } Line_2d;
/*---------------------------------------------------------------+
|    3-D Line Element (type 3)                                    |
+---------------------------------------------------------------*/
typedef struct line_3d
    {
    Elm_hdr  ehdr;        /* element header */
    Disp_hdr dhdr;        /* display header */
    Point3d  start;       /* starting point */
    Point3d  end;         /* ending point */
    } Line_3d;
/*---------------------------------------------------------------+
|    2-D Line String Element (type 4)                             |
|                                                                 |
|    Same structure represents 2-D Shape Elements (type 6), 2-D Curve |
|    Elements (type 11), and 2-D Conic Elements (type 13).  Shapes differ |
|    from line strings in that shape elements always start and end at |
|    the same point.  Curve and conic elements use the first and last |
|    vertices to establish the slope at the beginning and end.    |
+---------------------------------------------------------------*/
typedef struct line_string_2d
    {
    Elm_hdr  ehdr;          /* element header */
    Disp_hdr dhdr;          /* display header */
    short    numverts;      /* number of vertices */
    Point2d  vertice[1];    /* points */
    } Line_string_2d;
/*---------------------------------------------------------------+
|    3-D Line String Element (type 4)                             |
|    See comments for 2-D Line String Element.                    |
+---------------------------------------------------------------*/
typedef struct line_string_3d
    {
    Elm_hdr  ehdr;          /* element header */
    Disp_hdr dhdr;          /* display header */
    short    numverts;      /* number of vertices */
    Point3d  vertice[1];    /* points */
    } Line_string_3d;

/*---------------------------------------------------------------+
|    Reference File Attachment Element (type 5, level 9)          |
+---------------------------------------------------------------*/
typedef struct ref_file_type5
    {
```

```
    Elm_hdr  ehdr;                /* element header */
    Disp_hdr dhdr;                /* display header */
    short    file_chars;          /* number of characters in file spec */
    char     file_spec[65];       /* file specification */
    byte     file_num;            /* file number */
    Fb_opts  fb_opts;             /* file builder options mask */
    Fd_opts  fd_opts;             /* file displayer options mask */
    byte     disp_flags[16];      /* display flags */
    short    lev_flags[8][4];     /* level on/of flags */
    long     ref_org[3];          /* origin in reference file uors */
    double   trns_mtrx[9];        /* transformation matrix */
    double   cnvrs_fact;          /* conversion factor */
    long     mast_org[3];         /* origin in master file uors */
    short    log_chars;           /* characters in logical name */
    char     log_name[22];        /* logical name (padded) */
    short    desc_chars;          /* characters in description */
    char     description[42];     /* description (padded) */
    short    lev_sym_mask;        /* level symbology enable mask */
    short    lev_sym[63];         /* level symbology descriptor */
    long     z_delta;             /* Z-direction delta */
    short    clip_vertices;       /* clipping vertices */
    Point2d  clip_poly[1];        /* clipping polygon */
    } Ref_file_type5;
/*---------------------------------------------------------------+
|   Named view element (type 5, level 3)                         |
+---------------------------------------------------------------*/
typedef struct named_view_type5
    {
    Elm_hdr  ehdr;                /* element header */
    short    grphgrp;             /* graphics group number */
    short    attindx;             /* words between this and attrb linkage */
    short    properties;          /* property bits (always the same) */
#if !defined (mc68000)
    unsigned short num_views:3;   /* number of views */
    unsigned short reserved:13;   /* reserved for Intergraph */
#else
    unsigned short reserved:13;   /* reserved for Intergraph */
    unsigned short num_views:3;   /* number of views */
#endif
    char     viewdef_descr[18];   /* view definition description */
    byte     full_scr1;
    byte     full_scr2;
    Viewinfo view[1];
    char     rest_of_elem[1];     /* record has variable length */
    } Named_view_type5;
/*---------------------------------------------------------------+
|   Color table element (type 5, level 1)                        |
+---------------------------------------------------------------*/
typedef struct color_table_type5
    {
```

```
    Elm_hdr  ehdr;         /* element header */
    Disp_hdr dhdr;         /* display header */
    short    screen_flag;  /* screen flag */
    byte     color_info[1]; /* color table information */
    } Color_table_type5;
/*-------------------------------------------------------------------+
|    short pattern (type 5, level 0)                                 |
+-------------------------------------------------------------------*/
typedef struct short_pattern_type5
    {
    Elm_hdr  ehdr;         /* element header */
    Disp_hdr dhdr;         /* display header */
    short    indicator;
    long     name;
    double   scale;
    double   angle;
    long     row_spacing;
    long     column_spacing;
    } Short_pattern_type5;
/*-------------------------------------------------------------------+
|    long pattern (type 5, level 0)                                  |
+-------------------------------------------------------------------*/
typedef struct long_pattern_type5
    {
    Elm_hdr      ehdr;            /* element header */
    Disp_hdr     dhdr;            /* display header */
    short        indicator;
    long         name;
    double       scale;
    double       angle;
    long         row_spacing;
    long         column_spacing;
    Seven_wd_lknm  library;       /* file spec */
    Symbology     symbology;
    short         fbfdcn;
    byte          master_type;
    byte          request_type;
    Point2d       idpoint;
    Point2d       accpoint;
    } Long_pattern_type5;
/*-------------------------------------------------------------------+
|    Auxilliary Coordinate System (type 5, level 3)                  |
+-------------------------------------------------------------------*/
typedef struct aux_coordinate
    {
    Elm_hdr  ehdr;         /* element hdr (origin stored in range) */
    short    grphgrp;      /* graphics group number */
    short    attindx;      /* words between this and attrb linkage */
    short    properties;   /* property bits (always the same) */
#if !defined (mc68000)
```

```
    unsigned short type:3;           /* number of views */
    unsigned short reserved:13;  /* reserved for Intergraph */
#else
    unsigned short reserved:13;  /* reserved for Intergraph */
    unsigned short type:3;           /* number of views */
#endif
    char    description[18];     /* definition description */
    double  trans[3][3];
    short   attribute;           /* 0001000000000011 */
    short   user_id;             /* always 22 */
    long    name;                /* 6 characters stored RAD50 */
    } Aux_coordinate;

/*------------------------------------------------------------------+
|   2-D Text Node Element (complex element, type 7)                 |
+-------------------------------------------------------------------*/
typedef struct text_node_2d
    {
    Elm_hdr     ehdr;          /* element header */
    Disp_hdr    dhdr;          /* display header */
    unsigned short  totwords;  /* total words following (cmplx ele) */
    short           numstrngs; /* number of text strings in node */
    unsigned short  nodenumber; /* text node number */
    byte            maxlngth;  /* maximum length allowed */
    byte            maxused;   /* maximum length used */
    byte            font;      /* text font used */
    byte            just;      /* justification type */
    long            linespc;   /* line spacing */
    long            lngthmult; /* length multiplier */
    long            hghtmult;  /* height multiplier */
    long            rotation;  /* rotation angle */
    Point2d         origin;    /* origin */
    } Text_node_2d;
/*------------------------------------------------------------------+
|   3-D Text Node Element (complex element, type 7)                 |
+-------------------------------------------------------------------*/
/* Text Node Element (note: this is a complex element) */
typedef struct text_node_3d
    {
    Elm_hdr     ehdr;          /* element header */
    Disp_hdr    dhdr;          /* display header */
    unsigned short  totwords;  /* total words following (cmplx ele) */
    short           numstrngs; /* number of text strings in node */
    unsigned short  nodenumber;/* text node number */
    byte            maxlngth;  /* maximum length allowed */
    byte            maxused;   /* maximum length used */
    byte            font;      /* text font used */
    byte            just;      /* justification type */
    long            linespc;   /* line spacing */
    long            lngthmult; /* length multiplier */
```

```
    long          hghtmult;       /* height multiplier */
    long          quat[4];        /* quaternion rotations */
    Point3d       origin;         /* origin */
    } Text_node_3d;
```

/*---+
| Design file header (type 9) |
+---*/

```
typedef struct dgn_header
    {
    Elm_hdr       ehdr;           /* element header */
    short         tcbinfo[1];     /* tcb information */
    } Dgn_header;
```

/*---+
| Complex string (type 12, complex) |
+---*/

```
typedef struct complex_string
    {
    Elm_hdr       ehdr;           /* element header */
    Disp_hdr      dhdr;           /* display header */
    unsigned short totlength;      /* total length of surface */
    unsigned short numelems;       /* number of elements in surface */
    short         attributes[4];  /* to reach minimum elem size */
    } Complex_string;
```

/*---+
| 2-D Ellipse Element (type 15) |
+---*/

```
typedef struct ellipse_2d
    {
    Elm_hdr       ehdr;           /* element header */
    Disp_hdr      dhdr;           /* display header */
    double        primary;        /* primary axis */
    double        secondary;      /* secondary axis */
    long          rotation;       /* rotation angle */
    Dpoint2d      origin;         /* origin */
    } Ellipse_2d;
```

/*---+
| 3-D Ellipse Element (type 15) |
+---*/

```
typedef struct ellipse_3d
    {
    Elm_hdr       ehdr;           /* element header */
    Disp_hdr      dhdr;           /* display header */
    double        primary;        /* primary axis */
    double        secondary;      /* secondary axis */
    long          quat[4];        /* quaternion rotations */
    Dpoint3d      origin;         /* origin */
    } Ellipse_3d;
```

/*---+
| 2-D Arc Element (type 16) |

```
+--------------------------------------------------------------------*/
typedef struct arc_2d
    {
    Elm_hdr       ehdr;
    Disp_hdr      dhdr;
    long          startang;       /* start angle */
    long          sweepang;       /* sweep angle */
    double        primary;        /* primary axis */
    double        secondary;      /* secondary axis */
    long          rotation;       /* rotation angle */
    Dpoint2d      origin;         /* origin */
    } Arc_2d;
/*------------------------------------------------------------------+
|    3-D Arc Element (type 16)                                      |
+--------------------------------------------------------------------*/
typedef struct arc_3d
    {
    Elm_hdr       ehdr;
    Disp_hdr      dhdr;
    long          startang;       /* start angle */
    long          sweepang;       /* sweep angle */
    double        primary;        /* primary axis */
    double        secondary;      /* secondary axis */
    long          quat[4];        /* quaternion rotations */
    Dpoint3d      origin;         /* origin */
    } Arc_3d;
/*------------------------------------------------------------------+
|    2-D Text Element (type 17)                                     |
+--------------------------------------------------------------------*/
typedef struct text_2d
    {
    Elm_hdr       ehdr;           /* element header */
    Disp_hdr      dhdr;           /* display header */
    byte          font;           /* text font used */
    byte          just;           /* justification type */
    long          lngthmult;      /* length multiplier */
    long          hghtmult;       /* height multiplier */
    long          rotation;       /* rotation angle */
    Point2d       origin;         /* origin */
    byte          numchars;       /* # of characters */
    byte          edflds;         /* # of enter data fields */
    char          string[2];      /* characters */
    } Text_2d;
/*------------------------------------------------------------------+
|    3-D Text Element (type 17)                                     |
+--------------------------------------------------------------------*/
typedef struct text_3d
    {
    Elm_hdr       ehdr;           /* element header */
    Disp_hdr      dhdr;           /* display header */
```

```
    byte          font;           /* text font used */
    byte          just;           /* justification type */
    long          lngthmult;      /* length multiplier */
    long          hghtmult;       /* height multiplier */
    long          quat[4];        /* quartion angle */
    Point3d       origin;         /* origin */
    byte          numchars;       /* # of characters */
    byte          edflds;         /* # of enter data fields */
    char          string[2];      /* characters */
    } Text_3d;
/*------------------------------------------------------------------+
|    Surface (type 18, complex)        3d only                      |
+------------------------------------------------------------------*/
typedef struct surface
    {
    Elm_hdr       ehdr;           /* element header */
    Disp_hdr      dhdr;           /* display header */
    unsigned short  totlength;/* total length of surface */
    unsigned short  numelems; /* number of elements in surface */
    byte          surftype;       /* surface type */
    byte          boundelms;      /* number of boundary elements */
#ifdef unix
    short         filler;         /* needed for proper alignment */
#endif
    short         attributes[4];  /* attribute data */
    } Surface;
/*------------------------------------------------------------------+
|    2-D  B-Spline pole element (type 21)                           |
+------------------------------------------------------------------*/
typedef struct bspline_poles_2d
    {
    Elm_hdr       ehdr;           /* element header */
    Disp_hdr      dhdr;           /* display header */
    short         numpoles;       /* number of poles */
    Point2d       poles[1];       /* points */
    } Bspline_pole_2d;
/*------------------------------------------------------------------+
|    3-D  B-Spline pole element (type 21)                           |
+------------------------------------------------------------------*/
typedef struct bspline_pole_3d
    {
    Elm_hdr       ehdr;           /* element header */
    Disp_hdr      dhdr;           /* display header */
    short         numpoles;       /* number of poles */
    Point3d       poles[1];       /* points */
    } Bspline_pole_3d;


/*------------------------------------------------------------------+
|    Circular truncated cone  (type 23)      3-D files only         |
+------------------------------------------------------------------*/
```

```
        typedef struct cone_3d
            {
            Elm_hdr        ehdr;           /* element header */
            Disp_hdr       dhdr;           /* display header */
            struct
                {
        #if !defined (mc68000)
            unsigned short          type:3;         /* cone type */
            unsigned short          rsrv:12;        /* reserved */
            unsigned short          surf:1;         /* 0 = solid, 1 = surface */
        #else
            unsigned short          surf:1;         /* 0 = solid, 1 = surface */
            unsigned short          rsrv:12;        /* reserved */
            unsigned short          type:3;         /* cone type */
        #endif
                } b;
            long           quat[4];        /* orientation quaternion */
            Dpoint3d       center_1;       /* center of first circle */
            double         radius_1;       /* radius of first circle */
            Dpoint3d       center_2;       /* center of second circle */
            double         radius_2;       /* radius of second cirele */
            } Cone_3d;
        /*-------------------------------------------------------------------+
        |   Bspline flags                                                    |
        +-------------------------------------------------------------------*/
        typedef struct     bspline_flags
            {
        #if !defined (mc68000)
            unsigned short order:4;              /* order - 2*/
            unsigned short curve_display:1;      /* curve display flag */
            unsigned short poly_display:1;       /* polygon display flag */
            unsigned short rational:1;           /* rationalization flag */
            unsigned short closed:1;             /* closed curve flag */
            unsigned short curve_type:8;/* curve type */
        #else
            unsigned short curve_type:8;/* curve type */
            unsigned short closed:1;             /* closed curve flag */
            unsigned short rational:1;           /* rationalization flag */
            unsigned short poly_display:1;       /* polygon display flag */
            unsigned short curve_display:1;      /* curve display flag */
            unsigned short order:4;              /* order - 2 */
        #endif
            } Bspline_flags;
        /*-------------------------------------------------------------------+
        |   Bspline surface flags                                            |
        +-------------------------------------------------------------------*/
        typedef struct bsurf_flags
            {
        #ifndef mc68000
            unsigned short v_order:4;                    /* b-spline order - 2 (v Direction)*/
```

```
    unsigned short reserved1:2;             /* reserved */
    unsigned short arcSpacing:1;            /* rule lines spaced by arc length */
    unsigned short v_closed:1;              /* closed curve flag */
    unsigned short reserved2:8;             /* reserved */
#else
    unsigned short reserved2:8;             /* reserved */
    unsigned short v_closed:1;              /* closed curve flag */
    unsigned short arcSpacing:1;            /* rule lines spaced by arc length */
    unsigned short reserved1:2;             /* reserved */
    unsigned short v_order:4;               /* b-spline order (v Direction)*/
#endif
    } Bsurf_flags;
/*-----------------------------------------------------------------+
|   Bspline surface header (type 24)                               |
+-----------------------------------------------------------------*/
typedef struct bspline_surface
    {
    Elm_hdr         ehdr;           /* element header */
    Disp_hdr        dhdr;           /* display header */
    long            desc_words;     /* # words in description */
    Bspline_flags   flags;          /* miscellaneous flags */
    short           num_poles_u;    /* number of poles */
    short           num_knots_u;    /* number of knots */
    short           rule_lines_u;   /* number of rule lines */
    Bsurf_flags         bsurf_flags;    /* bspline surface flags */
    short           num_poles_v;    /* number of poles */
    short           num_knots_v;    /* number of knots */
    short           rule_lines_v;   /* number of rule lines */
    short           num_bounds;             /* number of boundaries */
    } Bspline_surface;
/*-----------------------------------------------------------------+
|   B-spline Surface boundary (type 25)                            |
+-----------------------------------------------------------------*/
typedef struct bsurf_boundary
    {
    Elm_hdr         ehdr;           /* element header */
    Disp_hdr        dhdr;           /* display header */
    short           number;         /* boundary number */
    short           numverts;       /* number of boundary vertices */
    Point2d         vertices[1];    /* boundary points (in UV space) */
    } Bsurf_boundary;
/*-----------------------------------------------------------------+
|   B-spline weight factor (type 26)                               |
+-----------------------------------------------------------------*/
typedef struct bspline_weight
    {
    Elm_hdr         ehdr;           /* element header */
    Disp_hdr        dhdr;           /* display header */
    long            weights[1];     /* bspline weights (variable length) */
    } Bspline_weight;
```

```
/*------------------------------------------------------------------+
|    B-spline curve header   (type 27)                              |
+------------------------------------------------------------------*/
typedef struct bpsline_curve
    {
    Elm_hdr        ehdr;              /* element header */
    Disp_hdr       dhdr;              /* display header */
    long           desc_words;        /* # words in description */
    Bspline_flags  flags;             /* miscellaneous flags */
    short          num_poles;         /* number of poles */
    short          num_knots;         /* number of knots */
    } Bspline_curve;
/*------------------------------------------------------------------+
|    B-spline knot vector (type 28)                                 |
+------------------------------------------------------------------*/
typedef struct bspline_knot
    {
    Elm_hdr        ehdr;              /* element header */
    Disp_hdr       dhdr;              /* display header */
    long           knots[1];          /* knots (variable length) */
    } Bspline_knot;
/*------------------------------------------------------------------+
|    Shared Cell Instance (type 35) - complete definition unpublished |
+------------------------------------------------------------------*/
typedef struct scOverride
    {
    unsigned short level:1;   /* level override (true for pnt cells)  */
    unsigned short relative:1;/* relative or absolute*/
    unsigned short class:1;   /* class value */
    unsigned short color:1;   /* color of all components */
    unsigned short weight:1;  /* weight of all components */
    unsigned short style:1;   /* style of all components */
    unsigned short assocPnt:1;/* origin of cell is associative point */
    unsigned short unused:9;
    } scOverride;
/*------------------------------------------------------------------+
| name             element_union - union of all element types       |
+------------------------------------------------------------------*/
typedef union msElementUnion
    {
    Cell_Lib_Hdr   cell_lib_hdr;
    Cell_2d        cell_2d;
    Cell_3d        cell_3d;
    Line_2d        line_2d;
    Line_3d        line_3d;
    Line_String_2d line_string_2d;
    Line_String_3d line_string_3d;
    Text_node_2d   text_node_2d;
    Text_node_3d   text_node_3d;
    Complex_string complex_string;
```

```
    Ellipse_2d      ellipse_2d;
    Ellipse_3d      ellipse_3d;
    Arc_2d          arc_2d;
    Arc_3d          arc_3d;
    Text_2d         text_2d;
    Text_3d         text_3d;
    Cone_3d         cone_3d;
    Surface         surf;
    Bspline_pole_2d bspline_pole_2d;
    Bspline_pole_3d bspline_pole_3d;
    Bspline_curve   bspline_curve;
    Bspline_surface bspline_surface;
    Bspline_weight  bspline_weight;
    Bspline_knot    bspline_knot;
    Bsurf_boundary  bsurf_boundary;
    short           tmp[768];
#if defined (ip32)
    short           buf[780];
#else
    short           buf[780];
#endif
    Extlev_hdr      extlevhdr;
    Elm_hdr         ehdr;
    Header          hdr;
    } MSElementUnion, MSElement;
/*------------------------------------------------------------------+
|    Element Descriptor structure                                   |
+------------------------------------------------------------------*/
typedef struct msElementDescr MSElementDescr;
struct msElementDescr
    {
    struct
    {
    MSElementDescr *next;        /* ptr to first entry in list */
    MSElementDescr *previous;    /* ptr to last entry in list */
    MSElementDescr *myHeader;    /* ptr to my hdr (NULL = not cmplx) */
    MSElementDescr *firstElem;   /* ptr to first element if header */
    int            isHeader;     /* is this a complex header */
    int            isValid;      /* INTERNAL USE ONLY */
    long           userData1;    /* available for user */
    long           userData2;    /* available for user */
    } h;
    MSElement      el;           /* elem data (hdr only if complex) */
    };
```

```
/*----------------------------------------------------------------------+
|    scanner.h -- Typedefs and Defines for using the design file        |
|       "scanner".  The scanner can quickly locate elements             |
|               based on predefined criteria.                           |
+----------------------------------------------------------------------*/
/* bits used in scantype */
#define ELEMDATA      0x0001 /* if true, store data */
#define NESTCELL      0x0002 /* if true, cell is treated as one element */
#define PICKCELL      0x0004 /* if true, compare cell name */
#define PROPCLAS      0x0008 /* if true, compare on properties and class */
#define GRPHGRP       0x0010 /* if true, compare on graphics group */
#define MULTI         0x0020 /* if true, there are multiple scan ranges */
#define SKEW          0x0040 /* if true, do a skew scan */
#define BOTH          0x0080 /* if true, get both pointers and data */
#define ONEELEM       0x0100 /* if true, get only one element */
#define ATTRENT       0x0400 /* if true, compare on attrb linkage entity */
#define ATTROCC       0x0800 /* if true, compare on attrb occurence # */
#define STOPSECT      0x1000 /* if true, check stop sector */
#define LEVELS        0x2000 /* if true, compare on levels */
#define ELEMTYPE      0x4000 /* if true, compare on element type */
/* bits used in extendedtype */
#define RETURN3D      0x0001 /* if true, return 3D elements from 2D file */
#define FILEPOS       0x0002 /* if true, return file pos, not block/byte */
#define MEMPTRS       0x0004 /* if true, return mem pointers or elements */
#define EXTATTR       0x0008 /* if true, do extended attribute scan */
/* Properties Indicators */
#define ELELOCKED     0x0100 /* set if locked */
#define ELENEW        0x0200 /* set if new */
#define ELEMOD        0x0400 /* set if modified */
#define ELEATTR       0x0800 /* attribute data present */
#define ELERELTVE     0x1000 /* set if relative to database */
#define ELEPLANR      0x2000 /* set if planar */
#define ELESNAP       0x4000 /* set if element is snappable */
#define ELEHOLE       0x8000 /* set if element is a hole */
/* Scanner error messages */
#define           END_OF_DGN        10
#define           BUFF_FULL         11
#define           READ_LIMIT        12

typedef struct scanrange
    {
    unsigned long   xlowlim;
    unsigned long   ylowlim;
    unsigned long   zlowlim;
    unsigned long   xhighlim;
    unsigned long   yhighlim;
    unsigned long   zhighlim;
    } Scanrange;
typedef struct
    {
```

```
    int             filePos;
    unsigned short  *element;
    } PtrPair;
typedef struct
    {
    short           numWords;    /* number of words of attr data to consider */
    unsigned short  extAttData[32];
    } ExtendedAttrBuf;
typedef struct extScanlist
    {
    short           sllen;       /* scan list length */
    unsigned short  scantype;    /* scan type (see bit definitions above) */
    unsigned short  tplval;      /* value for type/plane/level register */
    unsigned short  tplmsk;      /* mask for type/plane/level */
    unsigned long   xlowlim;     /* lower limit (main scan range) */
    unsigned long   ylowlim;
    unsigned long   zlowlim;
    unsigned long   xhighlim;    /* upper limit */
    unsigned long   yhighlim;
    unsigned long   zhighlim;
    union
        {
        unsigned short          propval;
        unsigned short          cell0;
        } pcl;
    union
        {
        unsigned short          propmsk;
        unsigned short          cell1;
        } pch;
    unsigned short  grgroup;
    unsigned short  sector;      /* sector at start */
    unsigned short  offset;      /* byte at start */
    short           ellength;    /* len of elmnt that wont fit (not used) */
    unsigned short  entity;
    unsigned short  clasmsk;
    unsigned short  levmask[8];
    unsigned short  typmask[8];
    long            occurnce;
    unsigned short  stopsector;  /* stop on this sector */
    unsigned short  extendedType; /* extended scan type bits */
    Dpoint3d        skewVector;  /* skew direction vector */
    Scanrange       exrange[8];  /* extended range blocks */
    ExtendedAttrBuf *extAttrBuf; /* extended attribute scanning */
    } ExtScanlist, Scanlist;
typedef struct
    {
    ExtScanlist scanlist;
    short       extrawords[100];
    } ScanContext;
```

```
/*-------------------------------------------------------------------+
|    tcb.h -- Typedefs and Defines for the MicroStation "terminal    |
|         control block".  This data structure basically contains    |
|         all of the "current" information about the design file      |
|         being edited.                                              |
+-------------------------------------------------------------------*/
#define MSVERSION        0x400    /* MicroStation Version 4.0.0 */

typedef struct ext_dimflags
     {
#if !defined (mc68000)
     unsigned joiner:1;
     unsigned boxtext:1;
     unsigned semiauto:1;
     unsigned leading_zero:1;
     unsigned trailing_zeros:1;
     unsigned decimal_comma:1;
     unsigned captext:1;
     unsigned superscriptLSD:1;
     unsigned roundLSD:1;
     unsigned omitLeadingDelimeter:1;
     unsigned colorOverride:1;
     unsigned weightOverride:1;
     unsigned textColorOverride:1;
     unsigned textWeightOverride:1;
     unsigned fontOverride:1;
     unsigned levelOverride:1;
     unsigned textSizeOverride:1;
     unsigned compatible:1;           /* If set place as IGDS primitives */
     unsigned arrowhead:2;            /* 0=Open, 1=Closed, 2=Filled */
     unsigned useRefUnits:1;          /* 1-use reference file units */
     unsigned relDimLine:1;
     unsigned underlineText:1;
     unsigned styleOverride:1;
     unsigned noAutoTextLift:1;
     unsigned arrowOut:1;             /* Reverse terminators (JIS) */
     unsigned unused2:6;
#else
     unsigned unused2:6;
     unsigned arrowOut:1;
     unsigned noAutoTextLift:1;
     unsigned styleOverride:1;
     unsigned underlineText:1;
     unsigned relDimLine:1;
     unsigned useRefUnits:1;
     unsigned arrowhead:2;
     unsigned msDimensionElm:1;
     unsigned textSizeOverride:1;
     unsigned levelOverride:1;
     unsigned fontOverride:1;
```

```
    unsigned textWeightOverride:1;
    unsigned textColorOverride:1;
    unsigned weightOverride:1;
    unsigned colorOverride:1;
    unsigned omitLeadingDelimeter:1;
    unsigned roundLSD:1;
    unsigned superscriptLSD:1;
    unsigned captext: 1;
    unsigned decimal_comma:1;
    unsigned trailing_zeros:1;
    unsigned leading_zero:1;
    unsigned semiauto:1;
    unsigned boxtext:1;
    unsigned joiner:1;
#endif
    } Ext_dimflags;

typedef struct dim_template
    {
#if !defined (mc68000)
    unsigned first_term:3;
    unsigned left_term:3;
    unsigned right_term:3;
    unsigned bowtie_symbol:3;
    unsigned pre_symbol:3;
    unsigned stacked:1;
    unsigned post_symbol:3;
    unsigned above_symbol:3;
    unsigned left_witness:1;
    unsigned right_witness:1;
    unsigned vertical_text:1;
    unsigned nofit_vertical:1;
    unsigned centermark: 1;
    unsigned centerLeft:1;
    unsigned centerRight:1;
    unsigned centerTop:1;
    unsigned centerBottom:1;
    unsigned reserved:1;
#else
    unsigned reserved:1;
    unsigned centerBottom:1;
    unsigned centerTop:1;
    unsigned centerRight:1;
    unsigned centerLeft:1;
    unsigned centermark:1;
    unsigned nofit_vertical:1;
    unsigned vertical_text:1;
    unsigned right_witness:1;
    unsigned left_witness:1;
    unsigned above_symbol:3;
```

```
      unsigned post_symbol:3;
      unsigned stacked:1;
      unsigned pre_symbol:3;
      unigned bowtle_symbol:3;
      unsigned right_term:3;
      unsigned left_term:3;
      unsigned first_term:3;
#endif
    } Dim_template;

typedef struct autodim1
    {
    byte        english;    /* english format accuracy  */
    byte        metric;     /* metric format accuracy   */
    struct
      {
#if !defined (mc68000)
      UShort    level:8;    /* auto dimensioning placement level */
      UShort    parallel:2;
      UShort    automan:1;
      UShort    term:1;
      UShort    witness:1;
      UShort    just:2;
      UShort    labang:1;
#else
      unsigned  labang:1;
      unsigned  just:2;
      unsigned  witness:1;
      unsigned  term:1;
      unsigned  automan:1;
      unsigned  parallel:2;
      unsigned  level:8;    /* auto dimensioning placement level    */
#endif
      } mode;
#if defined (unix)
    short dummy1;
#endif
    struct
      {
#if !defined (mc68000)
      UShort    actlev:8;      /* active level */
      UShort    metric:1;      /* use metric system as primary */
      UShort    dual:1;        /* dimensioning measurement system */
      UShort    tolerance:1;   /* tolerance generation */
      UShort    tolmode:1;     /* tolerancing mode */
      UShort    embedded:1;    /* text placement mode */
      UShort    horizontal:1;  /* horizontal text */
      UShort    aec:1;         /* mechanical or aec dimensioning */
      UShort    reserved:1;
#else
```

```
        unsigned  reserved:1;
        unsigned  aec:1;              /* mechanical or aec dimensioning */
        unsigned  horizontal:1;       /* horizontal text */
        unsigned  embedded:1;         /* text placement mode */
        unsigned  tolmode:1;          /* tolerancing mode */
        unsigned  tolerance:1;        /* tolerance generation */
        unsigned  dual:1;             /* dimensioning measurement system */
        unsigned  metric:1;           /* use metric system as primary */
        unsigned  actlev:8;           /* active level */
#endif
        } params;                     /* auto dimensioning parameters  */

#if defined (unix)
    short dummy2;
#endif

    struct
        {
#if !defined (mc68000)
        UShort    adres2:8;
        UShort    ref_mastersub:2;
        UShort    ref_decfract:1;
        UShort    adp_subunits:1;
        UShort    adp_label:1;
        UShort    adp_delimiter:1;
        UShort    reserved:2;
#else
        unsigned  reserved:2;
        unsigned  adp_delimiter:1;
        unsigned  adp_label:1;
        unsigned  adp_subunits:1;
        unsigned  ref_decfract:1;
        unsigned  ref_mastersub:2;
        unsigned  adres2:8;
#endif
        } format;
#if defined (unix)
    short dummy3;
#endif
    } Autodim1;

typedef struct autodim2
    {
    byte            arrfont; /* font for active arrowhead terminator */
    byte            arrhead; /* active arrowhead */
    byte            oblqfont; /* font number for oblique terminator  */
    byte            oblique;  /* oblique terminator */
    byte            cofont;   /* font # for common origin terminator */
    byte            comorg;   /* common origin terminator */
    byte            diamfont;     /* font number for diameter terminator */
```

```
    byte            diam;              /* diameter terminator */
    ULong           txheight;          /* text height */
    long            lowtol;            /* lower tolerance */
    long            uptol;             /* upper tolerance */
    } Autodim2;

typedef struct
    {
    byte            angle;             /* angle readout specification */
    byte            refdispl;          /* refresh display  */
    } Autodim3;

typedef struct autodim4
    {
    double          toltxt_scale;      /* Size of tolerance text    (*th) */
    double          witness_offset;    /* Length of witness offset  (*th) */
    double          witness_extend;    /* Length or witness extension (*th) */
    double          dimension_scale;   /* Text value scale factor   (*th) */
    double          text_margin;       /* Minimum leader with text inside(*th) */
    Ext_dimflags    ext_dimflg;        /* 32 bit bit field */
    Dim_template    dim_template[24];  /* Dimension command/tool settings */
    long            stack_offset;      /* Optional stack offset (uors) */
    long            dimcen;            /* Optional center mark size (uors) */
    short           curr_dimcmd;       /* Dimension command/template index */

    struct
      {
      char          main_prefix;       /* Optional prefix char for main text */
      char          main_suffix;       /* Optional suffix char for main text */
      char          tol_prefix;        /* Optional prefix char for tolerance */
      char          tol_suffix;        /* Optional suffix char for tolerance */
      char          upper_prefix;      /* Optional prefix char for upper text */
      char          upper_suffix;      /* Optional suffix char for upper text */
      char          lower_prefix;      /* Optional prefix char for lower text */
      char          lower_suffix;      /* Optional suffix char for lower text */
      } dimtxt;

    byte            dim_color;         /* Optional dimension element color */
    byte            dim_weight;        /* Optional dimension element weight */
    byte            dimtxt_color;      /* Optional dimension text color */
    byte            dimtxt_weight;     /* Optional dimension text weight */
    byte            dimfont;           /* Optional dimension text font */
    byte            bowtie_font;       /* Optional font for joint terminator */
    byte            bowtie_symbol;     /* Optional char for joint terminator */
    byte            dim_style;         /* Optional dimension element style */
    } Autodim4;

typedef struct
    {                                  /* *th - Units = text height      */
    double                      textMarginV;/* Text dist above dimension line (*th) */
```

```
    double              textMarginH;/* Text dist from leader end       (*th) */
    double              tolMarginV; /* Tolerance dist from text base   (*th) */
    double              tolMarginH; /* Space from text to tolerance    (*th) */
    double              tolSepV;    /* Vert space between tol values    (*th) */
    double              termHeight; /* Height of terminator tile       (*th) */
    double              termWidth;  /* Width of terminator tile        (*th) */
    ULong               textWidth;  /* Dimension text width (uors)          */
    struct
        {
        UShort          useWidth:1; /* If set use ad5 text width over active*/
    UShort    altStyle:1;           /* Use alt style */
    UShort    altWeight:1;          /* Use alt weight*/
    UShort    altColor:1;           /* Use alt color */
    UShort    useSecUnits:1;        /* Use optionsl secondary units */
    UShort    reserved1:11;
    UShort    reserved2:16;
        } flags;
    struct
        {
    UShort    style:3;      /* Alternate line style  */
    UShort    weight:5;     /* Alternate line weight */
    UShort    color:8;      /* Alternate line color */
        } altSymb;
    byte  reserved[2];
    struct                          /* Optional secondary unit definition */
        {                           /* for override in dual dimension */
    ULong     subPerMast;   /* Sub-units per master unit   */
    ULong     uorPerSub;    /* uors per sub unit    */
    char      mastName[2];  /* Master units name    */
    char      subName[2];   /* Sub units name */
        } secUnits;
    } Autodim5;

typedef struct             /* Replacement dimension symbols/terminators */
    {
    struct
        {                           /* Flag values:       */
    UShort    arrow:4;              /* 0 - None. Use built in terminator/symbol */
    UShort    stroke:4;             /* 1 - Symbol from font    */
    UShort    origin:4;             /* 2 - Shared cell  */
    UShort    dot:4;                /* */
    UShort    prefix:4;             /* Dimension prefix */
    UShort    suffix:4;             /* Dimension suffix */
    UShort    diameter:4;           /* Diameter symbol */
    UShort    plusMinus:4;          /* Plus/Minus symbol */
    UShort    res2:16;
    UShort    res3:16;
        } flags;

    long          arrow;       /* Cell name for replacement arrow (Radix50) */
```

```
        long        stroke;      /* Cell name for replacement stroke(Radix50) */
        long        origin;      /* Cell name for replacement origin(Radix50) */
        long        dot;         /* Cell name for replacement dot    (Radix50) */
        long        prefix;      /* Cell name for dimension prefix   (Radix50) */
        long        suffix;      /* Cell name for dimension suffix   (Radix50) */
        byte        preChar;     /* Replacement prefic character     */
        byte        preFont;     /* Replacement prefix font          */
        byte        sufChar;     /* Replacement suffix character     */
        byte        sufFont;     /* Replacement suffix font          */
        byte        pmChar;      /* Replacement Plus/Minus character */
        byte        res1[3];
        long        reserved[6];
        } Autodim6;

typedef struct
        {
        UShort    style:3;            /* Optional line style    */
        UShort    weight:5;           /* Optional line weight   */
        UShort    color:8;            /* Optional line color    */
        UShort    useStyle:1;         /* Use optional style     */
        UShort    useWeight:1;        /* Use optional weight    */
        UShort    useColor:1;         /* Use optional color     */
        UShort    capInArc:1;         /* Show cap inner arcs    */
        UShort    capOutArc:1;        /* Show cap outer arcs    */
        UShort    capLine:1;          /* Show cap line      */
        UShort    useClass:1;         /* Use class bit over display header */
        UShort    reserved:1;
        UShort    level:7;            /* Optional line level (0 for default)  */
        UShort    conClass:1;         /* Line is construction class  */
        } MlineSymbology;

typedef struct
        {
        long            dist;   /* Line distance from work line       */
        MlineSymbology symb;    /* Line symbology      */
        } MlineProfile;

typedef struct                  /* Current Multiline settings         */
        {                       /* ** TYPEDEF IS USED IN STYLE FILE    */
        double          orgAngle;     /* Origin cap angle     */
        double          endAngle;     /* End cap angle     */
        MlineProfile    profile[16];  /* Profiles          */
        MlineSymbology  orgCap;       /* Origin cap symbology */
        MlineSymbology  endCap;       /* End cap symbology*/
        MlineSymbology  midCap;       /* Joint line symbology*/

        long            orgRadius;  /* Origin cap arc radius */
        long            endRadius;  /* End cap arc radius*/
        long     height;    /* Multiline height (in z direction)*/
        byte     nLines;    /* Number of lines per segment */
```

```
    byte        fillColor;  /* Color for filled multilines       */
    struct
      {
      UShort    compatible:1;/* Place multilines as IGDS primitives */
      UShort    filled:1;
      UShort    reserved:14;
      } flags;
    byte              reserved2[4];
    } MultilineTCB;

typedef struct        /* Information about current element    */
    {                 /*      filled in by locate function    */
    Dpoint3d   point;             /* Point on located element   */
    ULong      filePos;           /* File position of located element */
    byte       elemType;          /* Type of element located    */
    short      elemNumber;        /* Number of element (if compound) */
    union                         /* Element specific information */
        {
      double          reserved[12];
        struct                    /* Line string locate information */
          {
          Dvector3d segPoints;    /* Closest segment points */
          byte      vertex;       /* Closest vertex to locate point */
          byte      segment;      /* Located segment (zero based)*/
          } lineString;

        struct                    /* Multiline locate information */
          {
          Dvector3d segPoints;    /* Closest segment to locate point  */
            byte    vertex;       /* Closest vertex to locate point   */
            byte    segment;      /* Located line segment (zero based) */
            byte    lineNo;       /* Profile line number        */
            byte    capNo;        /* 0-None, 1-origin, 2-mid, 3-end */
            } mline;

        struct                    /* Dimension locate information */
            {
            Dvector3d segPoints;  /* Closest segment to locate point */
            double    stackHeight;  /* StackHeight at locate */
            byte      pointNo;    /* Closest point in dimension element*/
            byte      segment;    /* Selected dimension segment */
            byte      elemType;   /* Primitive element type located */
            byte      component;  /* Dimension component (witness, text..)*/
            } dim;
        struct                    /* Bspline locate information   */
          {
          boolean   polygonSnap;
          double    u;
          double    v;
          } bspline;
```

```
        } u;
    } LocateInfo;

typedef struct dyntable
    {
    double          zoom;        /* dynamic zoom factor */
    short           panx;        /* dynamic pan factors */
    short           pany;
    } Dyntable;

typedef struct
    {
    Seven_wd_lknm   name;        /* file spec */
    short           levels[4];   /* level bit map */
    unsigned short  endsect;     /* ending sector */
    } Oldref;

typedef struct cntrlwd
    {
#if !defined (mc68000)
    unsigned        grid_lock:1;     /* grid lock in effect */
    unsigned        unit_lock:1;     /* unit lock in effect */
    unsigned        rsrv3:1;         /* reserved */
    unsigned        stream_mode:1;   /* point/stream mode */
    unsigned        delay_pattrn:1;  /* delayed patterning */
    unsigned        dis_asp:1;       /* display aspect ratio */
    unsigned        rsrv2:2;         /* reserved */
    unsigned        inh_msg:1;       /* inhibit CF, ST and PR messages */
    unsigned        inh_err:1;       /* inhibit err msgs (except fatal) */
    unsigned        rsrv1:4;         /* reserved */
    unsigned        wind_alt:1;      /* display window altered */
    unsigned        overview:1;      /* overview on */
#else
    unsigned        overview:1;      /* overview on */
    unsigned        wind_alt:1;      /* display window altered */
    unsigned        rsrv1:4;         /* reserved */
    unsigned        inh_err:1;       /* inhibit err msgs (except fatal) */
    unsigned        inh_msg:1;       /* inhibit CF, ST and PR messages */
    unsigned        rsrv2:2;         /* reserved */
    unsigned        dis_asp:1;       /* display aspect ratio */
    unsigned        delay_pattrn:1;  /* delayed patterning */
    unsigned        stream_mode:1;   /* point/stream mode */
    unsigned        rsrv3:1;         /* reserved */
    unsigned        unit_lock:1;     /* unit lock in effect */
    unsigned        grid_lock:1;     /* grid lock in effect */
#endif
    } Cntrlwd;

typedef struct ext_locks
    {
```

```
#if !defined (mc68000)
    unsigned      axis_lock:1;
    unsigned      auxinp:1;
    unsigned      show_pos:1;
    unsigned      autopan:1;
    unsigned      axis_override:1;
    unsigned      cell_stretch: 1;
    unsigned      iso_grid:1;
    unsigned      obsolete1:1;
    unsigned      obsolete2:1;
    unsigned      iso_plane:2;      /* 0=Top, 1=Left, 2=Right, 3=ALL*/
    unsigned      selection_set:1;
    unsigned      auto_handles:1;
    unsigned      single_shot:1;    /* user selected single shot */
    unsigned      dont_restart:1;   /* cmd doesnt want to be restart*/
    unsigned      viewSingle_shot:1;
    unsigned      snapCnstplane:1;
    unsigned      cnstPlanePerp:1;
    unsigned      fillMode:1;
    unsigned      iso_lock:1;
    unsigned      extendedLevels:1;
    unsigned      intersectionSnap:1;
    unsigned      association:1;     /* let snap create associations */
    unsigned      sharedCells:1;     /* place cells in shared mode */
    unsigned      fenceVoid:1;
    unsigned      fastDynamics:1;
    unsigned      snappablePatterns:1;
    unsigned      unused2:5;
#else
    unsigned      unused2:5;
    unsigned      snappablePatterns:1;/* enable snappable patterns */
    unsigned      fastDynamics:1;   /* set dynamics slow/fast */
    unsigned      fenceVoid:1;       /* 0=inside, 1=outside */
    unsigned      sharedCells:1;     /* place cells in shared mode */
    unsigned      association:1;     /* lock as on/off */
    unsigned      intersectionSnap:1;/* lock snap intersection on/off */
    unsigned      extendedLevels:1;
    unsigned      iso_lock:1;        /* lock isoplane on/off */
    unsigned      fillMode:1;        /* set fill on/off */
    unsigned      cnstPlanePerp:1;   /* datapnts placed perp to con plane*/
    unsigned      snapCnstplane:1;   /* snap to construction plane */
    unsigned      viewSingle_shot:1;
    unsigned      dont_restart:1;    /* cmd doesnt want to be restart*/
    unsigned      single_shot:1;     /* single shot from palette */
    unsigned      auto_handles:1;    /* new elements have handles */
    unsigned      selection_set:1;
    unsigned      iso_plane:2;       /* 0=Top, 1=Left, 2=Right, 3=ALL*/
    unsigned      full_cursor: 1;    /* set cursor full */
    unsigned      iso_cursor:1;      /* set cursor isometric */
    unsigned      iso_grid:1;        /* active gridmode isometric */
```

```
        unsigned        cell_stretch: 1; /* lock cellstrech on/off */
        unsigned        axis_override:1; /* override active axis for blocks */
        unsigned        autopan:1;       /* unused */
        unsigned        show_pos:1;      /* unused */
        unsigned        auxinp:1;        /* set auxinput on/off */
        unsigned        axis_lock:1;     /* lock ax on/off */
#endif
    } Ext_locks;

typedef struct
    {
#if !defined (mc68000)
        unsigned        dragen:1;
        unsigned        dragact:1;
        unsigned        snpele:1;
        unsigned        allowuc:1;
        unsigned        noele:1;
        unsigned        inflin:1;
        unsigned        noout:1;
        unsigned        fcmail:1;
        unsigned        prompt_uc:1;      /* prompt even though in UC */
        unsigned        uc_messages:1;    /* use user cmd msg field */
        unsigned        inhibit_parse:1;  /* inhibit T,E and keyin parse */
        unsigned        spare:5;
#else
        unsigned        spare:5;
        unsigned        inhibit_parse:1;
        unsigned        prompt_uc:1;
        unsigned        uc_messages:1;
        unsigned        fcmail:1;
        unsigned        noout:1;
        unsigned        inflin:1;
        unsigned        noele:1;
        unsigned        allowuc:1;
        unsigned        snpele:1;
        unsigned        dragact:1;
        unsigned        dragen:1;
#endif
    } Outflg;

typedef struct
    {
    short       len;
    char        c[42];
    } Ucm_register;

/*-----------------------------------------------------------------+
|   This structure defines the portion of the TCB which is stored in |
|   the two type 9's in the design file.                             |
+------------------------------------------------------------------*/
```

```
typedef struct tcb
    {
    Cntrlwd        control;  /* control word                    1 */
    double         rndunit;  /* unit lock roundoff val in uors  2 */
    unsigned long  uorgrid;/* uors per grid                     6 */
    short          refgrid;  /* grid points per reference grid point8 */
    byte           vwfull1;  /* view # on scrn 1 (full scrn mode)9 */
    byte           vwfull2;  /* "    "    "    "  "    2         9 */
    Viewinfo       view[8];  /* view information for each view 10 */
    Viewinfo       dig;      /* digitizer information          482 */
    Viewinfo       aux;      /* auxiliary coord system information541 */
    unsigned long  mastunits;/* master units per design (unsigned) 600 */
    unsigned long  subpermast;/* sub-units per master (unsigned) 602 */
    unsigned long  uorpersub;/* uors per sub unit (unsigned) 604 */
    char           mastname[2];/* master units name            606 */
    char           subname[2];/* sub units name                607 */
    double         actangle; /* active angle                   08 */
    double         anglernd; /* angle round-off               612 */
    double         xactscle; /* active scale in x-axis        616 */
    double         yactscle; /* active scale in y-axis        620 */
    double         zactscle; /* active scale in z-axis        624 */
    double         rndscle;  /* scale lock roundoff value     628 */
    unsigned long  chheight;/* character height (uors)        632 */
    unsigned long  chwidth;/* character width (uors)          634 */
    unsigned long  nodespace;/* vert uors between text node chars 636*/
    byte           nodelen;  /* maximum line length in node    638 */
    byte           nodejust; /* text node justification value (0-14)638 */
    byte           actfont;  /* active font number             639 */
    byte           anglefmt; /* angle readout format           639 */
    unsigned short graphic;       /* next graphics group number640 */
    byte           txtjust;  /* text justification value (0-14)641 */
    byte           rfcntrl;  /* reference file control flag    641 */
    byte           tentmode; /* tentative point mode flag      642 */
    byte           tentsubmode;/* tentative point sub mode     642 */
    double         azimuth;  /* azimuth true north angle       643 */
    Autodim1       ad1;      /* automatic dimensioning flags   647 */
    short          props;    /* element properties word        651 */
    Symbology      symbology;/* element symbology word         652 */
    struct
        {
#if !defined (mc68000)
        unsigned   solidhole:1;     /* solid/hole flag */
        unsigned   scalelk:1;        /* scale lock on */
        unsigned   txnodelk:1;       /* text node lock */
        unsigned   anglelk:1;        /* angle lock */
        unsigned   snaplk:1;         /* snap lock */
        unsigned   mirrorch:1;       /* mirror characters */
        unsigned   design3d:1;       /* design 3-d bit */
        unsigned   library3d:1;  /* library 3-d bit */
        unsigned   linewidth:1;  /* lines with width */
```

```
        unsigned      fenceclip:1;     /* fence clip mode */
        unsigned      gglk:1;          /* graphic group lock */
        unsigned      levellk:1;       /* level lock */
        unsigned      assactatt:1;     /* assign active attribute */
        unsigned      padding:1;       /* pads to 16 bits */
        unsigned      attsrch:1;       /* attribute search enabled */
        unsigned      overlap:1;       /* overlap or inside fence lock */
#else
        unsigned      overlap:1;       /* overlap or inside fence lock */
        unsigned      attsrch:1;       /* attribute search enabled */
        unsigned      padding:1;       /* pads to 16 bits */
        unsigned      assactatt:1;     /* assign active attribute */
        unsigned      levellk:1;       /* level lock */
        unsigned      gglk:1;          /* graphic group lock */
        unsigned      fenceclip:1;     /* fence clip mode */
        unsigned      linewidth:1;     /* lines with width */
        unsigned      library3d:1;     /* library 3-d bit */
        unsigned      design3d:1;      /* design 3-d bit */
        unsigned      mirrorch:1;      /* mirror characters */
        unsigned      snaplk:1;        /* snap lock */
        unsigned      anglelk:1;       /* angle lock */
        unsigned      txnodelk:1;      /* text node lock */
        unsigned      scalelk:1;       /* scale lock on */
        unsigned      solidhole:1;     /* solid/hole flag */
#endif
    } fbfdcn;              /* fb/fd control word            653 */
    Point3d      low;      /* range - lo (reversed, unsigned)654 */
    Point3d      high;     /* range - high                  660 */
    Dpoint3d     globorg;  /* global origin - UORs          666 */
    Seven_wd_lknm celllib;       /* cell library name        678 */
    unsigned short cellendsec;/* ending sector of cell file 685 */
    short        cellendbyte;/* ending byte of cell file    686 */
    unsigned short grgrpbas; /* graphics group base number  687 */
    unsigned short nodebase; /* node base number            688 */
    unsigned short canode;   /* next node number            689 */
    Seven_wd_lknm parent;        /* parent design file name  690 */
    short        sysclass; /* system class bit map          697 */
    Seven_wd_lknm usercmd;/* user command index file name 698 */
    short        ucdata[16];     /* user command data        705 */
    Seven_wd_lknm dmrsfile;      /* DMRS file spec           721 */
    Oldref       oldref[3];/* old reference file space (dead)728 */
    char         linkgen;  /* linkage generation mode (DMRS) 764 */
    byte         dmrsflg;  /* DMRS flag                     764 */
    byte         tutview;  /* tutorial view number          765 */
    byte         iactfl;   /* initial active file number ?  765 */
    Autodim2     ad2;      /* second part of auto dim stuff 766 */
    Point3d      dynamicorg;/* dynamic area/volume origin   776 */
    Point3d      dynamicext;/* dynamic area/volume extent   782 */
    Dyntable     dytab[4]; /* dynamic zoom/pan factors for 4 views 788 */
    struct
```

```
        {
#if !defined (mc68000)
        unsigned    user_help:1;      /* user help mode */
        unsigned    boresite:1;       /* standard or boresite locate mode */
        unsigned    prj_key:1;        /* project or keypoint snap */
        unsigned    cnstplane:1;      /* enable construction aide */
        unsigned    stackfract:1;     /* enable stacked fractions */
        unsigned    cellgg:1;         /* reserved */
        unsigned    capsurf:1;        /* capped surface placement mode */
        unsigned    newElementsPresent4:1;  /* new 4.0 elements present */
        unsigned    rsrved:8;
#else
        unsigned    rsrved:8;
        unsigned    newElementsPresent4:1;  /* new 4.0 elements present */
        unsigned    capsurf:1;        /* capped surface placement mode */
        unsigned    cellgg:1;         /* reserved */
        unsigned    stackfract:1;     /* enable stacked fractions */
        unsigned    cnstplane:1;      /* enable construction aide */
        unsigned    prj_key:1;        /* project or keypoint snap */
        unsigned    boresite:1;       /* standard or boresite locate mode */
        unsigned    user_help:1;      /* user help mode */
#endif
        } cntrl1;            /* miscellaneous control flags    812 */
    Autodim3    ad3;         /* more auto dimensioning stuff   813 */
    short       auxtype;     /* type of auxiliary coord system 814 */
    Point3d     dyndwnext;          /* dynamic download extents 815 */
    short       fbfdcn2;    /* another control word (B-splines)821 */
    short       reserv[7];          /* nothing here in TCB     822 */
    short       tcbend;     /* marks end of tcb */

/*  ----- User Command variables -------- */
    short       uc_r[32]; /* R0, R1, ... R31 */
    short       uc_err;    /* ERR */
    short       uc_num;    /* NUM */
    long        uc_i[16]; /* I0, I1, ... I15 */
    short       uc_xdt;    /* XDT */
    short       uc_ydt;    /* YDT */
    long        uc_xur;    /* XUR */
    long        uc_yur;    /* YUR */
    long        uc_zur;    /* ZUR */
    short       uc_vno;    /* VNO */
    double      uc_a[16]; /* A0, A1, ... A15 */
    Ucm_register uc_c[18];/* C0, C1, ... C15, KEY, MSG */
    short       uc_fno;    /* FNO */

/*---------- NOT SAVED IN TYPE 9 ELEMENT --------------*/
    short       dgnfil[3];           /* design file name (RAD50) */
    short       dgnext;              /* design file extension */
    unsigned short  dfsect;              /* end_of_file sector */
    short       dfbyte;           /* end_of_file byte */
```

```
unsigned short  wwsect;                 /* working window start sect */
short           wwbyte;             /* working window start byte */
short           wwfile;             /* working window start file */
short           fence;              /* number of fence points */
Point2d         fenpts[101];        /* fence points */
Point3d         fenrng[2];          /* fence range (x,y,z lo-hi range) */
short           fenvw;              /* view number containing fence */
long            activecell;         /* active cell  (radix 50) */
unsigned short  actcell_sect;/* active cell sector */
short           actcell_byte;       /* active cell byte */
short           acorgf;             /* add cell origin flag */
Point3d         celor;              /* add cell origin */
long            activeterm;         /* active line terminator */
unsigned short  actterm_sect;/* active line terminator sector */
short           actterm_byte;       /* active line terminator byte */
double          actterm_scale;      /* active line terminator scale */
long            activepat;          /* active patterning cell */
unsigned short  actpat_sect;  /* active pattern cell sector */
short           actpat_byte;        /* active pattern cell byte */
double          actpat_scale;       /* active patterning scale */
double          actpat_angle;       /* active patterning angle */
long            actpat_rowspc;      /* active patterning row spacing */
long            actpat_colspc;      /* active patterning column spacing */
long            actpnt;             /* active point (radix 50) */
unsigned short  actpnt_sect;  /* active point sector */
short           actpnt_byte;        /* active point byte */
short           tpnpts;             /* number of tentative points in table */
Point3d         tptabl[2];          /* tentative point table */
short           tptvw[2];           /* views for tentative points in table */
unsigned short  dspsec;             /* sector of currently displayed elemnt */
short           dspbyt;             /* byte of same */
Outflg          outflg;

unsigned short  wssect;             /* working set sector */
unsigned short  lscans;             /* locate/snap sector pointer */
short           lscanb;             /* locate/snap byte pointer */
double          smobuf[9];          /* floating point scratch area */
short           snapfl;             /* file number for snap scan */
unsigned short  snapsc;             /* sector to start snap search */
short           snapby;             /* byte to start snap search */
double          tmatrx[9];          /* view transformation matrix */
short           dittol;             /* locate tolerance */
Point3d         lstpnt;             /* last data point entered */
short           lstvw;              /* view for last point */
unsigned short  curebl;             /* current element, block */
short           cureby;             /* current element, byte */
short           curefl;             /* current element file */
unsigned short  eleblk;             /* next element, block */
short           elecnt;             /* next element, byte */
short           propmsk;        /* properties mask */
short           propval;        /* properties value */
```

```
    short        dynamics;       /* NO LONGER USED    7/90 RBB */
    long         handle;         /* design file file handle */
    long         cellhandle;     /* cell library handle */
    short        tagdel;         /* tag increment binary delta */
    short        tagadr;         /* address of first char in tag field */
    short        taglen;         /* number of characters in tag field */
    short        tagbin;         /* binary value of tag increment */
    short        relerr;         /* error number for last command */
    unsigned short cugraf;       /* current graphics group, only in UCM */
    short        ndices;         /* # of axes, 2 or 3 */
    short        angbyt;         /* # of bytes in orientation (4 or 16) */
    short        trabyt;         /* cell xform matrix (16 or 36) */
    short        pntbyt;         /* bytes in a point (8 or 12) */
    short        of_elo;         /* element origin (0 or 12) */
    short        of_txn;         /* offset for text elements (0 or 8) */
    short        of_clr;         /* offset for cell rotation (0 or 8) */
    short        of_clo;         /* offset for cell origin (0 or 28) */
    unsigned long  strdelta;     /* stream delta */
    unsigned long  strtol;       /* stream tolerance */
    Point3d      prjpnt;         /* projected locate point */
    byte         prjseg;         /* projected segment */
    byte         prjvw;          /* projected view */
    short        dctchs;         /* terminal type (15=MicroStation) */
    char         dgnfilenm[MAXFILELENGTH];   /* design file name */
    char         celfilenm[MAXFILELENGTH];   /* cell library name */
    char         ucifilenm[MAXFILELENGTH];   /* User Command Index name */
    char         celindxnm[MAXFILELENGTH];   /* cell index file name */
    short        ustn_version;   /* MicroStation version */
    short        keypnt_divd;    /* divisor for keypoint snapping */
    unsigned short ae;           /* active entity database */
    unsigned long  mslink;       /* MSLINK key field of ae record */
    char         *db_cntrl;      /* database descriptors */
    unsigned long  record;       /* basis for ae, last record written */
    double       actpat_angle2;  /* second pattern angle (for x-hatch) */
    char         schema[MAXFILELENGTH];  /* database master control file */
    short        task_size;      /* number of K bytes to save for tasks */
    Point3d      iuor[4];        /* File Builder scratch */
    short        tutnam[2];      /* tutorial name (radix 50) */
    unsigned short tutsec;       /* tutorial sector */
    struct
       {
#if !defined (mc68000)
    unsigned short    offset:15; /* tutorial word offset */
    unsigned short    usertut:1; /* is tutorial in user library */
#else
    unsigned short    usertut:1; /* is tutorial in user library */
    unsigned short    offset:15; /* tutorial word offset */
#endif
       }         tutwrd;
```

```
    short          tutsiz;        /* tutorial size */
    Ext_viewflags  ext_viewflags[8];
    short          lev_sym_mask;   /* level symbology enable mask */
    short          lev_sym[63];    /* level symbology words */
#if defined (unix)
    short          prompt_color[4]; /* normal prompt, alt, tut infields */
#else
    short          prompt_color[6]; /* normal prompt, alt, tut infields */
#endif
    Ext_locks      ext_locks;
    double         axlock_angle;
    double         axlock_origin;
    char           fntfilenm[MAXFILELENGTH];/* font library file name */
    long           msgkey;         /* indfpi message key for fb_only */
    short          classmask[8];
    short          window_mode;     /* saves funcname in window command */
    byte           numScreens;
    byte           currentScreen;
    short          tutfont;        /* font used in tutorials */
    Transform      digtrans;
    short          emm_size;
    short          max_grdpnts;
    short          max_grdrefs;
    char           *refFileP;      /* pointer to reference file array */
    short          maxRefs;        /* maximum number of reference files */
    short          bios_screen;
    short          dimension_version;
    Autodim4       ad4;
    Autodim5       ad5;
    Autodim6       ad6;
    double         grid_ratio;
    long           dyno_buffsize;
    short          small_text;

    /* information about the currently parsed command */
    long           last_parsed_command;
    long           current_command;
    short          last_parsed_class;
    short          command_class;
    short          last_parsed_source;
    short          command_source;

    /* the following values contain default (last entered) values for
       commands that require input */
    double         chamfer_dist1;
    double         chamfer_dist2;
    double         autochain_tolerance;
    double         consline_distance;
    double         arc_radius;      /* for circles and arcs */
    double         arc_length;
```

```
    double          cone_radius1;    /* used for cones only */
    double          cone_radius2;
    double          polygon_radius;
    double          surrev_angle;
    double          extend_distance;
    double          fillet_radius;
    double          coppar_distance;
    double          array_row_distance;
    double          array_column_distance;
    double          array_fillangle;
    double          point_distance;
    short           polygon_edges;
    short           points_between;
    short           array_numitems;
    short           array_numrows;
    short           array_numcols;
    byte            array_rotate;
    byte            bspline_order;
    byte            disp_attr_type; /* displayable attribute type # */
    byte            aux_coord_def;  /* type of aux coord being def'd */
    short           searchType[8];  /* element locate type mask */
    long            searchFile[MAX_FILEMASK];         /* file locate mask */
    byte            updateorder[MAX_REFS+2];        /* update order for files */
#if defined (macintosh)
    union
        {
        short           s;
        MSText_Style    b;
        } textStyle;
    Dpoint2d        clipPasteScale;
    double          clipRotation;
    struct
        {
        unsigned    reserved:10;
        unsigned    transparentBitmaps:1;
        unsigned    pastePictFile:1;
        unsigned    rasterCopy:1;
        unsigned    graphicScale:1;
        unsigned    verticalFlip:1;
        unsigned    horizontalFlip:1;
        } clipMode;
#endif
    long            ucmget_command; /* command number (in GET statement) */
    short           ucmget_class;   /* command class (in GET statement) */
    short           ucmget_source;  /* command source (in GET statement) */
    short           help;
    Dpoint3d        currentPosition;
    Dpoint3d        currentDelta;
    double          currentAngle;
    double          currentDistance;
```

```
      struct
        {
        double reference;
        double master;
        } refScale;
    Dpoint3d      refAngle;
    Point3d       precisionPoint;
#if defined (macintosh)
    char          workFileName[MAXFILELENGTH];
#endif
    long          activeAuxSystem;      /* Radix-50 for active ACS */
    long          textAboveSpacing;     /* Space between characters above */
    double        arcTolerance;
    short         arcVectors;
    short         extendedLevels[8][4];
    short         useRangeTree;         /* TRUE r-tree should be used */
    double        snapTolerance;        /* tolerance for snap/locate */
    unsigned short locateHdrSector;     /* header for locate/snap */
    short         locateHdrByte;        /* header for locate/snap */
    unsigned short locateComponentSector;  /* sector of component */ed */
    short         locateComponentByte;     /* (curebl,cureby might be hdr)*/
    unsigned short snapComponentSector;  /* sector of primitive snapped */
    short         snapComponentByte;     /* (lscans,lscanb might be hdr)*/
    short         snap2ndFile;          /* Loc of intrsctng snap elm */
    unsigned short snap2ndSector;
    short         snap2ndByte;
    unsigned short snap2HdrSector;/* loc of hdr if inter elem cmplx */
    short         snap2HdrByte;
    byte          restartLocate;   /* restart location */
    byte          inDynamics;      /* we are in dynamics */
    byte          EDFieldChar;     /* enter data field character */
    byte          angleReadoutPrec;/* unused, use if a byte is needed */
    double        strokeTolerance;
    short         arcMinimum;
    char          backgroundFile[MAXFILELENGTH];
    ULong         componentOffset; /* offset from header for complex
                                      component on locate */

    /* Rendering information */
    short         stereoSeparation;
    short         maxPolygonSize;
    RenderFlags   renderFlags;
    RGBFactor     ambientIntensity;
    RGBFactor     flashIntensity;
    RGBFactor     solarIntensity;
    Dpoint3d      solarDirection;
    Latitude      latitude;
    Longitude     longitude;
    SolarTime     solarTime;
    short         filledEdgeColor; /* Filled edge color (-1 = no edges) */
```

```
MultilineTCB    multiline;        /* All current multiline settings  */
LocateInfo      locateInfo;       /* Info from last located element  */
short           formsMode;        /* database screen forms mode */
short           confirmMode;    /* database multi-row confirmation */
CameraInfo      camera[8];
short           platform;         /* so UC's can tell what platform */
byte            streamAccept;   /* show acceptance criteria for stream */
int             snapElmNumber;  /* elm number if compound snapped elm */
int             snap2ElmNumber; /* elm number if 2nd compound snapped */
} Tcb;
```

Index

M

N

O

P

Q

R

S

MicroStation Software Order Form

CGM2DGN - Convert CGM to DGN

CGM2DGN is a direct file conversion software from CGM (Computer Graphic Metafile) into MicroStation design files. Now you can get reports and diagrams from Harvard Graphics, Freelance or any other software that generates CGM output directly into MicroStation.

For a FREE evaluation of the conversion capabilities, send us your CGM file on a DOS floppy disk. US$1,000 for single CPU copy, available on DOS only.

REFMAN - Reference File Manager

REFMAN is the ultimate reference file manipulation tool! REFMAN has a user friendly, screen based interface and allows users to view an manipulate reference file attachments.

REFMAN lets you keep track of your reference files. View and/or edit reference file attachments including levels, display flags and symbology. Reference files can be deleted and deleted reference file attachments can even be reattached. Copy or move reference files to other directories, even other disks and REFMAN will take care of the reference files. Use REFMAN to obtain reports of all aspects of the reference files attached to your design files. REFMAN has powerful facilities for changing the path(s) of reference files. Be free at last to move your design files. All this and more with REFMAN.

REFMAN is the design and reference file management tool you have been looking for! Site licences and demonstration versions available. US$300.00 for single CPU copy. Available on DOS only.

Pen And Brush Publishers
2nd Floor, 94 Flinders Street
Melbourne Vic 3000
AUSTRALIA

Tel: (03) 818 6226
Fax: (03) 818 3704
International Fax: +61 3 818 3704

Check Out These Other MicroStation Titles Available from OnWord Press

OnWord Press Products are Available Directly From

1. Your Local MicroStation Dealer or Intergraph Education Center
2. Your Local Bookseller
3. In Australia, New Zealand, and Southeast Asia from:
   Pen & Brush Publishers
   2nd Floor, 94 Flinders Street
   Melbourne Victoria 3000
   Australia
   Phone 61 (0)3 818 6226
   Fax   61(0)3 818 3704

4. .... Or Directly From OnWord Press
   (see ordering information on the last page.)

Upgrading to MicroStation 4.X from an earlier version? OnWord Press has Upgrade Tools!

The MicroStation 4.X Delta Book

Frank Conforti
A Quick Guide To Upgrading to 4.X on all Platforms from Earlier Versions of MicroStation

This short and sweet book takes you from 3.X versions of MicroStation into the new world of MicroStation 4.X.

Did you know that there are now over 950 commands in MicroStation? Have you seen the new graphical user interface (GUI)? Are you ready for dialog boxes? Associative dimensioning? Palettes? The new MicroStation Manager?

Intergraph's release notes don't tell the whole story. Sure they let you know about a few new features.

But the MicroStation 4.X Delta Book gets you up and running with these new productivity tools fast.

Highly graphic, the MicroStation 4.X Delta Book doesn't just tell you, it shows you!

Written by Frank Conforti, author of best-selling INSIDE MicroStation, the MicroStation 4.X Delta Book will have you turning out MicroStation 4.X productivity in no time.

Price: **US$19.95** (Australia A$29.95)
Pages: 200
Illustrations: 75+
ISBN: 0-934605-34-3

Cut Your Learning Curve... With

MicroStation 4.X Upgrade Training Video Series

MicroStation version 4.0 is the most comprehensive release to date, enabling users to shorten their production cycles and gain a competitive edge. Now you can cut your learning curve on all the newest features in version 4.0 by using the MicroStation Version 4.0 Upgrade Training Video Series.

The training video contains 12 lessons designed for the experienced MicroStation user. Written by qualified Microstation trainers at Intergraph Corporation, this complete training video series provides hands-on training on the latest MicroStation has to offer. It is a convenient way for MicroStation users to come up to speed on many of the capabilities in version 4.0.

MicroStation users will notice a completely new look in version 4.0 with the new GUI. You will find everything you need on the screen at your fingertips from icon-based tool palettes and dialog boxes to context sensitive help. The training video will walk you through the user interface, showing you a new way of accessing old and new commands and features, plus how to make them work for you.

The lessons in the video will show you how to use Microstation's B-spline surfacing tools, new 2D element placement commands, associated dimensioning, expanded rendering capabilities, multi-line placement, shared cells, named levels, plus view and file manipulation and control, and much more.

Price: **US$149.00**
Three 1/2 Hour VHS Tapes
Video Tapes, Index

Tap the power of MicroStation 4.X
with these new books from
On Word Press.

INSIDE MicroStation

Frank Conforti
The Complete MicroStation Guide
Second Edition, Release 4.X, Supports all 4.X and 3.X Platforms including DOS, Unix, Mac, and VMS

Completely updated for release 4.0!

This easy to use book serves as both a tutorial and a lasting reference guide. Learn to use every MicroStation command as well as time saving drawing techniques and tips. Includes coverage of 3-D, modelling and shading. This is the book that lets you keep up and stay in control with MicroStation.

With a complete update for MicroStation 4.X, this book covers all the new GUI features, additional 2D element placement, associative dimensioning, multi-line placement, shared cells, and more.

The first half of the book concentrates on personal productivity with lessons on basic MicroStation screen, menu, drawing and file control. Here you'll find tutorial information on creating, editing, detailing, and plotting your design work.

The second half of the book gives you the concepts and practical tools for workgroup productivity including advanced editing, cell library work, reference files, and 3D design. You'll also find examples of menu control, DXF transfers, networking, and applications development.

INSIDE MicroStation takes you beyond stand-alone commands. Using real world examples it gives you practical and effective methods for building good working habits with MicroStation.

Frank Conforti is an independent MicroStation consultant based in Delray Beach Florida. Formerly CAD Manager at Keith and Schnarrs Engineers, Frank managed a network of VAX-based IGDS and MicroStation systems running workstations, PCs and MACs. Conforti has been using CAD, IGDS and MicroStation for 16 years. He is an avid writer, trainer, and user group sponsor. He is co-author of the Macintosh CAD/CAM book.

✆ Optional INSIDE MicroStation Disk: **US$14.95** (Australia A$29.95) Includes the tutorial example design files, menus, listings, examples and more.

Price: **US$29.95** (Australia A$54.95)
Pages: 550
Illustrations: 220+
ISBN: 0-934605-49-1

The INSIDE MicroStation Companion Workbook

Michael Ward and Support From Frank Conforti
32 Steps to MicroStation -- A self-paced tutorial workbook
for individual or classroom use.
First Edition, Release 4.X, Supports all 4.X and 3.X Platforms including DOS, Unix, Mac, and VMS

This highly readable hands-on text is your guide to learning MicroStation. As a companion to the INSIDE MicroStation book, the workbook gives you practical exercises for developing MicroStation skills.

The INSIDE MicroStation Companion Workbook is set up for self-paced work alone, or in classroom or group training. The workbook comes setup for three types of training scenarios. You can work through the exercises and test yourself. Or you can organize the course into a three or four day professional or 10 - 14 week semester course. Or you can make up your own grouping from the 32 basic training units.

The workbook course takes you through at least two paths to develop your proficiency with MicroStation. First, you are taught basic functions and given exercises to develop your skills. Second, you can select from an architectural, civil, or electrical engineering "real life" professional drawing that you work on during the length of the course.

✆ The INSIDE MicroStation Companion Workbook training Disk comes with the book (5.25" DOS standard, other formats available on request). On the disk you will find exercise tools, exercise drawings, plot files, even a diploma!
✍ Also included in the package are several professional blueprints used as part of the training course.
Price: **US$34.95** (Australia A$54.95)
Pages: 400 (Includes DOS 5.25" Disk and Blueprints)
Illustrations: 75+
ISBN: 0-934605-42-4

Optional INSIDE MicroStation Companion Workbook Teacher/Trainer's Guide.

This 75 page instructor's guide to the INSIDE MicroStation Companion Workbook is geared for the professional trainer, college professor, or corporate training department. Filled with teaching tricks, organization tools and more, the instructor's guide is a must for anyone in an instructor's position.

Price: **US$9.95** (Australia A$18.95)
NOTE: The Teacher/Trainer's Guide is **FREE** to any group ordering 10 copies or more of the workbook. Contact OnWord Press for ordering information.
Pages: 75
ISBN: 0-934605-39-4

The MicroStation Productivity Book

Kincaid, Steinbock, Malm
Tapping the Hidden Power of MicroStation
Second Edition, Release 4.X, Supports all 4.X and 3.X Platforms including DOS, Unix, Mac, and VMS

With this book beginning and advanced users alike can take big leaps in productivity, job security and personal satisfaction. Thirty-six step-by-step chapters show you how to take charge of MicroStation.

Completely updated for MicroStation 4.X, the MicroStation Productivity book now includes complete information on MDL, using MicroStation with Oracle, 100 pages of new 3D tools, and more.

This book is really two books in one. The first half is "The Power Users Guide to MicroStation". Use the tools and tutorials in these chapters to go beyond the basic MicroStation menus and commands. Power drawing, power editing, automation of repetitive tasks, working in 3D, this section teaches you how to get the most out of MicroStation.

Turn to the second half "The Unofficial MicroStation Installation Guide" to take charge of your MicroStation installation. Here you'll find tools to supercharge your software installation, customize command environment, build menus, manage your files and make DXF transfers. There is even a chapter on the undocumented EDG editor that tells you how to fix corrupted design files.

Learn how to write user commands and immediately put to work the "Ten User Commands for Everybody" and "Our Ten Favorite User Commands". Take advantage of attribute data with links to database programs including dBASE and ORACLE. This book shows you how.

Appendices include listing of all TCB variables, command names, and the syntax you need to know to be a power user.

John Kincaid and Bill Steinbock are MicroStation installation managers for the U.S. Army Corps of Engineers, Rock Island and Louisville districts respectively. They are avid writers and MicroStation bulletin board aficionados. Rich Malm managed the Corp's Intergraph/MicroStation procurement efforts until he recently retired to devote his time to consulting and MicroStation database applications. Between them, the authors have over 40 years of CAD, IGDS and MicroStation experience.

✪   Optional Productivity Disk: **US$49.95** (Australia A$79.95) Includes all of the user commands in the book, design file and tutorial examples, menus for user commands, custom batch files, and the exclusive MicroStation 3D menu.

Price: **US$39.95**   (Australia A$69.95)
Pages: 850
Illustrations: 220+
ISBN: 0-934605-53-X

MicroStation Reference Guide, Pocket Edition

John Leavy
Everything you want to know about MicroStation -- Fast!
Second Edition, Release 4.X, Supports all 4.X and 3.X Platforms including DOS, Unix, Mac, and VMS

Finally, all of MicroStation's commands are in one easy to use reference guide. Important information on every MicroStation command is at your fingertips (including some that even Intergraph/Bentley don't tell you about!).

This book gives you everything you need to know about a command including:

    How to find it
    How to use it
    What it does
    What happens in an error situation

The book includes all commands, key-ins, ACTIVES, and environmental settings. Also you'll find background on such important concepts as coordinate entry, PLACE commands, and drawing construction techniques. Actual screens and examples help you get up and drawing now.

Now completely updated for 4.X, the MicroStation Reference Guide covers over 950 commands (The last edition of the book had only 400 commands!). Every user and every workstation should have one of these books handy.

The new edition features hundreds of command illustrations including the new 4.X GUI palettes for command operations.

John Leavy is president and chief Intergraph/MicroStation consultant with Computer Graphic Solutions, Inc. His specialty is MicroStation training and applications development. Leavy spent 12 years with Intergraph before moving into the private consulting world.

🅐 Optional MicroStation Reference Guide, Pocket Edition Disk: **US$14.95** (Australia A$19.95) The MicroStation Online Reference Guide disk puts this book online with MicroStation.

Price: **US$18.95** (Australia A$26.95)
Pages: 320
Illustrations: 200+
ISBN: 0-934605-55-6

The Complete Guide To MicroStation 3D

David Wilkinson
First Edition, Release 4.X, Supports all 4.X and 3.X Platforms including DOS, Unix, Mac, and VMS (Published by Pen & Brush Publishers, Distributed by OnWord Press)

If you are a MicroStation 2D user wanting to advance into the "real-world" of 3D, then this is the book for you. It is both a tutorial and a reference guide. Written especially for MicroStation 2D users, it teaches you how to use the 3D capabilities of MicroStation. Diagrams (over 220 in total) are used extensively throughout this book to illustrate the various points and topics.

Chapters 1 and 2 incorporate the basic tutorial section. Here you are introduced to the 3D environment of MicroStation and shown how to place elements in 3D. This is explained with simple exercises, graphically illustrated to avoid any confusion.

From this basic introduction you can advance, step-by-step, through complex problem solving techniques. This can be accomplished at your own pace. Having learned to create a 3D model, you are shown methods for extracting drawings and how to create rendered (shaded) images.

MicroStation version 4 tools are covered comprehensively, along with those for version 3.3 (PC version for 286 machines).

Among topics covered are the following:

* Basic placement and manipulation of elements
* Views and view rotation
* Projection and Surface of Revolution
* B-Spline Surface Constructions (version 4)
* Rendering (for both versions 3.3 and 4)

🅐 Optional Complete Guide to MicroStation 3D Disk: **US$19.95** (Australia A$29.95) Includes examples from the book as well as tips and tricks for 3D work, model building, shading and rendering.

Price: **US$39.95** (Australia A$69.95)
Pages: 400
Illustrations: 200+
ISBN: 0-934605-66-1 (Australia ISBN: 0-646-01678-4)

101 MDL Commands

Bill Steinbock
First Edition, Release 4.X, Supports all 4.X and 3.X Platforms including DOS, Unix, Mac, and VMS

This is the book you need to get started with MDL!

With MicroStation 4.0 comes the MicroStation Development Language or MDL. MDL is a powerful programming language built right in to MicroStation.

MDL can be used to add productivity to MicroStation or to develop complete applications using MicroStation tools. Virtually all of the 3rd party applications vendors are already using MDL for their development.

Now you can too, with 101 MDL Commands.

The first part of this book is a 100 page introduction to MDL including a guide to how source code is created, compiled, linked, and run. This section includes full discussion of Resource Files, Source Codes, Include Files, Make Files, dependencies, conditionals, interference rules, command line options and more.

Learn to control MicroStation's new GUI with dialog boxes, state functions, element displays and file control.

The second part of the book is 101 actual working MDL commands ready-to-go. Here you will find about 45 applications with over 101 MDL tools. Some of these MDL commands replace user commands costing over $100 a piece in the 3.0 market!

Here's a sampling of the MDL applications in the book and on the book:

        MATCH - existing element parameters
        Creation - create all the new element types from MDL
        Multi-line - convert existing lines and linestrings to multi-line elements
        CALC - Dialog box calculator
        DATSTMP - Places and updates filename and in-drawing date stamp
        PREVIEW - previews a design file within a dialog box
        Text - complete text control - underline, rotate, resize, upper/lower, locate text
             string, import ASCII columns, extract text
        Fence - complete fence manipulations including patterning, group control,
             circular fence and more
        3D surfaces - complete projection and surface of revolution control
        Cell routines - place along, place view dependent cell, scale cell, extract to
             cell library
        Dialog boxes - make your own using these templates!
        Search Criteria - delete, fence, copy, etc based on extensive search criteria.

Use these MDL commands to get you started with the power of MicroStation MDL. You can put these tools to work immediately, or use the listings to learn about MDL and develop your own applications.

   ☉   Optional 101 MDL Commands Disk: **US$101.00** (Australia A$155.00) Includes all of the MDL commands from the book in executable form, ready to be loaded and used.

Price: **US$49.95**   (Australia A$85.00)
Pages: 680
Illustrations: 75+
ISBN: 0-934605-61-0

   ☉   Optional 101 MDL Commands Source Disk 1: **US$59.95** Includes:

Element Creation Functions
Program 1: ELLIPSE

Program 2: EXTRUDE
Program 3: GRID
Program 4: LEADER
Program 5: PLBLKC
Program 6: POLY
Program 7: REVOLVE

Ⓐ   Optional 101 MDL Commands Source Disk 2: **US$59.95** Includes:

Element Manipulation
Program 8: COPYA
Program 9: CVT2VD
Program 10: MOVSEG
Program 11: SETZ
Program 12: UNPATLIN
Fence Commands
Program 17: CIRFEN
Program 18: FENGG
Program 19: FENSEA

Ⓐ   Optional 101 MDL Commands Source Disk 3: **US$59.95** Includes:

Text Functions
Program 20: CHNGFT
Program 21: IATXT
Program 22: LOCKTXT
Program 23: TEXTMOD
Program 24: TEXTTX
Program 25: ULTXT
Program 26: UPPER

Ⓐ   Optional 101 MDL Commands Source Disk 4: **US$59.95** Includes:

Cell Routines
Program 13: CELLALNG
Program 14: CELLMOD
Program 15: CELLPLOT
Program 16: CELLX
Active Parameters
Program 29: MATCH
Program 30: SHOW

Ⓐ   Optional 101 MDL Commands Source Disk 5: **US$59.95** Includes:

Utilities
Program 35: CALC
Program 36: CLOCK
Program 37: DATSTMP
Program 38: PREVW
Returning Values to the Design
Program 27: AREATXT
Program 28: NE

Ⓐ   Optional 101 MDL Commands Source Disk 6: **US$59.95** Includes:

Placing Elements With External Data Files
Program 31: TEXTCOL
Program 32: XYPLOT
Program 33: XYZCELL
Program 34: XYZLINE

Ⓐ   **ALL SIX 101 MDL Commands Source Disks:** *ONLY* US$299.95

Bill Steinbock's
Pocket MDL Programmers Guide

Bill Steinbock
First Edition, Release 4.X, Supports all 4.X and 3.X Platforms including DOS, Unix, Mac, and VMS

Intergraph/Bentley's MDL documentation is over 1000 pages!

Bill's Steinbock's Pocket MDL Programmers Guide gives you all the MDL tools you need to know for most applications in a brief, easy-to-read format.

All the MDL tools, all the parameters, all the definitions, all the ranges -- in a short and sweet pocket guide.

If you're serious about MDL, put the power of MicroStation MDL in your hands with this complete quick guide.

Includes all the MDL commands, tables, indexes, and a quick guide to completing MDL source for MDL compilation.

Price: **US$24.95**   (Australia A$39.95)
Pages: 256
Illustrations: 75+
ISBN: 0-934605-32-7

MDL-Guides

CAD Perfect
First Edition, Release 4.X, Supports all MDL 4.X Platforms Runs under DOS only.

1000 Pages of Intergraph MDL Documentation On-Line at Your Fingertips!

The Intergraph MDL Documentation is voluminous, to say the least. MDL-GUIDES puts the MDL and MicroCSL documentation in a hypertext TSR for reference access while you are programming or debugging in MDL.

This terminate-and-stay-ready program was sanctioned by Intergraph as the practical way to find out all the MDL information you need in an easy format.

The program is environment friendly, works with high DOS memory space to leave room for your other applications, and is quick.

The package includes the hypertext software, the complete set of MDL and MicroCSL Intergraph documentation in hypertext format, and a proper set of installation instructions.

MDL-GUIDES
For DOS Formats only (Other formats available on request from CAD Perfect)
Includes Disk and User's Manual
Disk Includes all MDL Documentation formatted for use on-line
Price: **US$295.00**
ISBN 0-934605-71-8

Programming With MDL

Mach Dinh-Vu
For Intergraph MicroStation
Supports all 4.X Platforms including DOS, Unix, Mac, and VMS. Will work with all 4.X versions of MicroStation.
(Published by Pen & Brush Publishers, Distributed by OnWord Press)

Programming With MDL is an indispensable tool for MDL command newcomers and programmers alike. This book serves as both a tutorial guide and handbook to the ins-and-outs of MDL.

Step-by-step explanations and examples help you create MDL programs to speed the design and drafting process. Learn how to attach "intelligence" to the drawing with or without database links. Take control of your menu, dialog, and command environment and customize it for your own application.

MicroStation Development Language is already built into your copy of MicroStation or IGDS. Put it to work for you today with Programming With MDL.

✪ Programming With MDL Disk: **$40.00** (Australia A$55.00) Includes all of the MDL Command examples in the book in a ready-to-use form. Use them as they are, or modify them with your own editor to get a jump-start on MDL programming.

Price: **US$49.95** (Australia A$85.00)
Pages: 320
Illustrations, Tables, Examples: 120+
ISBN: 0-934605-59-9 (Australia ISBN: 0-646-01679-2)

Programming With User Commands

Mach Dinh-Vu
Second Edition
For Intergraph IGDS and MicroStation
Release 3.X, Supports all 4.X and 3.X Platforms including DOS, Unix, Mac, and VMS. Will work with all 4.X versions of MicroStation.
(Published by Pen & Brush Publishers, Distributed by OnWord Press)

Programming With User Commands is an indispensable tool for user command newcomers and programmers alike. This book serves as both a tutorial guide and handbook to the ins-and-outs of UCMs.

Step-by-step explanations and examples help you create menus and tutorials to speed the design and drafting process. Learn how to attach "intelligence" to the drawing with or without database links. Take control of your menu and command environment and customize it for your own application.

Learn how to add your own functions to MicroStation's built in commands. You can do things like: save the current cell library, attach another, and then restore the previous one; or locate, add, move and modify elements -- all from User Commands.

The User Command language is already built into your copy of MicroStation or IGDS. Put it to work for you today with Programming With User Commands. Most users think UCMs are too complicated, too much like "programming". This book shatters that myth and makes User Commands accessible to every user.

Mach Dinh-Vu is an Intergraph and MicroStation CAD specialist in Engineering, Architectural, and Public Utility applications. His background includes six years of Intergraph experience, first on the VAX, but now on MicroStation and MicroStation DOS, VAX, and UNIX networks.

⊗   Programming With User Commands Disk: **$40.00** (Australia A$55.00) Includes all of the User
     Command examples in the book in a ready-to-use form. Use them as they are, or modify them
     with your own editor to get a jump-start on User Command programming.

Price: **US$65.00**   (Australia A$80.00)
Pages: 320
Illustrations, Tables, Examples: 120+
ISBN: 0-934605-45-9 (Australia ISBN: 0-7316-5883-3)

101 User Commands

Brockway, Dinh-Vu, Steinbock
Putting user commands to work on all Intergraph MicroStation and IGDS Platforms.
For Intergraph MicroStation & IGDS Users
Supports all versions of MicroStation and IGDS under DOS, Mac OS, UNIX and VMS

With this book user and programmers alike can jump ahead with MicroStation or IGDS productivity.
101 User Commands gives you 101 programs to automate your CAD environment.

Never programmed with user commands before?
This book shows you how. With the program listings, input and output variables, prompting sequences and more, you will be using user commands in no time.
Or copy the program listings from the optional disk into your word processor or line editor and you
will be programming in no time.

Already an experienced user command programmer?
Here you'll find some of the finest in the business. Each user command is built from basic building
blocks to help you organize your programs.
Mix and Match programs or subroutines to put together your own set of user commands.

This book has seven types of user commands:
Element Placement, Element Manipulations, Symbology and Attributes, Sub-Routines, Utilities, Feature Codes, and Civil Engineering Applications.

⊗   The Optional 101 User Command Disk **US$101.00** (Australia A$155.00) Includes all the user
     commands in the book in ready-to-go format. Edit them with your own word processor or compile
     them for immediate run-time programs.

Price: **US$49.95**   (Australia A$85.00)
Pages: 400
Illustrations, Tables, Examples: 75+
ISBN: 0-934605-47-5

Also Available from CAD News Bookstore:
Teaching Assistant for MicroStation

An Online Tutorial
This computer-aided-instruction package will have you learning Micro~Station by using MicroStation!
The Teaching Assistant is a series of five lessons that runs within MicroStation (PC Version 3.0 and
later).

All aspects of the program are covered from screen layout and menus to drawing layout and concepts,
to advanced editing and dimensioning. Self-paced and reusable, this courseware is a great tool for beginning users and a good refresher for casual users.

This is the perfect training material for IGDS users who need to know more about Micro~Station. The course takes average users six to ten hours to complete.
Published: May 1990 Through Version DOS 3.3 (Call for availability of 4.X Version)
Two 5 1/4 or 3 1/2" disks plus workbook.
Price: **US$449.95**

CAD Managers: Know Before You Hire!
The MicroStation Evaluator

MicroStation Operator Proficiency Training
The MicroStation Evaluator is an on-screen, reusable MicroStation test, designed to help employers select quality computer personnel. The evaluator asks 100 multiple choice questions, covering basic to advanced knowledge.

The Evaluator automatically grades the test and creates a report for the employer, including test scores, time taken, and work history. Because each operator's training is unique and every company's needs are different, the questions are placed in specific categories. The report gives scores in each category indicating the operator's strengths and weaknesses.

Even employers who are not familiar with Micro~Station can easily interpret category scores and compare candidates. The Evaluator produces graphic and written reports.
Through Version DOS 3.3 (Call for availability of 4.X Version)
Published: June 1990
Price: **US$149.00**

Order MicroStation 4.X Tools From OnWord Press Now!

Ordering Information:

On Word Press Products are Available From

1. Your Local MicroStation Dealer
2. Your Local Bookseller
3. In Australia, New Zealand, and Southeast Asia from:
   Pen & Brush Publishers
   2nd Floor, 94 Flinders Street
   Melbourne Victoria 3000
   Australia
   Phone 61(0)3 818 6226
   Fax   61(0)3 818 3704

4. .... Or Directly From OnWord Press:

To Order From On Word Press:

Three Ways To Order from OnWord Press

1. Order by **FAX** 505/587-1015
2. Order by **PHONE:** 1-800-CAD NEWS™ Outside the U.S. and Canada
   call 505/587-1010.
3. Order by **MAIL:** OnWord Press/CAD NEWS Bookstore, P.O. Box 500,
   Chamisal NM 87521-0500 USA.

Shipping and Handling Charges apply to all orders: 48 States: $4.50 for the first item, $2.25 each additional item. Canada, Hawaii, Alaska, Puerto Rico: $8.00 for the first item, $4.00 for each additional item. International: $46.00 for the first item, $15.00 each additional item. **Diskettes are counted as additional items.** New Mexico delivery address, please add 5.625% state sales tax.

Rush orders or special handling can be arranged, please phone or write for details. Government and Educational Institution POs accepted. Corporate accounts available.

MDL Books and Tools

Use This Form If Ordering Directly From OnWord Press

Quantity	Title	Price	Extension
	101 MDL Commands	$49.95	
	101 MDL Commands Disk/Executables	$101.00	
	101 MDL Commands Disk/Source Disk 1	$59.95	
	101 MDL Commands Disk/Source Disk 2	$59.95	
	101 MDL Commands Disk/Source Disk 3	$59.95	
	101 MDL Commands Disk/Source Disk 4	$59.95	
	101 MDL Commands Disk/Source Disk 5	$59.95	
	101 MDL Commands Disk/Source Disk 6	$59.95	
	ALL SIX 101 MDL Commands Source Disks	$299.95	
	Bill Steinbock's MDL Pocket Programmer's Guide	$24.95	
	MDL-GUIDES	$295.00	
	Programming With MDL	$49.95	
	Programming With MDL Disk	$40.00	
	Shipping & Handling*		
	5.625% Tax - State of New Mexico Delivery Only		
	Total		

AD CODE M49

Name_____

Company_____

Street_____
(No P.O. Boxes Please)

_____

City, State_____

Country, Postal Code _____

Phone _____

Fax_____

If Ordering Disks, Please Note

Disk Type _____

Payment Method

____ Cash ____ Check ____ Amex

____ MasterCARD ____VISA

_____
Card Number

Expiration Date _____

_____
Signature

FAX TO: 505/587-1015
or MAIL TO:
OnWord Press
Box 500, Chamisal NM 87521 USA

MicroStation Books and Tools

Use This Form If Ordering Directly From OnWord Press

Quantity	Title	Price	Extension
	MicroStation 4.X Delta Book	$19.95	
	MicroStation 4.X Upgrade Video Series	$149.00	
	INSIDE MicroStation	$29.95	
	INSIDE MicroStation Disk	$14.95	
	INSIDE MicroStation Companion Workbook	$34.95	
	Instructor's Guide: INSIDE MicroStation Companion Workbook	$9.95	
	MicroStation Productivity Book	$39.95	
	MicroStation Productivity Disk	$49.95	
	MicroStation Reference Guide	$18.95	
	MicroStation Reference Disk	$14.95	
	The Complete Guide to MicroStation 3D	$39.95	
	The Complete Guide to MicroStation 3D Disk	$19.95	
	Programming With User Commands	$65.00	
	Programming With User Commands Disk	$40.00	
	101 User Commands	$49.95	
	101 User Commands Disk	$101.00	
	Teaching Assistant for Micro~Station	$449.95	
	The MicroStation Evaluator	$149.00	
	MicroStation For AutoCAD Users	29.95	
	MicroStation For AutoCAD Users Disk	14.95	
	Shipping & Handling*		
	5.625% Tax - State of New Mexico Delivery Only		
	Total		

AD CODE M49

Name_____

Company_____

Street _____
(No P.O. Boxes Please)

_____

City, State_____

Country, Postal Code _____

Phone _____

Fax_____

If Ordering Disks, Please Note

Disk Type _____

Payment Method

____ Cash ____ Check ____ Amex

____ MasterCARD ____VISA

_____

Card Number

Expiration Date _____

_____

Signature

FAX TO: 505/587-1015
or MAIL TO:
OnWord Press
Box 500, Chamisal NM 87521 USA

MDL Books and Tools

Use This Form If Ordering Directly From OnWord Press

Quantity	Title	Price	Extension
	101 MDL Commands	$49.95	
	101 MDL Commands Disk/Executables	$101.00	
	101 MDL Commands Disk/Source Disk 1	$59.95	
	101 MDL Commands Disk/Source Disk 2	$59.95	
	101 MDL Commands Disk/Source Disk 3	$59.95	
	101 MDL Commands Disk/Source Disk 4	$59.95	
	101 MDL Commands Disk/Source Disk 5	$59.95	
	101 MDL Commands Disk/Source Disk 6	$59.95	
	ALL SIX 101 MDL Commands Source Disks	$299.95	
	Bill Steinbock's MDL Pocket Programmer's Guide	$24.95	
	MDL-GUIDES	$295.00	
	Programming With MDL	$49.95	
	Programming With MDL Disk	$40.00	
	Shipping & Handling*		
	5.625% Tax - State of New Mexico Delivery Only		
	Total		

AD CODE M49

Name_____

Company_____

Street_____
(No P.O. Boxes Please)

_____

City, State_____

Country, Postal Code _____

Phone _____

Fax_____

If Ordering Disks, Please Note

Disk Type _____

Payment Method

____ Cash ____ Check ____ Amex

____ MasterCARD ____VISA

Card Number _____

Expiration Date _____

Signature _____

FAX TO: 505/587-1015
or MAIL TO:
OnWord Press
Box 500, Chamisal NM 87521 USA

MicroStation Books and Tools

Use This Form If Ordering Directly From OnWord Press

Quantity	Title	Price	Extension
	MicroStation 4.X Delta Book	$19.95	
	MicroStation 4.X Upgrade Video Series	$149.00	
	INSIDE MicroStation	$29.95	
	INSIDE MicroStation Disk	$14.95	
	INSIDE MicroStation Companion Workbook	$34.95	
	Instructor's Guide: INSIDE MicroStation Companion Workbook	$9.95	
	MicroStation Productivity Book	$39.95	
	MicroStation Productivity Disk	$49.95	
	MicroStation Reference Guide	$18.95	
	MicroStation Reference Disk	$14.95	
	The Complete Guide to MicroStation 3D	$39.95	
	The Complete Guide to MicroStation 3D Disk	$19.95	
	Programming With User Commands	$65.00	
	Programming With User Commands Disk	$40.00	
	101 User Commands	$49.95	
	101 User Commands Disk	$101.00	
	Teaching Assistant for Micro~Station	$449.95	
	The MicroStation Evaluator	$149.00	
	MicroStation For AutoCAD Users	29.95	
	MicroStation For AutoCAD Users Disk	14.95	
	Shipping & Handling*		
	5.625% Tax - State of New Mexico Delivery Only		
	Total		

AD CODE M49

Name_____

Company_____

Street _____
(No P.O. Boxes Please)

_____

City, State_____

Country, Postal Code _____

Phone _____

Fax_____

If Ordering Disks, Please Note

Disk Type _____

Payment Method

____ Cash ____ Check ____ Amex

____ MasterCARD ____VISA

_____

Card Number

Expiration Date _____

_____

Signature

FAX TO: 505/587-1015
or MAIL TO:
OnWord Press
Box 500, Chamisal NM 87521 USA

MDL Books and Tools

Use This Form If Ordering Directly From On Word Press

Quantity	Title	Price	Extension
	101 MDL Commands	$49.95	
	101 MDL Commands Disk/Executables	$101.00	
	101 MDL Commands Disk/Source Disk 1	$59.95	
	101 MDL Commands Disk/Source Disk 2	$59.95	
	101 MDL Commands Disk/Source Disk 3	$59.95	
	101 MDL Commands Disk/Source Disk 4	$59.95	
	101 MDL Commands Disk/Source Disk 5	$59.95	
	101 MDL Commands Disk/Source Disk 6	$59.95	
	ALL SIX 101 MDL Commands Source Disks	$299.95	
	Bill Steinbock's MDL Pocket Programmer's Guide	$24.95	
	MDL-GUIDES	$295.00	
	Programming With MDL	$49.95	
	Programming With MDL Disk	$40.00	
	Shipping & Handling*		
	5.625% Tax - State of New Mexico Delivery Only		
	Total		

AD CODE M49

Name_____

Company_____

Street _____
(No P.O. Boxes Please)

_____

City, State_____

Country, Postal Code _____

Phone _____

Fax_____

If Ordering Disks, Please Note

Disk Type _____

Payment Method

____ Cash ____ Check ____ Amex

____ MasterCARD ____VISA

Card Number _____

Expiration Date _____

Signature _____

FAX TO: 505/587-1015
or MAIL TO:
OnWord Press
Box 500, Chamisal NM 87521 USA

MicroStation Books and Tools

Use This Form If Ordering Directly From On Word Press

Quantity	Title	Price	Extension
	MicroStation 4.X Delta Book	$19.95	
	MicroStation 4.X Upgrade Video Series	$149.00	
	INSIDE MicroStation	$29.95	
	INSIDE MicroStation Disk	$14.95	
	INSIDE MicroStation Companion Workbook	$34.95	
	Instructor's Guide: INSIDE MicroStation Companion Workbook	$9.95	
	MicroStation Productivity Book	$39.95	
	MicroStation Productivity Disk	$49.95	
	MicroStation Reference Guide	$18.95	
	MicroStation Reference Disk	$14.95	
	The Complete Guide to MicroStation 3D	$39.95	
	The Complete Guide to MicroStation 3D Disk	$19.95	
	Programming With User Commands	$65.00	
	Programming With User Commands Disk	$40.00	
	101 User Commands	$49.95	
	101 User Commands Disk	$101.00	
	Teaching Assistant for Micro~Station	$449.95	
	The MicroStation Evaluator	$149.00	
	MicroStation For AutoCAD Users	29.95	
	MicroStation For AutoCAD Users Disk	14.95	
	Shipping & Handling*		
	5.625% Tax - State of New Mexico Delivery Only		
	Total		

AD CODE M49

Name_____

Company_____

Street _____
(No P.O. Boxes Please)

_____

City, State_____

Country, Postal Code _____

Phone _____

Fax_____

If Ordering Disks, Please Note

Disk Type _____

Payment Method

____ Cash ____ Check ____ Amex

____ MasterCARD ___VISA

_____

Card Number

Expiration Date _____

_____

Signature

FAX TO: 505/587-1015
or MAIL TO:
OnWord Press
Box 500, Chamisal NM 87521 USA